Experimental Human–Computer Interaction

Experiments that require the use of human participants are time consuming and costly: it is important to get the process right the first time. Planning and preparation are key to success. This practical book takes the human–computer interaction researcher through the complete experimental process – from identifying a research question, to designing and conducting an experiment, to analyzing and reporting the results.

The advice offered in this book draws on the author's 20 years of experience in conducting experiments. In describing general concepts of experimental design and analysis, she refers to worked examples that address the real practicalities and problems of conducting an experiment, such as managing participants, obtaining ethical approval, preempting criticism, choosing a statistical method, and dealing with unexpected events.

DR. HELEN C. PURCHASE is a Senior Lecturer in the School of Computing Science, University of Glasgow. She is the recipient of Teaching Excellence awards from both the University of Queensland and the University of Glasgow. Her research has been published in numerous journals, including *IEEE Transactions on Visualization and Computer Graphics*, *International Journal of Human–Computer Studies*, *Information Visualization*, *Graph Drawing Conference*, and *ACM SIGCSE Bulletin*. Her research focuses on visual aesthetics, collaborative learning in higher education, and sketch tools for design.

Experimental Human–Computer Interaction

A Practical Guide with Visual Examples

HELEN C. PURCHASE
University of Glasgow

CAMBRIDGE
UNIVERSITY PRESS

CAMBRIDGE
UNIVERSITY PRESS

Shaftesbury Road, Cambridge CB2 8EA, United Kingdom

One Liberty Plaza, 20th Floor, New York, NY 10006, USA

477 Williamstown Road, Port Melbourne, VIC 3207, Australia

314–321, 3rd Floor, Plot 3, Splendor Forum, Jasola District Centre, New Delhi – 110025, India

103 Penang Road, #05–06/07, Visioncrest Commercial, Singapore 238467

Cambridge University Press is part of Cambridge University Press & Assessment,
a department of the University of Cambridge.

We share the University's mission to contribute to society through the pursuit of
education, learning and research at the highest international levels of excellence.

www.cambridge.org
Information on this title: www.cambridge.org/9780521279543

First published 2012

A catalogue record for this publication is available from the British Library

Library of Congress Cataloging-in-Publication data
Purchase, Helen C.
Experimental human-computer interaction : a practical guide with
visual examples / Helen C. Purchase, University of Glasgow.
pages   cm
ISBN 978-1-107-01006-2 (hardback)
1. Human-computer interaction.   I. Title.
QA76.9.H85P87   2012
004.01´9–dc23   2012004419

ISBN   978-1-107-01006-2   Hardback
ISBN   978-0-521-27954-3   Paperback

To my father

Contents

List of experiments

Acknowledgements

This book emerged from a tutorial that was prepared and delivered in 2009 at the Laboratoire Bordelais de Recherche en Informatique at the University of Bordeaux. I am grateful to Guy Melançon, who funded that visit (and others besides), and to Mats Daniels, who kindly provided resources at Uppsala University for an intensive writing period over the summer of 2011.

Over the past 10 years, I have attended several seminars and workshops at the Leibniz Center for Informatics at Schloss Dagstuhl. Many of the discussions I had there with colleagues in graph drawing, information visualisation, and aesthetic computing have inspired this book, and I am thankful to the German federal government, which generously funds this excellent facility for computer science research.

This book (and indeed much of my research career) would not be possible without the encouragement of Peter Eades and Julie McCredden, who first set me on an experimental research path; the support of other research colleagues (in particular David Carrington and John Hamer); and students who allowed me to use their assessed projects as a way of trying out different experimental ideas (in particular, Irvin Colquhoun, Eve Hoggan, Carolyn Salimun, Amanjit Samra, and Joshua Worrill).

Several colleagues generously gave me permission to use their experiments as examples in this book, in many cases permitting the reproduction of data and images: Daniel Archambault, Romain Bourqui, Johan Kildal, Pierre-Yves Koenig, Guy Melançon, and Peter Rodgers.

In the production of this book, I have greatly benefitted from the help and advice of Allan Brown, Alistair Donaldson, Euan Freeman, John Hamer, Mhari Macdonald, Marilyn McGee-Lennon, Paddy O'Donnell, and Oliver Rundell. John Hamer prepared many of the images. Lauren Cowles, David Jou, and their Cambridge team have been both efficient and very helpful in the production of my first book.

The cover image was inspired by the work of New Zealand artist Holly Mackinven. I extend my thanks to her, to the Sanderson Gallery in Parnell (which, through its own "experiment" brought her work to my attention), and to Susan Brown for permission to use this image on the cover.

With personal thanks to friends who have seen less of me and are still friends (Adam, Alex, Alice, Andrew, Jennifer, and Olly), and to John (who does the cooking).

Preface

Some years ago, I presented a retrospective of the graph drawing (and related) experiments I had conducted since 1995 to an audience of information visualisation researchers, describing the process I went through in defining a new experimental research area and learning to run human–computer interaction experiments. This was an honest and reflective seminar in which I highlighted the mistakes I had made, the good and bad decisions, and how my knowledge of experimental design had increased and improved with every experiment. At the end of my presentation, a member of the audience asked, "So, Helen, what is the 'Black Art'? What is it that you have learned about running experiments that we should all know?"

This started me thinking about how much expertise is embodied in experience and seldom communicated apart from in a master/apprentice model. PhD supervisors can advise students on how to formulate and conduct experiments, psychology and HCI research texts can be read, and other experiments in the research literature can be copied, but the actual step-by-step process of designing and running an experiment is rarely written down and communicated widely. Although I believe that one can never understand the process of conducting experiments without experiencing the process oneself, I also believe that experiences can (and should) be shared and that advice resulting from others' experiences can always be useful.

This, therefore, is my "Black Art" book. Based on my own experimental experiences, it aims to introduce researchers to the process of defining and running formal human–computer interaction experiments. It is a practical book, taking the reader through the entire process from the initial research idea, through experimental design and procedure and data analysis, and, finally, to reporting.

The material in this book is based on my own experiences, rather than on any textbook material (apart from a few basic common concepts) or other research available in the literature. It is therefore unique in that all examples are primary sources: I was personally involved in some way in all 21 of the experiments described here. Taking this approach allowed me to discuss the challenges and complexities of putting together these experiments, including the successes, mistakes, and failures. Such behind-the-scenes insight is seldom presented in secondary-source research publications. Most of these experiments have been published elsewhere, but some have not – they are included as a means of illustrating the experimental concepts and processes that I have adopted in my journey of learning how to conduct effective experiments.

As a consequence, the examples naturally relate to my own research area: information visualisation, and, in particular, the representation of relational information using graphs. However, the experimental principles illustrated by these examples are widely applicable to other HCI areas, including (but not limited to) mobile and multimodal devices, collaborative systems, games technology, and interface design.

Some advice offered here may seem trivial (e.g., clearly define a research question, ensure that there are no interruptions to the experiments, make sure that the software is robust, verify that data are being collected and stored correctly). Such seemingly trite advice is included here simply because I have suffered by NOT doing these things and then paid for it later (typically by having to throw away hard-fought-for data).

This book does not claim to be the only or final word on the topic of experimental design or statistical analysis – indeed, there are several other fine books in this area, most notably, Field and Hole's *How to Design and Report Experiments* (2003), Cairns and Cox's *Research Methods for Human–Computer Interaction* (2008), and Hinton's *Statistics Explained: A Guide for Social Science Students* (2nd ed.) (2004). As with any endeavour, advice from a wide range of other sources is recommended.

This book aims to be useful to anyone who wants to enter the exciting world of experimentation in HCI, and, in particular, PhD students, early career researchers, and industrial research scientists. It will also be useful as a text for an advanced undergraduate or taught postgraduate course in experimental HCI.

1

Introduction

This book describes the process that takes a researcher from identifying a human–computer interaction (HCI) research idea that needs to be tested, to designing and conducting a test, and then analysing and reporting the results. This first chapter introduces the notion of an "HCI idea" and different approaches to testing.

1.1 Assessing the worth of an HCI idea

Imagine that you have an HCI idea, for example, a novel interaction method, a new way of visualising data, an innovative device for moving a cursor, or a new interactive system for building games. You can implement it, demonstrate it to a wide range of people, and even deploy it for use – but is it a "good" idea? Will the interaction method assist users with their tasks? Will the visualisation make it easier to spot data trends? Will the new device make cursor movement quicker? Will users like the new game building system?

It is your idea, so of course you believe that it is wonderful; however, your subjective judgement (or even the views of your friends in the research laboratory) is not sufficient to prove its general worth. An objective evaluation of the idea (using people not involved in the research) is required. As Zhai (2003) says in his controversial article, "Evaluation is the worst form of HCI research except all those other forms that have been tried," the true value of the idea cannot be determined simply by "subjective opinion, authority, intimidation, fashion or fad."

If your idea were, for example, a new constraint satisfaction algorithm that you believe is faster than others, you could deploy vast amounts of computing power to run computational tests on different data sets to prove your point. Unfortunately, ideas that necessarily include human activity cannot be tested

1

so easily – there is no "ISO standard human" (Lieberman, 2003) against which the idea can be tested to prove its worth for all humanity. Because we do not have robust and complete models or theories of human behaviour against which we can test the idea, the participation of other humans is needed to assist us in checking our own intuitions (Zhai, 2003).

The phrase "HCI idea" is used here very generally to mean any idea that, once implemented and used, involves interaction between humans and technology. Possible categories of HCI ideas, with examples, include the following:

1. A type of interaction device associated with new hardware:
   - stylus input, vibratory output, olfactory output.
2. A method of perception using devices that target particular senses:
   - feedback mechanisms (e.g., vibration, sound, peripheral vision);
   - visualisation of data (e.g., different types of data charts, colour coding methods).
3. A method for system interaction usually embedded within other software:
   - direction of text scrolling (e.g., horizontal, vertical, page turning);
   - navigation method (e.g., site map, tabs, hierarchy diagram).
4. An interactive system designed to support a complex task:
   - a system to manage the proposal, preference collection, and allocation of student projects;
   - a sketch-based system for drawing project management scheduling charts.

Occasionally, new HCI ideas are quickly adopted into everyday use by a large number of people, and this wide-scale adoption is sufficient proof of their worth. For example, it seems superfluous to try to prove that mobile phones are more convenient than pay phones, that Google's interface is sufficient for online search tasks, or that Facebook is a good way for people to keep in touch.

Unfortunately, most HCI researchers (and, in particular, PhD students) do not have the luxury of time to wait and see if their novel idea takes off and is adopted at large. Proving that their HCI idea is a "good" one will need to be done in the context of a test that involves other people who try out the idea.

There are two different types of HCI test: formal comparative *experiments* and exploratory usability *evaluations*.

Experiments are objective tests that aim to demonstrate that the idea produces better results than an existing idea that performs the same function. Experiments are more appropriate for ideas in categories 1–3 in the preceding list (i.e., small, specific ideas for which alternatives can readily be found and that are usually associated with well-defined tasks). The outcome of an experiment is a conclusion indicating which idea results in better user performance. As such, experiments can be considered summative, although in many cases the experience of running the experiment reveals useful improvements, and so also contributes to a formative process (Ellis and Dix, 2006).[1]

Evaluations are exploratory tests that aim to show that the idea works in practice, in the context of typical uses. Such evaluations (also called "usability studies") are more appropriate for category 4 in the preceding list (i.e., larger, more complex pieces of interactive software for which it is difficult or impossible to find alternatives that fulfil identical functions and that typically support a wide range of user tasks). The outcome of an evaluation is a list of suggestions for system improvement (as part of a formative test), or it can be confirmation that the system performs its function sufficiently well for it to be deployed.

1.2 Experiments: Assessing worth by comparison

It is not uncommon for papers to be written that report that an idea is "good" because, for example, experimental participants reached a "high" level of performance. An experiment that investigated the parameters that could be used for representing information in vibrotactile devices (Brown, Brewster, and Purchase, 2005) reported an overall 71% recognition rate, with tactile "rhythms" being correctly identified more than 90% of the time and tactile "roughness" identified 80% of the time. Although these are impressive and interesting results, they do not tell us whether presenting information in a tactile manner is better or worse than any other medium, or whether the 80% recognition rate of roughness is sufficient for practical use – it may be the case that this rate is actually too low to be useful. In experiments like these, unless you get a result of 100%, it is difficult to make definite claims about the worth of the idea.

HCI experiments are therefore typically about comparison. They aim to prove that one HCI research idea is better than another that fulfils the same function. Note that it may be the case that neither (or both) of the ideas may be the experimenter's own, and neither (or both) may be new. What is key is the idea of comparing the "goodness" of one idea with another by measuring their relative performance.

This is not to say that experiments should be entirely focussed on a single conclusion; indeed, the value of running an experiment often arises from the process of conducting it – defining its rationale and motivation, deciding between the appropriateness of different experimental methods and activities, and investigating the different types of data collected.

---

[1] Summative tests are those whose only aim is to produce a conclusion; formative tests are those whose intention is to make recommendations for improvement.

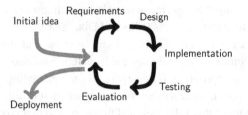

Figure 1.1: Iterative system development cycle.

In some cases, tests that do not entail comparison are the only type that can be run, simply because the technology used is so advanced that there are no viable alternatives, the HCI idea is extremely revolutionary, or the alternatives are so different that any comparison would be meaningless (e.g., comparing speech recognition technology with keyboard typing). In such cases, proving the worth of the idea may rather be done through descriptions of the design rationale, existence proofs, detailed scenarios of use or case studies, or participatory critique (Greenberg and Buxton, 2008).

An experiment is here defined in terms of comparison: a test that pits one or more alternatives against each other.

1.3 Evaluations: Assessing worth by use

Evaluations typically focus on determining the usability of a new interactive system. "Usability" is defined by the International Organization for Standardization (ISO) standard for the "ergonomics of human system interaction" (ISO 9241-11:1998; ISO 1998) as the "Extent to which a product can be used by specified users to achieve specified goals with *effectiveness*, *efficiency* and *satisfaction* in a specified context of use" (my emphasis: p 2). Evaluations entail potential users using the system, and the recording of their activities and comments.

Evaluations are an important stage of the iterative system development cycle (Figure 1.1). They not only produce useful feedback and suggestions for improvement that feed into the next requirements and design stages, but they are also crucial in determining when sufficient iterations have been completed and the system is ready to be deployed. In some cases, the system is deployed after testing as part of an external evaluation process; in this case, beta versions of software are released for a limited period of time so as to obtain feedback from a more extensive set of external potential users.

It is not usual for evaluations to be comparative as they tend to focus on one system and the experience of its potential users, their purpose being to provide feedback to improve a system within a development cycle. Often, they may not be considered "research" and may not be publishable in the serious research literature. However, evaluations are often part of a larger research project where once the system has been shown to be ready for deployment, it may subsequently be used in an experiment to demonstrate its worth in comparison against its competitors – this is more likely to be considered a research activity.

1.4 Focus of this book

It is tempting to associate other common terms with experiments and evaluations as a way of distinguishing them: experiments are sometimes considered "formal," producing "quantitative," "objective" results, and evaluations are "informal," producing "qualitative," "subjective" results.

Using these terms in this way can be misleading because evaluations can be formal and produce quantitative and objective results, whereas experiments may collect subjective data (although experiments are unlikely to be "informal"). The key distinguishing features of these two types of HCI test are as follows:

- Experiments are comparative and focus on producing data to demonstrate the worth of an HCI idea;
- Evaluations are not comparative and focus on producing feedback to either improve a system or confirm its readiness for deployment.

This book considers both experiment and evaluation tests as it follows the process from designing the test, conducting it, and collecting and analysing the data, to reporting the results.

Getting the design of an experiment right the first time is more important than doing so for an evaluation. An evaluation is a stage within the iterative development cycle, and its outcome (the feedback on system usability) feeds into the next design stage. This feedback helps designers in making design choices within given constraints. During the development of the system, several evaluations may be performed, perhaps with only a few potential users[2] and tasks in the first iteration (when it is likely that substantial changes will be suggested), an increased number in the second, and a much larger group when

---

[2] We distinguish here between "participants" (who take part in experiments) and "potential users" (who take part in evaluations).

the development team believes that the system is nearly ready for deployment, and only needs tweaking. Even if the design of an evaluation is flawed (e.g., by forgetting to ask potential users to use a particular contentious interface feature or to comment on a novel data entry method), useful feedback will still undoubtedly be produced from this evaluation, and the next round of evaluations can correct the previous flaws.

In contrast, an experiment is a one-off activity. It requires the cooperation of a large number of participants, all following the same experimental process. Once it has started, it cannot be interrupted to correct any flaws in its design – not unless the whole experiment is to be redesigned and run again. It is therefore important that an experiment be very carefully designed because errors can cost a great deal of time and effort.

The primary focus of this book is therefore on experiments because their design is more complex and more risky than evaluations. In addition, good experimental design requires knowledge and skills typically not taught in a computer science or software engineering curriculum in the same way that usability evaluation is often covered as part of the iterative design cycle. All chapters in the book, however, conclude with a relevant section on evaluations.

1.5 Structure of this book

The chapters of this book follow the process of designing, conducting, analysing, and reporting experiments and evaluations, with the focus on experiments. The book is intended to be read from start to finish (perhaps with the exception of Chapter 5 on statistics), and preferably prior to designing an experiment, rather than used only as a reference book. Throughout the book, details are given of example experiments: most of these have been conducted by the author, and so provide a personal insight into the actual processes that led to their design and implementation – such insight is not typically available from secondary source published papers.

Chapter 2 highlights the importance of defining a clear research question. It describes the process of designing the experiment and includes a discussion on the generalisability of the results (in particular, with reference to the choice of experimental objects and tasks).

Chapter 3 describes the practicalities of conducting the experiment, based around a discussion of the participant experience. It includes hints on recruiting and managing participants, conducting pilot tests, adhering to ethical requirements, and performing pre- and postexperiment activities.

Chapter 4 deals with the collection of data, describing the range of different data types that can be collected, and focuses on methods for collecting and analysing qualitative data.

Chapter 5 addresses the analysis of quantitative data and presents a selection of statistical tests useful for analysing data produced by comparative experiments.

Chapter 6 gives advice on how best to report the results of the experiment for publication, proposing an appropriate structure for the report and accounting for the limits of the generalisability of the results. It also includes common reviewers' comments.

Chapter 7 discusses possible problems and pitfalls in running HCI experiments, and how to address them.

Chapter 8 concludes the book by presenting "six key principles" for conducting HCI experiments, as well as a model of HCI experimentation.

2
Defining the research

The first step in running an experiment is defining what you want to discover and how you will do so. This chapter presents an approach to experiments that begins by first defining a research question, and then basing the definition of the conditions, experimental objects, and tasks on that question. These elements will ultimately define the form of the experiment.

Several key concepts used throughout the book are introduced and defined in this chapter:

- *The research question:* a clear question that succinctly states the aim of the research;
- *Conditions:* the ideas of interest – these will be compared against each other;
- *The independent variable:* the set of conditions to be used in the experiment – there will always be more than one condition;
- *The population:* all the people who might use the idea; *the sample:* the set of people who will take part in the experiment;
- *Generalisability:* the extent to which experimental results can apply to situations not explicitly included in the experiment itself;
- *Experimental objects:* the way in which the ideas are presented to the participants – experimental objects embody the conditions so that they can be perceived;
- *Experimental stimulus:* the combination of an experimental object and a condition;
- *Experimental tasks:* what the participants will actually do with the experimental objects;
- *Experimental trial:* the combination of a condition, an experimental object, and a task.

2.1 The research question

Experiments are often run within the context of wider research projects.[1] Although these projects may have broad aims, for example, "Investigating the use of head-mounted eye gaze equipment" (as in San Augustin et al., 2009) or "Designing alternative methods for menu design," it is important that each individual experiment be clearly defined by a research question – with a clear "?" at the end. Defining a clear research question upfront is crucial to focussing the study, and it is the first step to ensuring that your experiment is designed to discover what you actually want to find out! A useful side effect of expressing your experiment aim as a clearly defined question is that it makes it much easier to explain your research interests to outsiders.

Examples of inappropriately phrased research questions are as follows:

- "To investigate the use of a visual mouse in a text reading task";
- "Asking people to draw graphs using a visual mouse and seeing if they like it";
- "Seeing if the visual mouse works."

These could be better stated as follows:

- "Is reading a piece of text using a visual mouse more efficient than when using a physical mouse?"
- "Do users prefer a visual mouse to a physical mouse when drawing graphs?"
- "How accurate is the use of a visual mouse when performing fine-grained interaction tasks?"

You can see that the latter three examples, expressed as questions, are much more focussed and include details (e.g., "more efficient," "drawing graphs") that will become important features of the experimental design.

Some researchers, especially those with a psychology background, prefer to express their experiment aims in terms of a null hypothesis statement that they will ultimately try to reject as being false (e.g., "There will be no efficiency difference when reading a piece of text between a visual mouse and a physical mouse"). Although this is a valid approach, I find that starting off with a clear, focussed research question is a better (and often less confusing) starting point.

---

[1] Ideally, of course, the experiment or evaluation should be conducted by someone (or a team) who has not been associated with developing the HCI idea, although this is seldom the case for academic research projects. Lieberman (2003) points out that it would be unthinkable for a new medical technique to be evaluated by the person who developed it.

Thus, before commencing the design phase of an HCI experiment, you need two things:

- A clearly defined HCI research idea – this may be a technique, method, technology, system, etc.;
- A clear research question that defines how the worth of this idea will be investigated.

2.2 Conditions for comparison

As mentioned in Chapter 1, the key to HCI experiments is the notion of comparison: we compare the performance of one HCI idea against another. One or more alternative ideas need to be identified. Importantly, the alternatives must offer the same functionality as the idea you want to test; otherwise, a comparison is unfair (as in "comparing apples to oranges").

The different alternatives (including the idea to be tested) are called the *conditions*. In many cases, alternatives will be easy to identify, especially if the new idea was devised as an improvement to an existing system. For example, if the idea is a new touch-based interaction method for turning pages when reading text on a screen, then an obvious alternative will be the common existing method of vertical scrolling. The experimenter might also want to include horizontal scrolling as one of the conditions, even though this is not so common.

In other cases, alternatives may need to be contrived. For example, if the idea is the use of olfactory output to present information about the people and situations in a set of photographs to the visually impaired, then an alternative, more common method for presenting this information (e.g., voice recordings) may need to be devised to enable appropriate comparison.

An *independent variable* comprises a set of at least two conditions; in the previous page turning example, the independent variable is "the method of turning pages", and its three conditions are "touch", "horizontal", and "vertical". These three methods allow for all text to be accessed, and so have equivalent functionality.

The experimenter has control over the conditions that comprise the independent variable, and they must be defined in advance of the experiment. They must

- be clearly defined;
- permit equivalent functionality.

Looking forward to the nature of our results (and it is always a good idea to look forward to the required form of the results at the end of the experiment), what

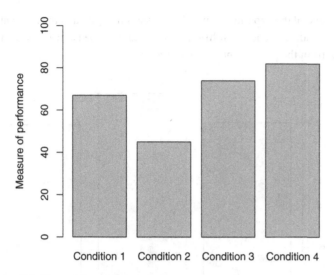

Figure 2.1: Form of the results required.

the experimenter is ultimately looking for is a bar chart similar to the one in Figure 2.1, where each condition is associated with summary data representing its performance.

Example 1: Orthogonal Corners Experiment

Research question: "Which shape of corners in orthogonal graph drawings is best for reading graph structure?" (Hoggan and Purchase, 2005)

For this experiment, Eve Hoggan defined three **conditions** (90-degree bends, Quadratic curves, and Smoothed bends) – each of which can be applied to the corners of a graph that has been drawn to emphasise the principle of "orthogonality" (i.e., fixing nodes and edges to an invisible grid). Applying each condition produces a slightly different graph, as shown in Figure 2.2. The experiment asked users to answer shortest path tasks on graphs drawn with all three types of corners.

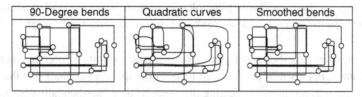

Figure 2.2: Three conditions for the Orthogonal Corners experiment.

At the end of the experiment, we obtained summary data of the mean number of errors made for each **condition** – this was the measure of performance obtained from the participants (Figure 2.3).

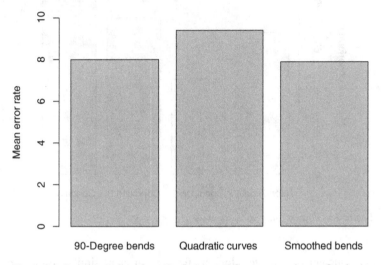

Figure 2.3: Results obtained from the Orthogonal Corners experiment. Quadratic curves produced significantly more errors than either 90-degree or Smooth bends.

Example 2: Web Page Aesthetics Experiment

Research question: "Does the visual layout of objects on a Web page affect participants' judgement of 'aesthetic'?" (Purchase et al., 2011)

In this case, Oran Ryan and Adrian Jamieson chose fifteen existing web pages as the **conditions** – they were carefully chosen so that each used a different layout of objects on the page. Each conformed to a quantitative measurement of a layout principle to a different extent (as defined by existing formulae) (Ngo, Teo, and Byrne, 2003). Example principles were Balance, Symmetry, Simplicity, and Proportion. The web pages were categorised according to four differing extents of the layout principles: minimum, low, high, and maximum.

Participants were asked to rank the pages in order of "aesthetically pleasing."

In the examples shown in Figure 2.4, each page exhibits a different amount of Balance. For each of the fourteen layout principles, a bar chart like that in Figure 2.5 was produced, indicating the mean relative "aesthetically pleasing" rankings given by the participants.

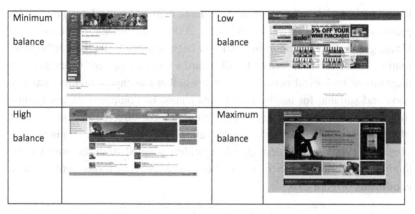

Figure 2.4: Four of the conditions used in the Web Page Aesthetics experiment, each with a different amount of visual Balance.

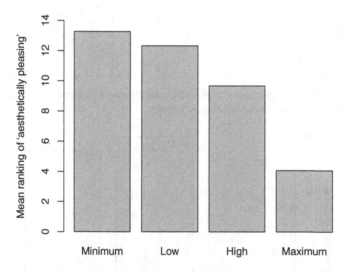

Figure 2.5: Summary results for "aesthetically pleasing" rankings for a set of web pages with different amounts of aesthetic Balance (a rank of 1 indicates the most aesthetic web site).

Example 3: Metabolic Pathways Experiment

Research question: "Which of three different layout algorithms best supports the interpretation of metabolic pathways?" (Bourqui, Purchase, and Jourdan, 2011)

Romain Bourqui developed a new algorithmic method for displaying metabolic pathways called MetaViz (Bourqui et al., 2006). This method was based on a planar graph drawing algorithm and had been adapted to include orthogonal routing on the external face of the diagram, a feature inspired by hand-drawn diagrams of biological networks. To test whether this layout method was any good and suitable for use by bioinformaticians, he compared its use against two other common popular layout algorithms: a force-directed algorithm, GEM (the Generalized Expectation-Maximization algorithm, Frick, Ludwig, and Mehldau, 1994), and a hierarchical algorithm adapted from the well-known Sugiyama algorithm (Auber, 2003). These three layout methods were his three **conditions** (Figure 2.6).

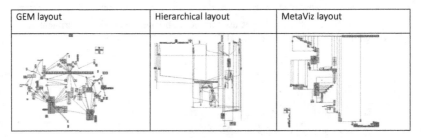

Figure 2.6: Three conditions in the Metabolic Pathways experiment: all three drawings represent the same metabolic pathway.

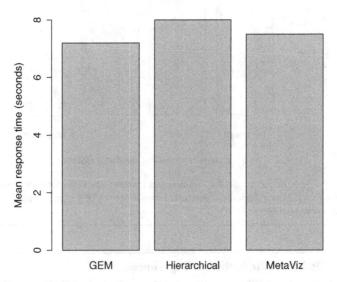

Figure 2.7: Summary results of response time for the Metabolic Pathways experiment.

This experiment revealed that the GEM and MetaViz layouts produced comparably good response time performance (i.e., the length of time participants took to perform tasks using these layouts), whereas the Hierarchical layout had the worst performance (Figure 2.7).

2.3 Designing experiments

Similar to other forms of design, experimental design is about making decisions. There are many choices to be made, and all alternatives should be considered. The concept of design space is useful here – a design space is an imaginary representation of the design options possible in a multidimensional space. Design is the process of analysing that multidimensional space to identify the best set of options, while taking into account constraints and the experimental aims.

However, it is important to note that *no experiment can be perfect*. The aim of the experiment is to investigate whether the values of the different conditions (the independent variable) have an effect on performance, satisfaction, enjoyment, usability, or anything that we can observe and record. The ideal experiment would ensure that only the independent variable is ever varied and that everything else in the experimental environment stays exactly the same. This is impossible – we cannot eliminate all extraneous factors that might affect the data collected.

For instance, in the Orthogonal Corners experiment (Example 1, p 11), the experiment was conducted in different locations on different computers at different times of the day; in the Web Page Aesthetics experiment (Example 2, p 12), the web pages contained different information content, which may have biased the participants' judgement of "aesthetics."

Experiments may be interrupted, software may crash, the sun might be shining on one day and not the next (affecting the perception of colours on a screen), participants might be in a bad mood (and not willing to give their best performance), and/or some might have useful background knowledge not possessed by others.

Extraneous factors such as these that might affect the reliability of the data are called *confounding factors*: some will be easy to identify (e.g., a computer that works slower than expected for some participants, the different content in Web page stimuli), and some will not (e.g., prior knowledge of each participant, whether a participant is tired or motivated that day).

Those aspects of the experimental environment that the experimenter *can* keep the same throughout the experiment are called *experimental controls*. For instance, in the Orthogonal Corners experiment, the same graph was used to present each type of corner, and the same experimental software was used to present each graph drawing; in the Web Page Aesthetics experiment, the web pages were printed at the same resolution on a single page from the same printer.

In designing the experiment, possible confounding factors should be taken into account as much as possible, but compromises will always have to be made. What is most important is to recognise when compromises have been made, and what effect they will have on the interpretation of the results. It is also important to acknowledge these compromises and limitations when writing up the results.

Thus, different factors of the experiment are

- deliberately varied (the independent variable);
- deliberately kept the same (the experimental controls); or
- accidentally varied (the confounding factors).

Experimental design decisions that we have considered so far are as follows:

- What is the research question? What is the key issue about this HCI idea that needs to be shown to be worthwhile?
- What are the alternatives? What can we compare this HCI idea against?

The rest of this chapter deals with other design decisions that need to be made:

- What objects should be used to embody the HCI idea and its alternatives?
- What will our participants do?
- What application domain or information content should be used to represent the HCI idea?

2.4 Generalisability

There will be a set of people who will ultimately be expected to make use of the HCI idea that is being tested – the *population*. The definition of the population may be broad (e.g., all people, present and future, who are expected to use a mobile phone), or limited (e.g., all people who will make use of aids for the visually impaired in the stadium during the men's 100-metre final at the next Olympics).

Very few HCI ideas have such a limited definition of the population that all its members can take part in the experiments. Experiments typically use a set of experimental participants (the *sample*), collect responses to the idea from these participants, and make *generalisations* from these responses (i.e., speculate about how the wider population would respond).

At one extreme, a sample of just one person will produce results that cannot reasonably be generalised to the population; at the other extreme, a large sample that includes all members of the population is complete, and does not need to be generalised. The larger and the more diverse the sample of people used, the more likely it is that the generalisation will be valid.

We can aggregate the individual results obtained by each participant in the sample to produce summary performance measures (e.g., the mean response time over all participants for a condition or the total number of errors). By doing this, we can speculate about what results would be obtained if the whole population had taken part. Statistical methods (see Chapter 5) can determine the probability of the sample results having been simply produced by chance, rather than as a consequence of the differing values of the independent variable.

However, it is useful to consider other relevant generalisations, in particular, what the participants are asked to do (the *experimental tasks*) and the means by which the abstract idea is instantiated in a concrete form (the *experimental objects*).

If we ask our participants to perform only one task using the new HCI idea, then the results can only be representative of performance with that one task. And, as with the previous sample/population difference, it is typically impossible to ask the participants to perform every possible task (apart from when testing very limited systems or ideas).

If we only use one instantiation of the HCI idea, then the results can only be representative of performance with that one instantiation. As before, it is typically impossible to ask the participants to use every possible instantiation of the idea. (This concept of *experimental objects* as different instantiations of an idea is explored in more detail in Section 2.5.)

For instance, in the Metabolic Pathways experiment (Example 3, p 13), it would have been impossible to use all existing metabolic pathways, neither could we ask our participants to perform all possible interpretation tasks. We therefore chose three representative metabolic pathways as our experimental objects and three variations of a motif-matching task as our tasks.

Just as we have a population of people (from which we select a sample), we also therefore have a population of possible tasks (from which we select a sample) and a population of experimental objects (from which we also select a sample). In the same way that we aggregate results over people (to generalise to the human population), we can also aggregate results over sample tasks and sample experimental objects to generalise the results to apply to more than one type of task and more than one type of experimental object. We can therefore speculate as to what results would have been obtained if a wider range of tasks or experimental objects had been used.

The more general the experiment, the more readily the results can be extrapolated outside the boundaries of the specific experiment. There needs to be, however, a balancing act between making the experiment as generalisable as possible, and ensuring that is it still focussed enough to be practical and to address the specific research question of interest.

2.5 Experimental objects

The HCI idea that is being tested, as well as the alternative conditions, need to be embodied in a perceivable experimental object: this is the way in which the idea is presented to the participants in a concrete manner, rather than as an abstract idea.

For example, if a new method for selecting objects on a screen is to be tested, then some items would need to be displayed on the screen for the participant to experience how this new method would work. If the experiment is testing a new interface for a program for managing personal finances, then some financial information (real or imaginary) would need to be loaded in the system for the users to be able to use the new interface. If a handheld mobile device is to be tested to determine whether it can be used effectively for navigation, then information about a given geographic area would need to be stored in the device. If a new horizontal scrolling method is to be tested, then some text needs to be used so that it can be scrolled.

Experimental objects are the concrete means by which a participant can experience the HCI idea and its alternatives. If only one experimental object is used in the experiment, then the results of the experiment will only pertain to that particular experimental object (in the preceding examples, the results will only apply to the particular set of items shown on the screen, the financial data used, the specified geographic area, or the given text) or objects of a similar nature, with comparable size, structure, and content. The conclusions we make from the results will not be generalisable to any other experimental objects.

It is a very easy objection for a reviewer of a research article to make: "The conclusions only hold for object [x], and so do not tell us anything useful about the usefulness of [the HCI idea being tested] more generally."

Because we want our results to be as generalisable as possible, we can use more than one experimental object, and this would allow us to extend our final conclusions to cover a wider range of object sizes, structures, or content. So we can use displays of, for example, three, five, and seven items to demonstrate the new screen selection method, five different sets of financial records, four different maps of surrounding areas, and a selection of six short stories.

Just like performance data are aggregated over the sample participants so as to permit generalisation to a larger population, so data can be aggregated over the experimental objects to allow for wider inferences to be made about the population of objects.

Example 4: Graph Algorithms Experiment
 Research question: "Which graph layout algorithm is best for interpreting graph structure?" (Purchase, 1998)

In this experiment, we aimed to determine which of the eight algorithms provided in the GraphEd system (Himsolt, 1994) produced graph drawings that are easiest to read. In this case, it was not that we wanted to test one particular new idea but simply that we wanted to compare several existing ideas. The eight algorithms were our **conditions**; we created eight different graph drawings of the same graph, one from each algorithm (Figure 2.8).

We asked our participants to perform some graph-theoretic tasks using each of the eight graph drawings, and aggregated the performance of all participants (Figure 2.9). As only one graph was used, there was only one **experimental object** in this experiment.

This experiment was limited in that only one graph was used: there was only one **experimental object**. The results are therefore only applicable to this one graph, or graphs of similar size and structure. Although we obviously could not have run the experiment using all graphs of all different sizes, using more than one graph would have made the results more generalisable. Figure 2.10 shows a suggestion for a more appropriate set of experimental objects for an experiment with a similar research question. It uses four different graphs of not-too-dissimilar sizes (all having between 20 and 25 nodes and between 40 and 50 edges), but with different structures. Each graph has been drawn under three algorithm **conditions** (hierarchical, orthogonal, and spring), as implemented in the yEd system (yWorks, 2012). This gives twelve drawings, with four drawings per condition.

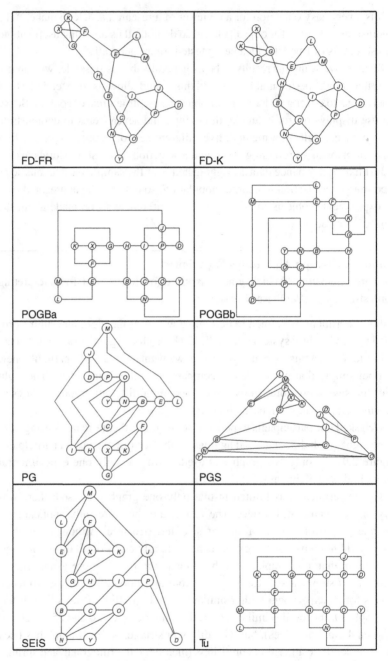

Figure 2.8: Experimental object represented using eight different layout algorithms, used in the Graph Algorithms experiment.

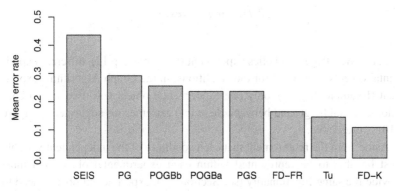

Figure 2.9: Performance comparison for the eight conditions.

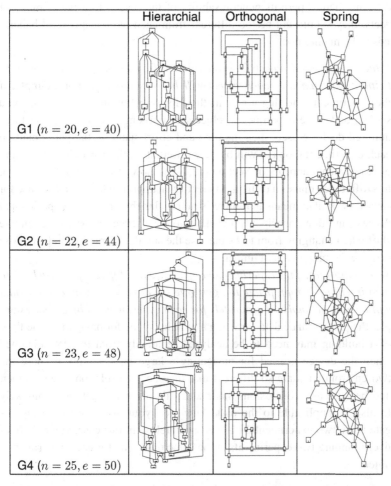

Figure 2.10: Better set of drawings for an experiment to determine which layout algorithm produces better performance, using four experimental objects. This set will allow for better generalisation of the results than in the Graph Algorithms experiment.

In the Web Page Aesthetics experiment (Example 2, p 12), different experimental objects were used for the conditions; in the Graph Algorithms experiment (Example 4, p 19), only one experimental object was used for all conditions. A middle ground between these two extremes (as suggested in Figure 2.10) is preferable.

Aside from the requirement that each condition of the independent variable must be able to be represented within each experimental object and must provide the same functionality (see Section 2.2), experimental objects need to be chosen carefully. Although it is true that having experimental objects of a differing nature permits generalisability of the results to a wider range of objects, they should not be too different from each other – a careful balance needs to be maintained:

- *If the experimental objects are too different from each other, then the participant experience of each object will be very different.* For example, if the experiment is testing a new method for selecting highlighted dots on a screen, and three experimental objects comprising five, twenty, and three hundred dots are used, then the time and effort spent by the participant on each experimental object will be very different. A discussion on the timing of experiments appears in Section 3.2.1. For now, it is enough to note that this difference makes it difficult to identify an appropriate time allowance for each task. It also means that there is no regular rhythm to the experimental process and that participants are likely to experience an extreme cognitive shift when changing from tasks that use the smaller number of dots to those that use the much larger number.
- *More important, if the experimental objects are too different from each other, then it will be inappropriate to aggregate the data over them, and the data will need to be analysed separately for each experimental object.* For example, the performance data for using a mobile device for navigating one floor of a building may need to be analysed separately from the data obtained when the device is used for navigating a large park, simply because the two environments are so different that they bear no relation to each other, and because any conclusions made about the floor navigation are unlikely to also be applicable to the park. However, your aim may be to investigate these two experimental objects separately – in this case, you are effectively running two experiments at the same time: one for each experimental object.

It is therefore a careful balancing act: choosing a set of experimental objects so that the results are not constrained, while ensuring a practical experimental process that does not inappropriately aggregate data from widely different user experiences.

In this vein, we can look back to the generalisability that is gained by using a varied sample of the population in the same way: if the sample of experimental participants is too diverse, then overall results may not be useful, and analysing the data separately according to participant demographics (e.g., age, ethnicity, prior experience) may be more appropriate (see Section 5.5.3).

Usually, each experimental object will be used several times, at least once for each condition. The combination of an experimental object with a condition is called a *stimulus*.

In the Metabolic Pathways experiment (**Example 3**, p 13), Bourqui used three different genuses of a bacterium called *Buchnera* as his **experimental objects**: *Buchnera APS*, *Buchnera aphidicola BP*, and *Buchnera aphidicola SG*. These were similar-size metabolic networks (503 nodes/526 edges, 558 nodes/538 edges, and 562 nodes/559 edges) and topologies. Using more than one metabolic pathway ensured some **generalisability** of his results to other metabolic pathways. When representing all conditions in each experimental object, he had a total of nine **stimuli** for his experiment.

Example 5: DAGMap Experiment

Research question: "How effective is the new DAGMap visualisation method in interpreting directed acyclic graphs?" (Koenig, 2007)

Pierre-Yves Koenig devised a new information visualisation method called DAGMap, which represented directed acyclic graphs in a similar manner to the way the TreeMap visualisation represents trees as nested rectangles (Shneiderman, 1992).

Figure 2.11 shows two visualisations of the same information: on the left, a graph representation (NodeLink), and on the right, the equivalent DAGMap representation.

In the experiment, three **experimental objects** were used, representing international companies and their subsidiaries. Three companies of comparable size were represented: Fiat, Nestlé, and Danone. The experiment had three **conditions**: DAGMap, NodeLink, and the combination of them both (the Combination condition) (Figure 2.12).

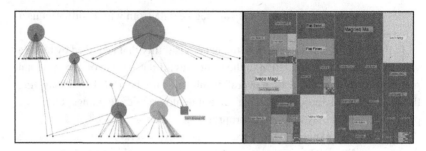

Figure 2.11: NodeLink and DAGMap representations of the same information.

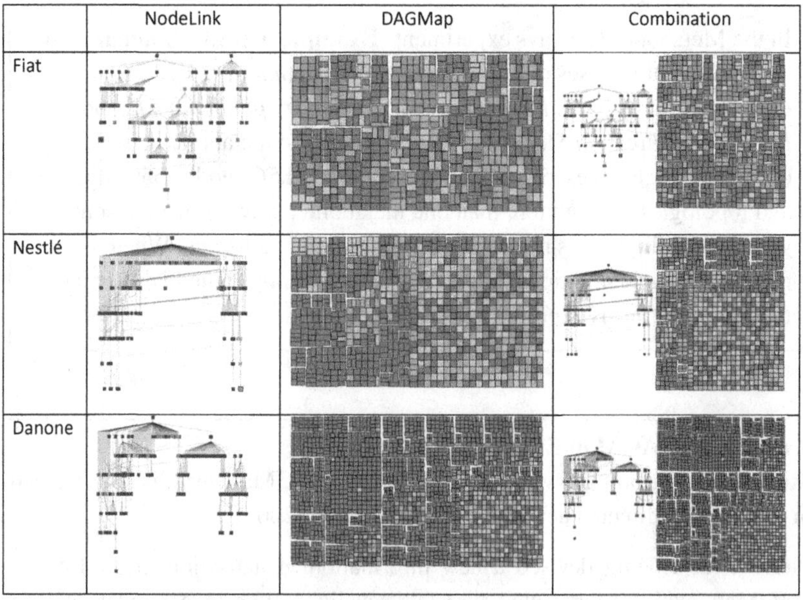

	NodeLink	DAGMap	Combination
Fiat			
Nestlé			
Danone			

Figure 2.12: Nine stimuli for the DAGMap experiment, each condition applied to each experimental object.

Example 6: Euler Diagrams Experiment

Research question: "Which well-formedness principles in the presentation of Euler diagrams, when broken, are easiest to understand?" (Rodgers, Zhang, and Purchase, 2011)

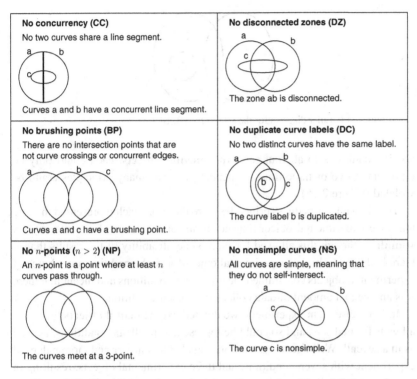

No concurrency (CC)	No disconnected zones (DZ)
No two curves share a line segment.	
Curves a and b have a concurrent line segment.	The zone ab is disconnected.
No brushing points (BP)	No duplicate curve labels (DC)
There are no intersection points that are not curve crossings or concurrent edges.	No two distinct curves have the same label.
Curves a and c have a brushing point.	The curve label b is duplicated.
No *n*-points ($n > 2$) (NP)	No nonsimple curves (NS)
An *n*-point is a point where at least *n* curves pass through.	All curves are simple, meaning that they do not self-intersect.
The curves meet at a 3-point.	The curve c is nonsimple.

Figure 2.13: Six well-formedness principles with examples of their violation used in the Euler Diagrams experiment.

Peter Rodgers investigated the use of different well-formedness principles in the use of Euler diagrams. These diagrams use closed curves to represent sets of items and their intersections. Assumptions are typically made about how Euler diagrams should best be presented, and there are several "well-formedness" principles that are considered most beneficial for understanding information about how sets of items relate to each other; these are best illustrated by showing their violation (Figure 2.13). These well-formedness principles were the **conditions** for the experiment.

In this experiment, the **experimental objects** were fourteen abstract descriptions of sets, each of which could be drawn using a Euler diagram; for example, the set [A, B, AB, BC] requires that four distinct zones (and only these zones) be represented, as in Figure 2.14.

None of the fourteen sets used in this experiment could be drawn without violating at least one of the principles, and none of them could be drawn while violating all six of the principles. It was therefore impossible to apply

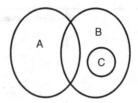

Figure 2.14: Euler diagram for the set [A, B, AB, BC].

all six conditions to all fourteen **experimental objects**: each could only be represented two or three times, depending on how many principles could be violated (Figure 2.15).

The six well-formedness principles were therefore each represented in more than one experimental object (but not in all of them), resulting in thirty-six **stimuli**. Although this allowed for more generalisability of the results than if there had been only one experimental object for each condition, our choice of experimental objects constrained the use of our conditions and meant that there was an unequal amount of data collected for each condition.

In our subsequent experiment, we defined **experimental objects** that were all well-formed sets, and so could be represented in all six conditions, as well as in a seventh Well Formed condition. This led to a neater and more balanced experiment with seven conditions and three experimental objects, resulting in twenty one **stimuli**.

Experimental object	Option 1	Option 2	Option 3
[A B AC BC]	Brushing point, nonsimple curve	Concurrency	Duplicated curve label
[A B AB AC BC ABC]	n-point	Disconnected zone	(No other options possible)

Figure 2.15: Two of the experimental objects, with their alternative represent-ations.

In most cases, experimental objects are clearly defined in advance of the experiment, and the conditions are applied to them in turn to produce the stim-uli. An interesting variation on this approach can be used when experimental software is used to present the stimuli. In this case, new experimental objects can be randomly generated during the experiment itself by changing the values of parameters. These parameters are chosen to ensure that the different conditions are represented in the experimental objects and that a wide variety of experimental objects are used. The advantage of generating objects randomly is that any biases or errors that might unintentionally be introduced in manual creation of objects can be avoided.

For example, if the experiment aims to determine whether different colours are naturally associated with different shapes (perhaps to test synaesthesia responses), then the experimental objects (polygons of varying size in different colours) can be generated randomly during the experiment. In this case, it is important that whenever a new object is created, the parameters that define the experimental object are carefully stored together with the participant's response because they will be needed for the data analysis later.

Example 7: Shortest Path Experiment
Research question: "What effect do path length and bendiness, number of edge crossings and branches, and angle of edge incidence have on performance of shortest path tasks?" (Ware et al., 2002)

Colin Ware created software that could generate random forty-two–node graphs for the **experimental objects**. The program took as input a desired path length (3, 4, or 5), and produced a graph structure and identifiers for two nodes: the graph was created such that it has a unique path of the desired length between the two nodes, and a random number of edges associated with each node (between 1 and 5).

The graph was then depicted (using a spring algorithm), ensuring that the conditions of interest were varied: the number of edge crossings over the shortest path, their incident angle, the bendiness of the path (angular deviation from a straight line), and the number of branches from intermediate nodes. In this way, a new **stimulus** was created for each trial (a trial is a combination of a stimulus and a task; see Section 2.7 for more detail on trials), and **experimental objects** were never used more than once.

This method of testing the effect of these conditions was better than the alternative approach of drawing several graphs in advance, each with a specified number of edge crossings, incident angles, etc. (the Graph Aesthetics experiment, Example 11, p 37). The variety and random nature of the experimental objects used made the results much more generalisable. Figure 2.16 shows two examples of drawings used in this experiment, with the nodes highlighted.

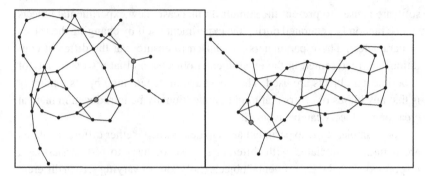

Figure 2.16: Two randomly generated stimuli used in the Shortest Path experiment. The left-hand one has a shortest path of 3 between the highlighted nodes; the shortest path on the right is 4.

2.6 Experimental tasks

The next step in the experimental design is to define what the participants will be asked to do with the stimuli.

The participants must do something for us to be able to collect data: they must perform a *task*. What they will be asked to do will depend on the type of HCI idea that is being tested and the research question. If, for example, different methods for on-screen page turning are being studied, then the participant will need to do something that requires pages to be turned. If the experiment is trying to identify which screen font allows for easier understanding of text, then the participants will need to look at text and demonstrate the extent to which they have understood it. If a new mobile device for searching the Internet is being tested, then the participants will have to access specified web pages. If the experiment is investigating different programming styles, the participants will be required to write a program (perhaps based on a given specification). In all experiments, participants need to be asked to perform specific, well-defined tasks.

The definition of the experimental tasks is often one of the most difficult aspects of experimental design, especially if a cognitive activity (e.g., analysis of a scenario, comprehension of a diagram) is involved. Tasks for more physical activities are easier: participants can be asked to select objects on a screen using a cursor, or wave a remote control device in the correct manner so as to turn on-screen pages. If we are interested in cognitive activities, then the tasks are more difficult to define. It is important to remember that we cannot ever measure what is actually going on in a participant's mind, we can only measure observable behaviour; therefore, we need to choose tasks that will produce behaviours that appropriately relate to the cognitive activity in which we are interested.

Experimental tasks need to satisfy a wide set of requirements. They must

- require the participant to use the experimental stimuli (i.e., if any participant can complete the task correctly, based simply on their prior knowledge, then the experiment will be pointless);
- require the participant to use all aspects of the stimuli that are being tested, not just part of them (i.e., if the answer can be obtained by using only some aspects of a stimulus, then conclusions cannot be made about it as a whole);
- be answerable using all conditions (otherwise, some conditions will be naturally favoured over the others);
- allow for a range of answers to be possible using the different experimental objects (i.e., if all answers are the same for all experimental objects, the participants will realise soon enough);
- ideally, relate to clearly definable cognitive activities (e.g., analysis, identification, description);
- be unambiguous and clear;
- be easy for the participant to indicate their answer: single digits or multiple-choice answers are better than anything that requires excessive typing (because the participant's typing skill will affect the speed and accuracy of answering);
- not be too hard or too easy – they should be hard enough to engage the participants, but not so hard that they give up trying.

The tasks should also be designed so as to avoid *ceiling* and *floor* effects. These occur when the tasks are so easy that participants get most of them right (Figure 2.17, left) or so difficult that they get most of them wrong (Figure 2.17, right). In this case, there is unlikely to be any variability in the data, and it will be impossible to say that the conditions have had any effect on performance.

For the same reason that we use more than one experimental object, it is a good idea to use more than one task to permit generalisability. If only one task is used, then your conclusions will hold for only that task. In some cases, performance in relation to only one task may actually be what you want; for example, if the sole function of a new eye-gaze pointer is to select an object on a screen, then the only suitable task would be of the form "Select the green object".

Because most new HCI ideas aim to support several different functions, a reasonable range of functions should be chosen as the experimental tasks – it may impossible to use them all, but a variety should be used. It is a very easy objection for a reviewer of a research article to make: "The conclusions

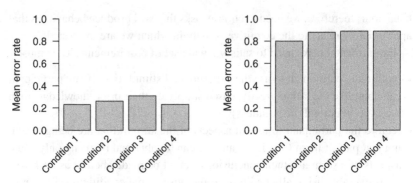

Figure 2.17: Ceiling and floor effects, showing no variation in error performance with respect to condition. On the left, the mean error rate for all conditions is very low, indicating that the tasks were very easy; on the right, the mean error rate for all conditions is very high, indicating that the tasks were rather difficult.

only hold for the task of [x], and so do not tell us anything useful about the usefulness of [the HCI idea being tested] more generally."

In the graph experiments (Example 4, p 19; Example 11, p 37) which consider the presentation of information in graph drawings (Purchase, 1997; 1998), the **tasks** were based on graph-theoretic tasks of interest to mathematicians. For example,

- How long is the shortest path between the two highlighted nodes?
- How many nodes need to be removed so that there is no path between the two highlighted nodes?
- How many edges need to be removed so that there is no path between the two highlighted nodes?

Note that in all cases, the form of the answer is simply a number. Alternative tasks, for example, "What is the shortest path between the two highlighted nodes?", would require a rather clumsy method of entering the answer because the labels for the intervening nodes on the shortest path would need to be specified.

Other **tasks** for similar experiments could include the following:

- How many nodes can the highlighted node reach using only three edges?
- How many edges are in the subgraph formed by the four highlighted nodes?

In all cases, the relevant nodes are highlighted in colour on the graph to allow for easy identification. Tasks such as "How many nodes can node 17 reach using only three edges?" would require additional visual search time while the participant scans the drawing to find the node with the label 17. This visual search time would then be included in the overall response time recorded for performing the task and would inappropriately exaggerate it.

The **tasks** used by Koenig in the DAGMap experiment (Example 5, p 23) were related to the domain of the visualisation: the structure of international companies and their subsidiaries:

- The two highlighted subsidiaries are A and B. At what level (above A and B) lies the company that has most direct control over both A and B?
- The highlighted company is A. In how many different countries (represented by different colours) are subsidiaries that are directly controlled by A?
- The highlighted company is A. What is the length of the shortest path separating it from its headquarters?

Example 8: Aural Tables Experiment

Research question: "Which is the better method of aurally depicting tabular data: sonification or speech?" (Kildal and Brewster, 2006)

Johan Kidal wanted to investigate methods for nonvisual users to explore two-dimensional tabular data. The system he developed allowed users to move a stylus over an interactive panel which represented a matrix of values. There were two experimental conditions: the system would either emit a sound (the pitch of which was related to the number under the stylus, the Sonification condition) or produce a spoken version of the number (the Speech condition).

Twenty-four different experimental objects were created, each of the same form (Table 2.1). The tables had seven columns (one for each day of the week) and twenty four rows (for each hour of the day). The numbers in the cells represented the number of times a fictional international website was accessed during the hour indicated. The **tasks** that the blindfolded participants were asked to perform were as follows:

- At which time of the day/day of the week does the web site get more/fewer visits?
- In which quadrant of the table (top-left, bottom-left, top-right, or bottom-right) are values highest/lowest?

Table 2.1: *Sample experimental object for the Aural Tables experiment*

	Mon	Tue	Wed	Thur	Fri	Sat	Sun
Midnight	68,697	70,660	71,119	71,180	71,728	68,458	70,930
1am	69,756	69,300	70,243	72,907	73,121	71,418	71,831
2am	71,966	72,264	70,900	72,872	72,958	72,186	71,940
3am	72,057	73,230	76,630	75,575	75,963	72,850	73,160
4am	73,818	74,185	73,562	76,049	74,033	73,336	75,009
5am	79,294	79,247	79,223	77,668	74,573	74,960	75,830
6am	80,757	79,494	81,236	79,310	75,880	81,014	75,603
7am	77,357	78,884	78,403	79,621	78,679	82,557	77,338
8am	81,238	83,197	83,780	79,206	82,885	83,867	81,232
...	...	...		...	...	...	...

The first **task** was a "local" task; it was very specific, requiring only a row or a column to be searched, and a precise answer given. The second **task** was more "global" because the whole table had to be scanned in both directions, and a less precise quadrant answer was expected.

Example 9: Screen Layout Experiment
Research question: "Does the layout of objects on a screen affect task performance?" (Salimun et al., 2010)

Carolyn Salimun investigated whether the positioning of objects on a screen affected participants' performance in a visual search task. Using layout aesthetic principles defined by formulae (the same as used in the Web Page Aesthetics experiment, Example 2, p 12), she presented participants with a simple visual search **task**. Her conditions were different levels of layout aesthetic principles (Figure 2.18).

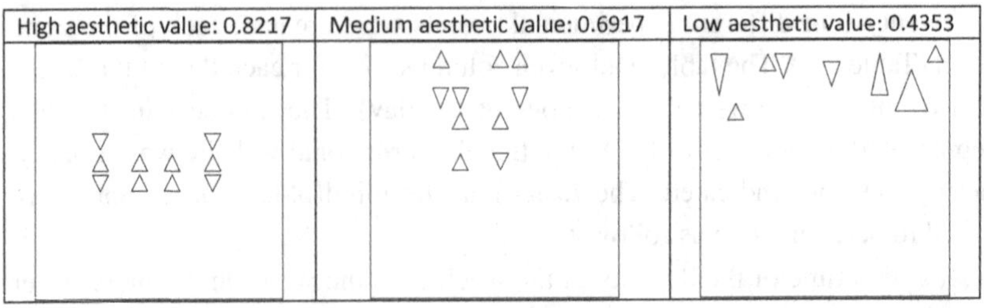

Figure 2.18: Three stimuli used for testing task performance based on layout, with high, medium, and low aesthetic values. The formulae used to calculate the values of the layout aesthetics are based on Ngo, Teo, and Byrne (2003) and range between 0 and 1, where 1 indicates a perfect instantiation of the aesthetic.

In this case, the **task** was simple: the participants had to count the number of triangles that were upright, and indicate the answer by selecting a multiple-choice option. Although interesting results were obtained showing that a higher aesthetic layout resulted in significantly improved performance, this conclusion is only specifically applicable to the **task** of identifying upright triangles.

In the Euler Diagrams experiment (Example 6, p 24), two **tasks** were presented:

- How many items are there in a given zone? (e.g., "How many items are there in zone AC?")
- Which zone contains a given number of items? (e.g., "Which zone contains five items?")

The first task requires a numeric answer, whereas the second requires a nominal answer; in both cases, on-screen multiple-choice options were provided to make it easy for participants to indicate their answers.

Sometimes it is difficult to devise tasks that ensure that the participant is using all aspects of the stimuli being tested – this is often the case when the stimuli are dynamic (i.e., are presented over time) rather than static. If the task can be performed without the participant looking at the whole stimulus, then it is not appropriate. For example, if the stimulus is a short movie and the task is to indicate whether a particular word is spoken, then participants can respond as soon as they hear the word and ignore the rest of the movie. This would be problematic if the condition that is being tested is one that affects the entire movie (e.g., the frame rate, style of the accompanying music, or shift in focus).

Example 10: Spring Dynamic Graph Experiment

Research question: "Does restricting the movement of nodes between time slices in a dynamic graph drawing assist in understanding evolving relational information?" (Purchase and Samra, 2008)

Amanjit Samra used an imaginary social network to represent changing relational information. Each time slice represented the phone calls made between a group of friends over the period of a week, and the whole graph represented 6 weeks. The layout of each time slice was based on the popular spring algorithm (Fruchterman and Reingold, 1991), and there were three conditions: "High Mental Map" (individual nodes did not move very far in the plane from one time slice to the next), "Low Mental Map" (nodes moved freely between time slices), and an interim "Medium Mental Map" condition (Figure 2.19).

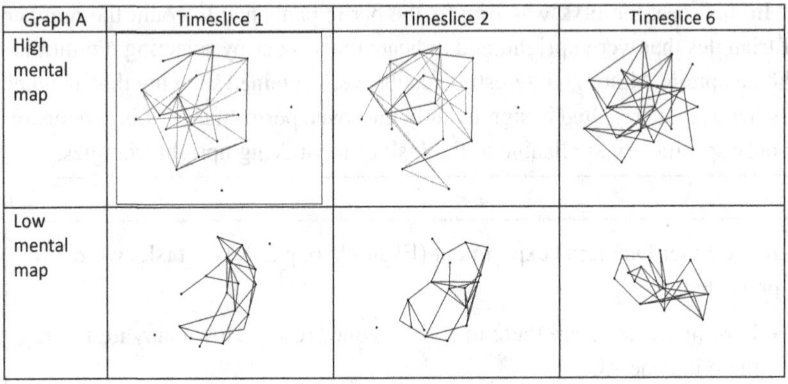

Graph A	Timeslice 1	Timeslice 2	Timeslice 6
High mental map			
Low mental map			

Figure 2.19: First two and final time slice for graph A, under High and Low Mental Map conditions.

She used the GraphAEL system for the creation of the three evolving graphs that were her experimental objects (Erten et al., 2004). The presentation of the time slices was animated, with smooth interpolation of node movement between each time slice. There were three different experimental objects: graphs A, B, and C.

There were several interesting **tasks** that initially seemed promising but could not be used in this experiment because they did not require the participant to watch the whole animation:

- Whose phone was disconnected three times?
- How many more people did Jan speak to in the second week compared to the first?
- Who called the most people in the fourth week?
- Which person was called most after the middle of the 6-week period?

In these cases, participants could have indicated a correct answer without seeing the whole **stimulus** (and therefore without experiencing the entire effect of the mental map condition).

Samra settled on the following **tasks**, all of which required that the whole animation be watched before an answer could be given:

- Who was called the least (overall) during the 6-week period?
  This was the node with the lowest overall degree over all time slices, excluding those people who were not called at all (it is easy to identify people who are never part of the network).
- Whose phone was disconnected during only 1 of the 6 weeks?
  Each experimental object was designed so that there was only one node with no connections in only one of the time slices.

- Who was called the most (overall) during the 6-week term?
  This was the node with the highest overall degree over all time slices.

These **tasks** all required participants to watch the whole animation.

Typically, the same task will be presented with the same experimental object several times, in each case with the experimental object embodying a different condition, thus providing data to determine whether the different conditions affect task performance. For example, Object1 may be represented in three conditions, giving three stimuli (Object1-C1, Object1-C2, Object1-C3), and the same task will be asked of all three stimuli.

However, if *exactly* the same task is asked, then it will always have exactly the same answer for each experimental object (regardless of condition) – and the participants will soon realise that the answer is always the same.

For example, if we are testing the three on-screen page-turning conditions of touch turning, horizontal scrolling, and vertical scrolling, then we might use four different short stories as our experimental objects, with two different tasks: who talks the most? and where does most of the action take place? If each story is presented three times, one for each condition, but the answer to the two tasks is the same in each case for each story, then as soon as the participant realises that the same task/experimental object combination has been presented, the response will be trivial, and the participant's performance will not relate to the condition.

We can therefore distinguish between *tasks* and *task variants*. A task may be presented in the same form several times, each time as a different variant that refers to different aspects of the experimental object: for example, different nodes can be highlighted for a shortest path task (the Shortest Path experiment, Example 7, p 27), different company subsidiaries can be selected for a subsidiary task (the DAGMap experiment, Example 5, p 23), or a different day of the week can be chosen for identifying visit frequency (the Aural Tables experiment, Example 8, p 31).

In addition, it may also be possible to apply a transformation to the stimulus – one that makes no difference to the use of the experimental conditions or the tasks. For example, a random 90-degree rotation could be applied to a DAGMap or a graph drawing, a Euler diagram may be rotated and flipped on an axis, or the labels associated with sets could be changed whenever the same Euler diagram is used (e.g., instead of using A, B, C, and D to represent sets in a Euler diagram experimental object, P, Q, R, and S could be used the second time it is presented). Such minor transformations will help in ensuring that the participants do not recognise repetitions of experimental objects.

2.7 Experimental trials

We have already noted that the combination of a condition and an experimental object is called a stimulus. The combination of a stimulus and a task is called a *trial*.

The DAGMap experiment (Example 5, p 23) had the following:

- Three **conditions** (NodeLink, DAGMap, Combination)
- Three **experimental objects** (Danone, Fiat, Nestlé)
- Three **tasks** (level of control, subsidiary countries, shortest path)

This experiment therefore had $3 \times 3 \times 3 = 27$ **trials**.

The Euler Diagrams experiment (Example 6, p 24) had the following:

- Six **conditions** (the six common Euler diagram well-formedness conditions)
- Fourteen **experimental objects** (different abstract descriptions of set relationships)
- Two **tasks** (identification of a zone by number of items, number of items in a zone)

In this case, not all conditions were appropriate for all experimental objects: eight objects had three conditions applied to them and six objects had two conditions applied to them. With there being two tasks, this resulted in a total of $2 \times [(8 \times 3) + (6 \times 2)] = 72$ **trials**.

The trials can be depicted as a tree structure, as shown in Figure 2.20 for the Aural Tables experiment (Example 8, p 31) and the Spring Dynamic Graph experiment (Example 10, p 33).

Performing the task should not require additional cognitive load or physical activity from the participant that is not directly related to the stimulus because it is only the performance using the stimulus that is of interest. So, for example, if the participant has to perform a visual search for two labelled objects on a screen before undertaking the experimental task itself, then the response time measured will include irrelevant search time. In this case, highlighting the objects so that they can be located quickly is preferable. The participant should be free to concentrate on the specific experimental task without having to do anything else.

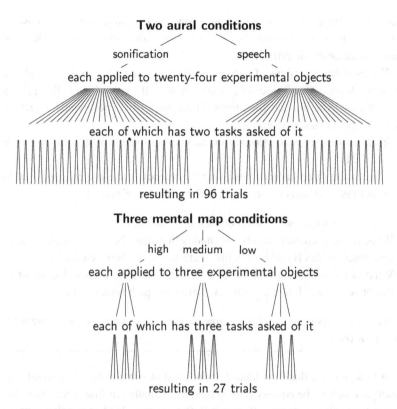

Two aural conditions

sonification   speech

each applied to twenty-four experimental objects

each of which has two tasks asked of it

resulting in 96 trials

Three mental map conditions

high   medium   low

each applied to three experimental objects

each of which has three tasks asked of it

resulting in 27 trials

Figure 2.20: Tree representations of the trials in the Aural Tables experiment and the Spring Dynamic Graph experiment with respect to conditions, experimental objects, and tasks.

Example 11: Graph Aesthetics Experiment

Research question: "Which graph drawing aesthetic is best for interpreting relational information?" (Purchase, Cohen, and James, 1995)

This experiment served as an initial pilot investigation of a new experimental area of study. Graphs can be drawn in many ways, and can conform to a lesser or greater extent to some well-established graph drawing aesthetics. In this preliminary version of the experiment, we investigated three common graph-drawing aesthetics as the conditions:

- minimising the number of edge bends;
- minimising the number of edge crossings;
- maximising the display of symmetry.

Each could have been investigated in a separate experiment, but we chose to look at the three of them together, thus allowing comparisons both within and between the aesthetic criteria.

We used three versions of each aesthetic: low, medium, and high aesthetic presence (called "few", "some", "many"); with three aesthetics, this gave a total of nine experimental conditions. There were two experimental objects: a dense graph and a sparse graph.

This resulted in nine **stimuli** for each experimental object, as shown in Figure 2.21.[2]

There were three **tasks** in this experiment; each of these were presented in different **task variants** that differed with the choice of nodes:

- How long is the shortest path between nodes J and P?
- What is the minimum number of nodes that must be removed in order to disconnect nodes B and F such that there is no path between them?
- What is the minimum number of edges that must be removed in order to disconnect nodes L and C such that there is no path between them?[3]

With two experimental objects, nine conditions, and three **tasks**, there were fifty-four **trials**.

If tasks require that item identifiers be used in stimuli, then they should, as much as possible, be equally easy to read and equally familiar, yet clearly distinguishable. This reduces differences in the cognitive load required in reading identifiers of different complexity or shape, and the additional time taken to compare two identifiers that look almost the same. It takes longer to read the name TOBIAS than it does to read TOM and longer to distinguish TIM from JIM than to distinguish JOHN from MARK, but it is easier to recognise Helen than HELEN. For instance, in the Spring Dynamic Graph experiment (Example 10, p 33), which depicted a social network, the people in the network were identified by three-letter names (to make them equally easy to read), and all

---

[2] There was a flaw in the use of aesthetic principles in defining these conditions in that it is generally assumed in the graph drawing community that a high level of symmetry will *increase* the ease of graph interpretation and a high level of edge bends or crosses will *decrease* ease of interpretation. Implicit in the design of the conditions in this experiment is that few = easy and many = difficult. This incorrect use of aesthetic definitions was corrected in the later (Purchase, 1997) version of this experiment.

[3] The tasks in this early experiment required that participants search for nodes by label, thus including irrelevant search time in the task completion time – contrary to advice given above. Later experiments corrected this flaw in the task design by highlighting the nodes relevant to the task.

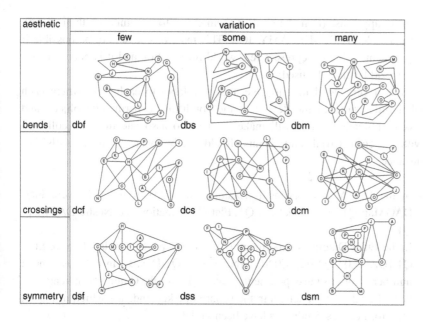

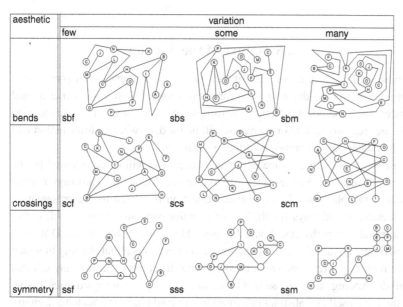

Figure 2.21: Stimuli for investigating the effect of common graph drawing aesthetics in the Graph Aesthetics experiment: the dense graph above and the sparse below.

were in uppercase (to make none of them easier to recognise by their shape): for example: TED, SUE, AMY, JOE. This may, of course, not be possible if experimental objects represent real world information and it is necessary for real world labels to be used.

It is a very good idea to give a unique label to each trial, where each label fully specifies the details of the condition, experimental object, and task combination – this will make it easier to associate the data collected with the correct trial. Participants should not be aware of these labels. For instance,

- In the DAGMap experiment (Example 5, p 23), trial labels were Fiat-DAGMap-Q1, Fiat-NodeLink-Q1, Fiat-Combination-Q1, Nestlé-DAGMap-Q1.
- In the Euler Diagrams experiment (Example 6, p 24), trial labels were E07-Q1-[DZ], E07-Q2-[C], E02-Q2-[N,B], E11-Q1-[NS,B]. In this case, the E number identifies the experimental object (1–14), the Q number indicates the task (1 or 2) and the letters in the square brackets indicate which of the six well-formedness conditions have been violated.

2.8 Nature of the domain

Before looking at the overall structure of the experiment in Chapter 3, it is appropriate to consider here the information content used in the experimental objects (i.e., the domain of the experiment). A choice needs to be made as to whether real world data or scenarios will be used, or whether information will be fabricated for the purposes of the experiment.

In some cases, the choice is obvious because it will be determined by the research question. For instance, if, like in the Metabolic Pathways experiment (Example 3, p 13) the research question is related to the presentation of metabolic pathways for the use of bioinformaticians, then it is clear that real metabolic pathways should be used. However, if, like in the DAGMap experiment (Example 5, p 23), the research question is about the way in which information is presented (regardless of what it represents), then any domain will do. Koenig chose to use real companies and their real subsidiaries, but he could have used any abstract information. He could have fabricated a scenario of the relationships between people and management in an imaginary large organisation, and this could have been used equally well to answer his research question comparing DAGMap with NodeLink representations.

Example 12: Small Multiples/Animation Experiment

Research question: "Which approach – Small Multiples or Animation – is best for reading graphs that evolve over time?" (Archambault, Purchase, and Pinaud, 2011)

To answer this question, Daniel Archambault defined two conditions for representing an evolving graph: Animation and a series of Small Multiple diagrams of each time slice (Figure 2.22). He collected data from two **real domains** for his two experimental objects, and when defining the tasks, he adapted both experimental objects to allow for tasks that were appropriate in difficulty and that applied to the whole extent of the evolving graph.

The first domain was a cell phone communication network where each node is a cell phone and an edge connects two nodes if the two phones called each other on a particular day. To make this information of appropriate size for use

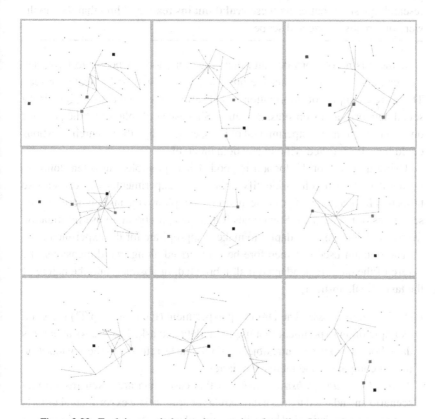

Figure 2.22: Evolving graph depicted as a series of small multiples.

in the experiment, the last 9 days of the cell phone network were used, and some nodes were randomly inserted and removed from the data set at each time slice. The other domain represented newsgroup discussions, where nodes are authors and two nodes are connected to each other if one author replied to the posting of another (Frishman and Tal, 2008) and the first nine time slices were chosen.

The tasks, however, were **not domain tasks**: they did not refer to the domain of the graphs at all. For example,

- Which node increases its degree over time?
- Which set of three nodes appear together exactly once?
- In this data set, does the number of nodes increase, decrease, remain constant, or fluctuate?

Thus, Archambault could have invented any evolving graph to address his research question, but using these **real domains** reassured him that the graphs were of a realistic size and scope.

If there is no obvious domain, then you can choose whether to have one. You can also choose whether the information used will be fabricated or real. There are examples of information visualisation experiments using imaginary social networks and web sites, as well as Shakespeare's plays and the postings on an online forum as experimental objects, even though the research questions could have been tested without any domain at all.

Using a "real world" domain is good if it is possible, but often doing so makes it more difficult to identify appropriate experimental objects, choose tasks that have a range of possible answers, and phrase the tasks in terms of the semantics of the domain. Sometimes it may be appropriate to use information from a real domain, but adapt it to make it appropriate for the experiment.

The domain used can therefore be categorised along two dimensions: the nature of the data (real, adapted real, fabricated, or abstract) and the nature of the tasks (real, abstract).

- *Real data, real tasks*. The DAGMap experiment (Example 5, p 23) is a good example of an experiment that used real data and asked real tasks about this data: both the experimental objects and the tasks referred to the organisation of real companies and their subsidiaries.
- *Adapted real data, abstract tasks*. In this case, data are taken from a real scenario and adapted to make it possible for appropriate experimental objects and tasks to be defined. The tasks do not relate in any way to the domain of the data. The advantage of this method is that the experimenter controls the

nature of both the data and the tasks, and is also sure that the structure of the data is of a realistic scope and structure. The Small Multiples/Animation experiment (Example 12, p 41) is a good example of this.

- *Fabricated data, real tasks.* In this case, a real domain is used, but the information itself is fabricated – thus, the perceivable form of the experimental objects match what might be found in the real world, but the information within these objects has been devised especially for the experiment. The tasks relate to the fabricated information depicted in the experimental objects. The advantage of this approach is that the results of the experiment can be said to apply to the domain, although with the caveat that the scope of the information embedded in the experimental objects may limit the generalisability of the results within that domain.

Example 13: Entity-Relationship Diagrams Experiment
Research question: "Which notation for the depiction of Entity-Relationship models is best for human comprehension of the structure of data?" (Purchase et al., 2004)

Two different notations were compared: the Chen notation (Chen, 1976) and SSADM (the Structured Systems Analysis and Design Method, Weaver, 1993). As we were investigating notations representing relationships between data, we needed to give labels to the data objects. Although we could have used abstract labels (e.g., A, D3, "foo"), we chose to use an **imaginary scenario** of project supervision and financing within an organisation. So, the domain in which the experimental objects were presented was real, but the actual information was not (Figure 2.23).

The tasks in this experiment required participants to match a given textual specification (a single page describing the objects and their relationships to each other) against the diagrams, indicating whether each diagram correctly matches the specification. Thus, the tasks in this case were **real tasks**, even if the information within the experimental objects was imaginary.

Example 14: UML Notation Experiment
Research question: "Which UML notational conventions best support understanding?" (Purchase et al., 2001)

This experiment, like the Entity-Relationship Diagrams experiment (Example 13), used a **real notation** (UML class diagrams), but **imaginary** content (project management) (Figure 2.24). The experimental task was a **real task**,

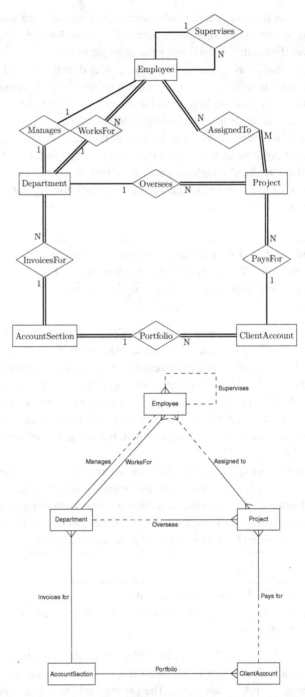

Figure 2.23: Two notations investigated in the Entity-Relationship Diagrams experiment, depicting project management in an imaginary organisation. The Chen notation is above, and the SSADM notation below.

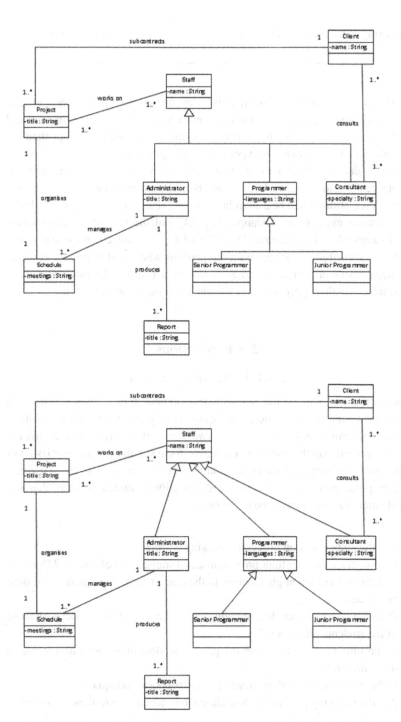

Figure 2.24: Two different notational conventions used in the UML Notation experiment.

requiring participants to indicate whether the UML diagrams matched a given textual specification.

- *Abstract data, abstract tasks.* This is by far the easiest approach to take because the experimenter has complete control over the information and the nature of the experimental objects and tasks, and can adapt them as necessary to improve the experimental design. It has the disadvantage in that it can be difficult to see how the experiment's results can apply to any real world scenario. In this case, both the experimental objects and the tasks are abstract and bear no relation to any real world concepts. The Euler Diagrams experiment (Example 6, p 24) and the two graph experiments (Example 4, p 19; Example 11, p 37) all fall into this category: the results tell us something about these representations when used to present abstract, meaningless information, and an assumption needs to be made that these results will also apply to situations when real information is used.

2.9 Evaluations

2.9.1 Evaluation question

Evaluations, as part of the iterative development cycle, are not concerned with answering research questions, being, as they are, focussed on a system. However, forming a specific *evaluation question* will ensure that the evaluation has a clear aim and that the feedback will be focussed on the particular issues of interest. For example, if we are evaluating a new piece of software to manage the proposal, preference collection, and allocation of student projects, then our evaluation questions might be as follows:

- Are the authentication processes working correctly?
- Can supervisors enter their project proposal suggestions efficiently? Does the system give sufficient guidance as to the correct format and number of their proposals?
- Does the system match the prerequisite skills required for a project with those of the students effectively?
- Is the time taken to calculate the project–student allocations acceptable to those involved?
- Is the interface for student viewing of the proposals adequate?
- Are the resulting project–student allocations acceptable to those involved?

This is much more preferable than evaluation studies that simply ask potential users to use the system to "see what happens."

Evaluations need to consider all the interactions with the system at some time during the development cycle, so the entire set of evaluation questions needs to include all interactive aspects of the system. It will be useful to remember the ISO definition of usability as "*effectiveness, efficiency* and *satisfaction* in a specified context of use" (ISO 9241-11:1998; ISO 1998), and ensure that all three are adequately covered in the set of evaluation questions. In the preceding list, the first three questions are associated with effectiveness, the fourth question is related to efficiency, and the final two are user satisfaction questions.

Because the expectation is that several such evaluations will be performed as part of an iterative cycle, it may be that different evaluations may focus on different aspects of the system at different times. Broader questions are more appropriate for the early evaluations in the cycle (e.g., "Are all the essential user tasks supported?", and "Is it clear to the user what stage of the workflow process the system is currently in?"). More limited and specific questions would be confined to the later evaluations (e.g. "Can the colour scheme be improved?", and "Are the input fields laid out in the best order on the screen?").

Telling the potential users in advance what the aim of the evaluation is means that they will focus on the particular aspects of the system in which you are interested. Feedback on colour, layout, terminology, etc., are often the first things on which users will comment. Unless you have told them specifically that you are interested in other, more fundamental aspects if the system (e.g., data modelling, interaction process), users will sometimes look no further than the less important features that are most immediately obvious to them. This is not to say that features such as font, colour, etc., are not important – because they most definitely are – but simply that it is useful to encourage users not to focus on the most obvious details when you are interested in more important aspects of the interaction model.

2.9.2 Design of the evaluation

Unlike experiments, evaluations do not depend on the definition of alternative conditions, and possible confounding factors do not need to be explicitly considered or avoided. It may be that the evaluation question asks which of several implementation features is most acceptable to users (e.g., whether the method of specifying the prerequisite skills for a project should be by textbox entry or selection from a prepopulated drop-down list). In this case, potential users would provide feedback on each method; however, because their feedback is unlikely to be analysed statistically (more detail on analysis of evaluation feedback is provided in Section 4.5), rigorous treatment of the conditions and confounds is not required.

Generalisability *is* important though – with respect to the nature of the potential users, the experimental objects, and the tasks, as before. As wide a range of potential users should take part in the evaluations, especially in the latter stages when the system is getting nearer to being ready for deployment.

As before, "experimental objects" are the different instantiations of the system with varying information content, and "tasks" are what the potential users are asked to do. In experiments, a task tends to be a direct question with a clear correct answer: this is not the case for evaluations, where the tasks tend to be longer and more complex, and the aim is for the potential users to experience the system, rather than get an answer correct. Evaluations are therefore more exploratory, as well as less constrained and controlled than experiments.

The combination of an experimental object and a task is, in this context, called a *scenario*. It is likely that different scenarios may be more appropriate for potential users with different *roles*. For example, potential project supervisors may be asked to enter project proposals of different lengths, with varying extents of completeness or validity, whereas potential students may be asked to enter conflicting or incomplete preferences, or misrepresent their existing skills.

A useful tip when defining scenarios is to specify as much of the details in advance as possible. If you want to get feedback on the ordering process for an online florist, then it is better to ask the potential user to "Order flowers for your mother on the occasion of her birthday," rather than "Order some flowers" – in the latter case, the potential user will spend additional time making up the name and address of someone to send the flowers to! This is wasted time because it is not relevant to the system. Being specific about the details also means that you can target particular areas of the system on which you want feedback. For example, if you are not sure that the way the system is representing the prices of the flowers is appropriate, then you might ask, "Order the second cheapest bunch of roses for your girlfriend."

The feedback from an evaluation will be most useful if

- clear evaluation questions are specified, and the potential users are aware of these questions;
- the set of questions includes efficiency, effectiveness, and user satisfaction;
- a wide range of realistic scenarios are used;
- a wide range of potential users take part, including representatives from all possible roles.

Further information on evaluation procedure appears at the end of Chapter 3, and on the nature of the data collected (and its analysis), at the end of Chapter 4.

Example 15: Aropä Evaluation

Evaluation question: "How efficiently and effectively can instructors set up assignments in the Aropä peer assessment system?" (Hamer and Purchase, 2009)

Aropä is an online system developed by John Hamer for conducting peer assessment activities in a class, allowing students to submit assignments, and then to review their peers' submissions using a marking rubric specified by the instructor.

One aspect of the evaluation of Aropä focussed on a **scenario** of an instructor setting up a peer assessment assignment for a class, looking in particular at how long different tasks within the overall activity took and how successful the instructors were in achieving the goal. Only one **scenario** was presented; potential users (taking the **role** of instructors) were asked to

- create a new assignment: potential users were given the parameters – an assignment name, submission date, and date by which reviews should be completed;
- specify the peer review parameters as follows: all authors are reviewers, there is no self-review, all reviews are anonymous, each student does two reviews;
- register a set of users: potential users were given a list of imaginary student identification numbers;
- create a marking rubric: potential users were asked to load and amend an existing rubric, and then save it;
- save and activate the assignment.

This evaluation gave us useful feedback on the Aropä system, which led to several improvements in the navigation facilities and the intuitiveness of the interaction objects. However, it was limited in its generalisability with respect to the use of only one variant of the **scenario** and in the choice of potential users – because this evaluation was conducted as part of a student project, the "potential users" were students playing the **role** of instructors.

Generalisability limitations like this would be a serious flaw in a comparative experiment; for an evaluation, they are less so – what matters is that feedback was obtained that could feed into the next iteration of the development cycle.

2.10 Summary

This chapter addresses the decisions that need to be made when designing an experiment or evaluation. Taking time over these decisions is crucial for the success of your test of the HCI idea – you will not regret spending time on thinking things through very carefully in advance![4]

It is important to note that, with such a range of decisions to be made, it is easy to (consciously or otherwise) make decisions that are biased towards a desired result. This could be done by choosing tasks or experimental objects that will naturally favour one condition over another – clearly inappropriate if the experiment is to be "fair."

Also note that there are many ways to skin a cat: two different researchers with the same research question may design very different experiments to address it – they may choose different experimental objects, different tasks, different domains, and different participants – and may produce equally valid results. There are often, therefore, differing opinions as to the "best" experimental method to use: researchers will tend to have their own favoured method and may argue against others. Ensuring that all decisions made are clearly justified and explained (as discussed in Chapter 6) will help support your own choices in any debate.

Having defined:

- the research question,
- the conditions,
- the experimental objects, and
- the tasks,

we now have a set of trials to present to participants.

The next step is to define the structure of the experiment – that is, what the participant experience will actually entail. We need to carefully specify each stage of the process: from when a participant starts the experiment to when it is complete. The decisions that need to be made about this process are discussed in Chapter 3.

---

[4] Many people only realise how important these decisions are *after* they have run their first (and hopefully last) flawed experiment – don't be one of them!

3

Experimental procedure

The definition of the conditions, tasks, and experimental objects is the initial focus of the experimental design, and must be carefully related to the research question, as described in Chapter 2. The experiment itself could be described simply as presenting the stimuli to human participants and asking them to perform the tasks. There are, however, still many other decisions to be made about the experimental process, as well as additional supporting materials and processes to be considered.

This chapter focuses on the nature of the participant experience, that is, what each participant will do between the start and end times of the experiment – a lot more happens than simply presenting the trials.

3.1 Allocating participants to conditions

As highlighted in Chapter 1, the key issue when running experiments is the comparison of performance between the conditions: does one condition produce better or worse performance than another? To determine "performance with a condition," human participants will need to perform tasks associated with the HCI idea being investigated, and measurements of the overall performance for each condition will be taken. Recall that we want to produce data like that in Figure 2.1, which summarises performance according to each experimental condition, with no explicit reference to tasks or experimental objects.

Each trial is associated with (usually) only one condition. One of the key decisions to be made is how the conditions will be allocated to the participants (i.e., will some participants perform all trials associated with one condition, while the others use the other conditions, or will all participants perform all trials relating to all conditions?). These two approaches are known

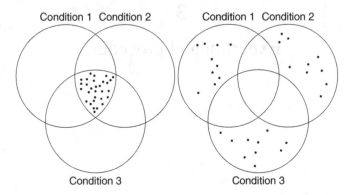

Figure 3.1: Within-participants experiment: each participant (represented by a dot) performs all trials, thus using all conditions (left). Between-participants experiment for three conditions: each participant performs the trials associated with only one condition (right).

as *between-participants* experiments and *within-participants* experiments. Figure 3.1 illustrates the difference between them.

As in all decision making, the advantages and disadvantages of each approach need to be weighed, and compromises may need to be made.

3.1.1 Between-participants experiments

In this case, the number of participants is divided by the number of conditions, and each participant is randomly allocated to one of the conditions, as a member of a *condition-group*. The trials are separated according to the conditions that they represent, and members of each condition-group are presented only with those trials that match their allocated condition. If conditions have been applied equally to the experimental objects, then the trials performed by a member of a condition-group will include instances of all experimental objects. The overall performance for a condition is then measured as the mean performance in all trials over all participants within that condition-group.

The disadvantage of this method is that people are different; that is, by chance, different condition-groups may contain people with different levels of ability or prior knowledge that may affect performance in the tasks. Thus, the participants in the condition-group associated with the condition Blue may have particular knowledge that enables them to perform well, whereas those allocated to the Green condition-group may not have the background knowledge to perform similarly well. It may therefore seem that the Blue condition produces better performance than the Green one, even though the difference in performance is not attributable to the different conditions.

Although a random allocation of participants to condition-group may go some way toward alleviating participant variability in a between-participants experiment, the only way to ensure that there are no problems is to assess participants' relevant skills prior to the experiment and allocate them to condition-groups so that each group has a comparable mix of abilities. This is difficult because this preexperiment assessment would need to evaluate all relevant skills (e.g., it may be easy to assess participants' prior knowledge of the Highway Code, but less so to evaluate the extent of their driving experience). A between-participants experiment that wants to determine the relative effects of two different road safety educational programmes on the understanding of traffic rules and conventions would therefore have to take into account the confounding factor (see Section 2.3) of driving experience.

Another important disadvantage of a between-participants experiment is that each participant produces data for only one condition: the time given by participants to take part in experiments is a precious resource (as discussed in Section 3.3), and the more data points that can be obtained from each participant, the better.

Example 16: Smalltalk Experiment
 Research question: "Which layout features best support the interpretation of software class diagrams?" (Grundon and Purchase, 1996)

Steve Grundon wanted to establish which common graph layout aesthetics would be most useful in displaying object-oriented class diagrams. We created two small Java programs representing the same functionality (storing and maintaining information about the keys used for several rooms in a building): these were our two experimental objects. One of the programs (PCent) stored the information centrally, and the other (PDist) used a distributed model of information storage.

 Four layout aesthetics were investigated – edge bends, edge crosses, orthogonality, and upward flow. These were our four independent variables, and each variable had three conditions, a different extent of the aesthetic (low, medium, and high), so there were twelve conditions in all.

 The class diagram for both programs was drawn twelve times, once for each condition, resulting in twenty-four stimuli (two stimuli per condition). Figure 3.2 shows four of these stimuli with two conditions applied to both PDist and PCent.

 The twelve PDist class diagrams were printed on green paper, and the PDist code listing on yellow. The twelve PCent class diagrams were printed on blue paper, and the PCent code listing on pink. Thus, each experimental trial

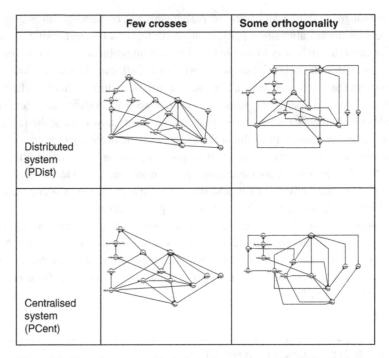

Figure 3.2: Class diagrams used in the between-participants Smalltalk experiment.

consisted of two code listings and two class diagrams all associated with one condition.

Each participant's task was to either match the code listings to the class diagrams by colour (e.g., by saying that the yellow code is represented by the blue diagram) or indicate that there was no appropriate match. Because experience gained by doing the task once would make it easier the second time, and because the task could take some time, we used a **between-participants** experiment. We had fifty-five participants, all members of a third-year computer science class, each of whom was randomly allocated to one of the twelve **condition-groups**; we kept the size of the groups the same, as much as possible. The data collected was the time taken for each participant to get the correct answer.

It should have come as no surprise to us that the data were meaningless, and that no conclusions could be made about the effectiveness, or otherwise, of the layout features. Despite our attempts to limit **participant variability** by restricting eligibility to only those students who were within the top quartile of the class in a midsemester test, it was clear that some participants simply knew more about class diagrams than others. This participant variability meant that, even if we had been able to establish that some **condition-groups** produced better performance than others (which we didn't), we would not have been able to conclude that this better performance was due to the experimental condition.

This was a good lesson to learn – if there is any chance that the participants may already have knowledge or skills that will affect their performance in the experimental task, then a **between-participants** experimental design is not appropriate.[1]

3.1.2 Within-participants experiments

In this case, *all* participants perform *all* tasks with *all* stimuli. Crucially, each participant's performance on one condition is then compared with their *own* performance on the other conditions. This solves the "participant variability" problem because it means that no comparisons are being made between the performances of participants who may have differing levels of skills: the comparison is always done according to exactly the same level of participant skill. This method also means that each participant produces performance data for all conditions.

There is, however, a key disadvantage of this method, which was hinted at in the Smalltalk experiment (Example 16, p 53). Because the participants will be performing the experimental tasks several times (at least as many times as there are trials), it is obvious that they will become more competent and their measured performance will improve – and this improvement will be unrelated to the different experimental conditions. Thus, although a participant's performance on a trial relating to condition 1 (presented at the start of the sequence) may be worse than his or her performance using condition 2 (presented at the end), this may not be as a result of the differing effect of the two experimental conditions. This is called the *learning effect*.

Although we cannot totally eradicate the learning effect, there are two ways in which the experimental design can attempt to mitigate and reduce its impact:

- *Participants are given the trials in random order*. Each participant's "high-performing" later trials will therefore appear earlier in the experiment for the other participants, randomly spread over time, and the results will not be biased by the effect of order. It is important that this is a *different* random order for each participant, not the same random order for all participants.[2]

---

[1] This is the first and last between-participants experiment I have ever conducted.
[2] Using the same random order for all participants is the kind of mistake you will only make once!

- *A set of "practice trials" are presented to participants at the start of the experiment.* This allows participants to get used to the tasks and to get over an initial learning period before starting on the real experimental trials. The practise trials are in exactly the same form as the experimental trials, and the data from them are simply thrown away. It is important that participants are not aware that these trials are just for practise, thus ensuring that they take them as seriously as the real experimental trials and engage effectively in a learning period.

Within-participants experimental design also raises the problem of the length of the experiment. If every participant is to be presented with every experimental trial, and there are lots of trials, then the experiment may take an unreasonable length of time. If each trial takes 5 minutes, and there are twenty trials, then this is too long to expect a participant to fully concentrate on the experiment. This may result in a *fatigue effect* – this is somewhat comparable to the learning effect except that performance in the later trials is worse than those on the earlier ones because the participant is either tired or bored (rather than because of the effect of the experimental conditions). The fatigue effect is, of course, also mitigated by the randomisation of trial order; however, lengthy experiments may raise ethical issues (see Section 3.7).

There is a therefore delicate balance that needs to be struck when deciding on the time allowed for each trial. Although reducing the time may permit more stimuli to be presented to the same participant, it may also mean that there is insufficient time for the participant to complete each task satisfactorily, which could result in a "floor effect" in the data (see Section 2.6).

In choosing either a between-participants or a within-participants approach, the key issues are as follows:

- the extent to which prior knowledge may be a confounding factor in task performance,
- the size and complexity of the experimental tasks.

Table 3.1 summarises the decisions to be made with respect to these two dimensions.

In general, a between-participants approach is the most appropriate for simple tasks that are unaffected by prior knowledge (e.g., low-level perception tasks such as colour recognition, pattern matching, and interpretation of vibrotactile messages) and that typically do not require any significant cognitive processing. In HCI experiments, however, it is rare not to have some meaningful content

Table 3.1: *Deciding how to allocate participants to conditions, based on two dimensions of prior knowledge and task complexity*

Is prior knowledge likely to affect the results?	Is the task large and time consuming?	Example	Suggested method
NO	NO	Identifying the coloured item among a collection of black items: the condition is the colour. Different experimental objects can be defined by using different numbers and shapes.	Can be done either **within** and **between**. **Within** would give more data points per condition; **between** would allow for a larger number of experimental objects to be used.
NO	YES	Sorting 100 items in order of size: the condition is the colour of the items in the set. Different experimental objects can be defined by using different shapes.	Best done **between**.
YES	NO	Finding the length of the shortest path between two nodes in a graph drawing: the condition is the layout of the drawing. Different experimental objects are different graph structures.	Best done **within**.
YES	YES	Answering questions about a short story: the condition is the typeface font. Different experimental objects are different stories.	There is no easy solution to these types of experiment: **within** may be possible if there are only a few conditions and experimental objects; **between** may be possible if you are certain that all participants have the same relevant prior knowledge.

associated with the experimental objects; in this case, between-participants experiments will be risky because it will be difficult to control for prior knowledge of that content.

It seems, therefore, that within-participants designs are preferable for HCI experiments (if they are feasible), provided that the timing is managed so that the experiment is of reasonable length, and sincere attempts are made to address any learning effect.

3.2 The experimental process: Defining the participant experience

The participant experience is the process that each participant will go through: it is best visualised as a timeline of stages (Figure 3.3).[3] The most important stage is the experiment itself. This, too, can be visualised on a timeline (Figure 3.4).

There are also several numeric parameters used when defining the participant experience (as shown in Figure 3.4):

1. The number of experimental trials (S) is fixed by the experimental design: a trial is the combination of a condition, a task, and an experimental object (as discussed in Section 2.7). If it is possible to present all S trials more than once (ideally, using different task variants while keeping the length of the experiment within reasonable time), then it is a good idea to do so. The parameter m (where $m > 0$) indicates the number of times each trial will be presented, and mS represents the total number of experimental trials presented.
2. The number of practice trials (P): from the participants' point of view, these should be indistinguishable from the experimental trials. (These may not be necessary in a between-participants experiment, although they will do no harm.)
3. The total number of trials (E): this is the number of experimental trials (mS) plus the number of practise trials (P).
4. The number of trials in each "block" (B): it is usual to divide the total number of trials (E) into blocks and allow participants to take a brief rest between each block. The final block does not have to have B trials in it if E is not exactly divisible by B.

---

[3] This and future sections in this chapter assume a within-participants experimental design, although most of the material is equally applicable to between-participants experiments.

Preexperiment activities		Experiment	Postexperiment activities	
Introduction	Preparatory events	Experimental trials	Additional data collection	Debrief
The participant is welcomed, the experimental process is briefly explained, and the consent form is signed.	These may include tutorials, worked examples of the experimental tasks, software demonstrations, and the opportunity for the participant to ask questions and seek clarification.	The participant performs the experimental trials in the order determined by the experimental method.	Participants may be asked to complete a questionnaire or take part in an interview.	The aim of the experiment is explained, and the participant has an opportunity to ask questions.

Time →

Figure 3.3: Typical stages in the participant experience.

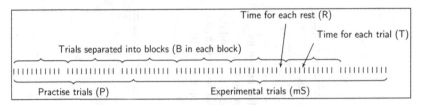

Figure 3.4: Process followed during the experiment itself.

5. The time allowed for each trial: this can be set in one of three ways:
   a. a fixed number of seconds for all trials (**T**): appropriate if the stimuli have been designed so that they are all expected to take approximately the same length of time;
   b. a different number of seconds for each trial (**Ts**): this is unusual, and participants will need to know how much time they have for each stimulus – unlike in item a, participants will not be able to get into a regular rhythm when performing the trials;
   c. unlimited time, with the participants indicating when they have finished each trial and moving on to the next at their own pace (**Tu**).
6. The time allowed for each rest break: this can be set in one of two ways:
   a. a fixed number of seconds (**R**);
   b. unlimited time, with the participants indicating when they are ready to continue (**Ru**).

3.2.1 The tricky issue of time

One of the main considerations is the length of time allocated to each trial: there is no golden rule for this, and it will depend on the nature and relative difficulty of the trials. In deciding how to manage time, it is important to remember that the desired outcome of the experiment is variation in the data: we want to collect data that indicate which of the conditions performs better than the others (collection of data is discussed in Chapter 4). If the participants' performance is uniformly high or uniformly low over all conditions, then there will be a ceiling or floor effect (Figure 2.17), neither of which will help in comparing conditions.

Limiting the time allowed for each trial means that participants' performance can be deliberately curtailed: the answer that participants give to some trials will be incorrect simply because the participants have not had time to answer them correctly, and we would expect that this would occur for the more "difficult"

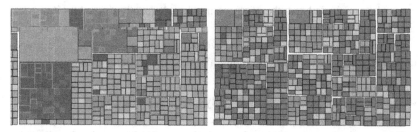

Figure 3.5: Two different levels of filtering of the Fiat company data used in the DAGMap experiment.

conditions. Putting the participants under time stress means that there is more likely to be variation in the accuracy data for the different conditions. Not everyone agrees with this method, however, because it is sometimes seen as "unfair" not to give participants sufficient opportunity to answer correctly. It does, nevertheless, help in measuring the relative difficulty of the conditions with respect to accuracy.

If participants are given unlimited time for each trial, then it is likely that most trials will be performed correctly, and there will be little variation in the accuracy data. In this case, we would hope that the length of time taken to complete the trials would provide data variation between the conditions, representing their relative "difficulty." Giving unlimited time, however, means that the experimenter has no control over the total length of the experiment, and participants who perform slowly, taking a long time with each trial to ensure that every answer is correct, may experience fatigue during the later stages. In addition, recruiting and timetabling participants (of which more is said in Section 3.6.1) may prove difficult if the experimenter cannot be sure how long each participant will take to complete their experimental session. In the Web Page Aesthetics experiment (Example 2, p 12) one participant was so eager to perform well that he took 80 minutes to complete the four ranking tasks, whereas the other participants took less than 20 minutes.

Tasks that require interaction with a system are typically best presented with unlimited time (e.g., if the participant needs to explore an interface using zooming or scrolling, or adjust the settings on a vibrotactile device). In this case, the time taken for interaction is included in the total task time. For instance, in the DAGMap experiment (Example 5, p 23) participants could interact with the system and use a filter to adjust the level at which the information was presented before they gave their answer; although they were not required to use this filter, they were able to if they wanted (Figure 3.5). Such interaction cannot be anticipated and, therefore, cannot be adequately catered for if a strict time limit is given for each trial.

There are some useful tricks, however, that allow participants to be given unlimited time, while encouraging them not to take too long with each trial:

- The participants are told that they only have a fixed time (e.g., 20 seconds), even though this limit is never enforced;
- The participants are told that they only have a fixed time; the time limit is enforced for the practise tasks (so that the participants can get into a rhythm), but not for the experimental tasks;
- The participants are told that they have unlimited time but that they are expected to complete each trial within a fixed number of seconds; although a brief audio alarm can be sounded after the fixed number of seconds has elapsed, the participants can still take as long as they want;
- The participants are told that they have unlimited time, but that the task will be easier if they do it quickly.

Example 17: Mental Model Experiment

Research question: "Which layout features of a graph drawing are most noticed and best remembered?" (Purchase et al., 2012)

We were interested in which of six visual features (selected according to existing theories of perception) were most readily internalised when people read graph drawings. These six features were the different conditions: Symmetry, Colinearity, Node Alignment, Parallel Lines, Horizontal and Vertical Lines, and Grid. We included a seventh Control condition, which explicitly did not conform to any of the six features, and an additional four conditions representing alternative topologies. These eleven conditions were embodied in four different graphs (the four experimental objects, Figure 3.6). There was only one task for each stimulus: the participant was required to draw the graph drawing from memory after viewing it for **3 seconds**.

We wanted the participants to draw what they could remember and have **sufficient time** to represent their memory of the drawings. However, we were concerned about both the possibility of their memory fading and the overall duration of the experiment. Participants were therefore told that they could **take as long as they wanted** to draw their memory of the graph drawing, but that the task would be easier if they drew the graphs **as quickly as possible**, before their memory faded.

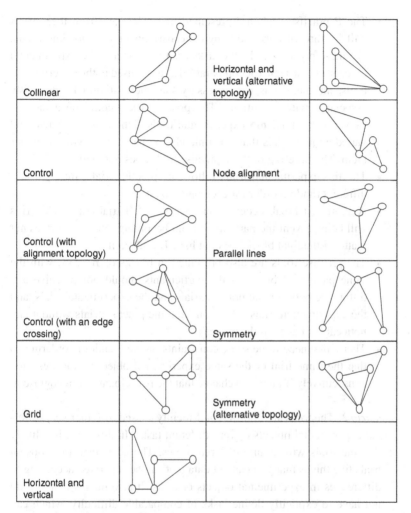

Figure 3.6: Experimental conditions applied to one of the experimental objects in the Mental Model experiment, producing eleven stimuli for that object.

3.2.2 Example participant experiences

The following scenarios illustrate a variety of issues to be considered, with reference to the experimental parameters defined previously:

Scenario 1: The trials are of comparable difficulty and require an identical interaction method. In this case, a predetermined time limit (**T**) can be set for each trial and a within-participants methodology used:

- The **P** practise trials are presented first. The data from these trials will be thrown away, although the participant will not know this. For these practise trials, the tasks are the same and the experimental objects are the same (or comparable) as those used in the experimental trials, although it is not necessary that these stimuli be explicitly associated with conditions. The practice trials could be a random subset of the total **mS** experimental trials if there are sufficient and varied enough trials that it is unlikely the participant will remember them. The ordering of these practise trials does not matter.
- The **mS** experimental trials follow the practise trials; they are in a different random order for each participant.
- A short rest break occurs after each set of **B** trials (a block). This will help prevent the participant from becoming fatigued. It does not matter if the final block does not have **B** trials in it.
- The practise trials are also presented in blocks of **B** tasks, with the same pattern of breaks – the participants should not perceive any difference between the practise trials and the experimental trials, and the experimental trials follow on from the practise trials without any noticeable change in the process.
- There may need to be some constraints on the "random" ordering so that the same trial or the same experimental object is not presented consecutively if there is a chance that the participant will recognise it.

Scenario 2: The trials are of different difficulty caused by either very different experimental objects or very different tasks. In this case, it is likely that the trials will require different times. The advantage of choosing trials like this is that you can get data that can be separated according to differences in experimental objects or tasks. It also means that you do not have to explicitly define tasks of comparable difficulty, which can sometimes be tricky. There are two choices to be made here:
- The same process as shown in Scenario 1 can be used, but with different time limits for each trial according to the nature of the task or experimental object. This may cause problems with the rhythm of the experiment because participants need to have some idea as to how long they have for each trial, and if this changes for each trial, it will be hard for them to set an "internal clock." Furthermore, if they are told that there will be a different time for each trial, then this is an additional cognitive load that they have to consider, and this may interfere with their performance. An audio warning indicating when the participants have, for example, 10 seconds remaining for a trial may help address this problem.

- It may be that the participants could be given unlimited time for these trials, but consideration would need to be given to the possible consequences of a ceiling effect and unreasonable length of total experimental time.

Scenario 3: The conditions require different interaction methods (e.g., one condition uses a mobile navigation device, whereas another condition entails looking at a map on paper). In this case, the cognitive shift required when moving from using one interaction method to another needs to be considered:

- The trials for each condition should be presented together, so that the participant does not have to change his or her means of interaction for every trial. Thus, the trials for condition 1 (mobile navigation) are presented before those for condition 2 (map).
- However, there is still a possibility of a learning effect, so participants should use the conditions in a different order. Thus, some participants will do the trials for condition 1 before those for condition 2, whereas some will do condition 2 trials before those for condition 1.

Participants are therefore randomly assigned to a *participant-group*; if there are **n** participants and **C** conditions, then there are **C** groups, each with **n/C** participants. Each participant-group uses the conditions in a different order. This means that each participant only shifts from one interaction mode to another **C-1** times, and randomisation within each condition (associated with, in this case, interaction mode) addresses any learning effect.

In cases like these, where the trials for each condition are presented separately, the condition order for each participant-group is often determined by a *Latin square*: a square where each symbol appears in only one row and one column.

In the DAGMap experiment (Example 5, p 23) the participants were not required to interact with the visual representations when performing the tasks. However, each of the three representational methods (the three conditions) used **different interaction and viewing methods** for scrolling and changing the visual level of detail. If the experiment were to be run again with tasks that asked participants to use the navigation facilities to explore the visualisations, the total number of participants would need to be divided into three **participant-groups**, each doing the trials for each condition in a different order (based on a 3 × 3 **Latin square**, Table 3.2).

Table 3.2: *Latin square for three conditions*

	First set of trials	Second set of trials	Third set of trials
Group1	DAGMAP	NODELINK	COMBINATION
Group2	NODELINK	COMBINATION	DAGMAP
Group3	COMBINATION	DAGMAP	NODELINK
Time →			

3.2.3 Filler tasks

The experimental process may include "filler tasks" – these are tasks that are unrelated to the experimental tasks and usually quite different in nature (e.g., small verbal puzzles, mazes). Their purpose is to engage the participant's attention between trials to prevent memory or performance effects from one trial being carried over to the next. Participants should, of course, have no idea that these filler tasks are not part of the experiment, thus ensuring that they take them seriously. Filler tasks should not be too difficult. If participants struggle with them, then they will get frustrated, and this frustration is likely to affect performance in the "real" trials.

In the Mental Model experiment (Example 17, p 62), the participants were asked to draw the graph drawing that they had just seen from memory (and to take as long as they needed to do so) before being presented with the next drawing. It was important that their visual memory buffer was cleared as much as possible before looking at the next stimulus, or else the memory of one drawing might affect the perception of the next. A small **spot-the-difference puzzle** was presented between each drawing to ensure that visual memory was cleared – it was presented for 10 seconds, and participants were asked to count aloud the number of differences they saw (Figure 3.7).

3.2.4 Distracter tasks

One problem with asking participants to do a series of trials is that this is a very artificial environment: throughout the experiment, the participant is doing only one type of activity, is totally focussed on that activity, and is always awaiting the next similar activity.

	Stimulus (3 seconds)	Task (unlimited time)	Filler task (10 seconds)	Next stimulus (3 seconds)
Instruction	Look at the diagram	Draw the diagram as exactly as you can	Count aloud the number of differences between these two pictures	Look at the diagram
Display/activity	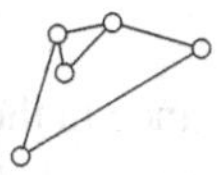	*[Participant draws the graph on the tablet PC, and indicates when finished]*		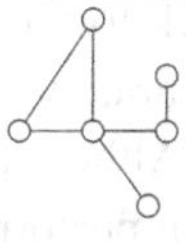
		Time →		

Figure 3.7: Extract from the Mental Model experiment, showing a stimulus, the task, a filler task, and the next stimulus.

To make the environment a bit more realistic, it is sometimes appropriate to ask participants to perform a secondary "distracter" task concurrently with the primary task. Doing so increases cognitive load and can therefore simulate the fact that, in real contexts, users are often thinking about more than one thing at a time. This is often done in experiments by asking the participant to continually perform a secondary task, during which time they are interrupted to perform the primary experimental trials. Participants do not, of course, know the experimental distinction between these tasks.[4]

For example, if the research question is to investigate which of a set of data visualisation methods is best for representing economics data, then, as well as asking the participants to interpret the stimuli (the primary task), they could also be asked to read through a list of recent stock prices and identify those that have increased in the past week (the secondary task). They would then be interrupted by the primary task at randomly spaced intervals.

The distracter task must be chosen so that the additional cognitive activity is relevant – asking participants to juggle balls is obviously inappropriate for visual interpretation experimental tasks, but may be less so for an experiment that is investigating the form and positioning of manual controls in an airplane cockpit. Asking participants to walk around a room is a common secondary

---

[4] Thus, from the participants' point of view, the "secondary" task is the main task that they are being asked to perform, and the "primary" task (the basis of the research question) is a distraction.

task for experiments that investigate the use of mobile devices; reading aloud may be used in an experiment investigating the perception of speech.

Like filler tasks, the secondary task should not be too difficult because this will cause frustration for the participant. Depending on the nature of the secondary task, this may mean calibration for individual participants: McGee-Lennon, Wolters, and McBryan (2007) used a secondary task that required participants to memorise a series of digits presented on a screen and repeat them back to the experimenter – the appropriate number of digits was determined separately for each participant in a pretest.

Although the focus is on the participants' performance in the primary tasks, their performance in the secondary task should also be recorded because it may also prove to be interesting. If participants take a longer time to recover their secondary task performance after completing experimental trials associated with one condition than with another, then this may indicate a difference in the difficulty of the two conditions.

3.3 Pilot experiments

In an ideal world, we would be able to specify all experimental parameters in advance, prepare the experiment, and then run it successfully. Sadly, it is seldom the case that an experiment runs correctly the first time.

Experimental parameters (the timing, number of practise tasks, length of rest breaks, ordering, etc.) can be tested and refined by pilot tests. Pilot tests enable the participant experience to be tried out to ensure that it is appropriate for both the research question and the participants. Pilot tests, like real experiments, require the help of people not involved in the development of the HCI idea being tested or in the design and conduct of the experiment. Data from pilot tests are discarded.

The key motivation for piloting is that participants are typically difficult to come by, and "participant time" is a scarce resource. Collecting data from a poorly designed experiment simply wastes participant time. And if the experiment goes wrong for the first participant, then subsequent scheduled experimental sessions may need to be cancelled or postponed, and it may be difficult to persuade participants to reschedule for a later date. As a result, even more precious participant time would be wasted.

Each pilot test entails conducting a version of the experiment with a single participant. Improvements can then be made to the experiment after each pilot test. It is sometimes useful to divide the piloting process into "pre-pilot" and "pilot" tests.

Pre-pilot tests are typically run with members of the research team to ensure that experimental equipment or software works correctly. Pilot tests are typically run with people outside the research team who do not know the experimental aims – these pilots focus more on ensuring that the participant experience will produce appropriate data.

Running pilot tests will ensure that the experimental method is robust before collecting real experimental data. Early pilots may not use complete versions of the intended experiment, but they are useful in getting timely feedback before too many experimental design decisions are set in concrete (and therefore difficult to change). Later pilots should be run as if they were the real experiment. Ultimately, everything that is to be used in the real experiment (stimuli, filler tasks, consent forms, questionnaires, etc.) should have gone through the piloting process before the experiment starts.

The main advantages of pilot tests are as follows:

- *The experimenter can interview the pilot participants at the end of the experiment to determine whether there are any problems with the method and then make the appropriate changes*. Once the real experiment starts, no further changes should be made to the experimental method or materials. For example, a pilot participant might comment that some stimuli were much easier than others, that it was difficult to know how to go about finding the answer for some tasks, that the timing was too short/too long, that there were errors in the introductory material, that questions on the questionnaire were ambiguous, etc. The pilot tests for the Spring Dynamic Graph Experiment (Example 10, p 33) revealed that it was difficult for participants to identify the different time slices during the animation (labels identifying the weeks were added to the screens), that there was a mistake in the answer options provided for one of the tasks (this was corrected), and that the tasks were too easy (the tasks were changed to make them more difficult).
- *The experimenter can determine appropriate values for the experimental parameters (e.g., size of blocks, time for each task, timing of rest breaks) based on observation of the process and the opinion of the pilot participants.*
- *Looking at the data obtained from pilots may identify whether there are likely to be problems with a "ceiling" or "floor" effect due to the difficulty and timing of the trials.*
- *Any bugs in the software, materials, procedure, data collection process, etc., can be identified and corrected.* For example, a pilot test for the Mental Model experiment (Example 17, p 62) revealed the obscure fact that the video recording software we used only works on the tablet device if the screen is rotated before the software is launched, not afterward.

- *The most appropriate means of communication between the experimenter and the participant can be tested.* Pilot tests for the Mental Model experiment (Example 17, p 62) suggested that the experiment would flow more easily if the experimenter and the participant each had their own stylus (rather than using one stylus between the two of them).
- *The physical location of the experiment and the comfort of the participant can be tried out, ensuring that the chosen venue is quiet and that the participant is comfortable using the equipment.*
- *Pilot tests allow the experimenter to gain practise in the process of conducting the experiment, so that it later can be conducted with confidence when using real experimental participants.* Although this is particularly important for first-time experimenters, it is useful for all.

It is extremely rare that no problems are identified with the experimental method during piloting. If this does happen (exceptionally),[5] then the pilot data can be included with the real experimental data, provided that no changes (at all) are subsequently made to the materials or method.

There is no golden rule for the number of pilot experimental sessions to run – as many as are needed to ensure the smooth running of the experiment and the appropriate collection of data: no more and no less. The Euler Diagrams experiment (Example 6, p 24) needed nine participants to take part in a pilot experimental session before the parameters could be appropriately set. It is a good idea to plan for around four or five pilot sessions, of which at least two are run as "late" pilots, following exactly the same process as the intended experiment.

A word of caution about pilot tests though: don't make all the changes the pilot participants suggest! If pilot participants complain that the tasks are too difficult or there is insufficient time to answer, then making them easier (or giving more time) may result in ceiling effects (see Section 2.6). We want the participants to perform some perceptual or cognitive processing; if the tasks are too easy, our performance measures will not be able to record anything meaningful. A careful balance needs to be struck between making the tasks too easy and making them so difficult that the participants get frustrated and abandon any attempt at performing the task correctly.

In contrast, do take seriously any feedback that suggests that the overall experiment is too long and that participants started to get tired near the end: this may mean changing the experimental design so that it uses fewer trials,

---

[5] This has never happened to me!

perhaps reducing the number of tasks or experimental objects (or even the number of conditions).

The secret of experimental success is preparation. Before participants are recruited and timetabled into scheduled experimental sessions, the experimenter must be confident that the entire process will run smoothly and that the data collected will be appropriate.

It is easy to forget that the participants know nothing about the experiment when they start. The participant experience should be designed so that a participant is always confident that he or she knows exactly what he or she should be doing at every stage in the experiment. If a participant becomes frustrated or confused at any time, performance may be affected.

The key to a good experiment is ensuring that the participant experience is so seamless and comfortable that the participants' performance is in no way affected by any external factors.

3.4 Experimental materials: Software

Most HCI experiments will use software of some sort, and participants will typically be asked to interact with a system in some way. Experimental software should, of course, be robust (unexpected crashes will waste participant time) and should store the participants' data correctly, reliably, and securely.

Importantly, any experimental software should be easy to use – if the participant experiences any problems (however minor) with its use, then the experimental data will be compromised. If the software clearly guides the participant through the experiment process step by step, then so much the better. For example, the software used in the Mental Model experiment (Example 17, p 62) included screens that simply told the participants when they should pick up and put down the stylus.

The best experimental software does not require excessive additional interaction from the participant that may distract from the experiment itself: participants should not have to load files, compile programmes, change or move windows, rename files, etc. Any additional participant activities not associated with the experimental trials will confound the data and may confuse novices. In the Mental Model experiment, we needed to be sure that every diagram drawn was saved; so, instead of asking participants to explicitly save each diagram (which they may forget to do), the "clear panel" button (which had to be pressed before the next diagram could be drawn) performed an automatic save action as well.

Any additional cognitive activities required of the participants may distract them from the tasks. For example, they should not be asked to keep track of the number of stimuli they have seen, the length of time available for doing the task for each stimuli, or the order in which stimuli are presented, etc. If necessary, such administration should be done by the supporting software.

Example 18: Clustering Experiment

Research question: "Does using path-preserving clusters in the depiction of large graphs improve the readability of graphs?" (Archambault, Purchase, and Pinaud, 2010)

For this experiment, Daniel Archambault produced **experimental software** that performed two functions. First, it permitted the participant to explore the visualisation by clicking on the graph to open and close metanodes, or to zoom in and out. In addition, it provided the experimental facilities for the participants to enter their answers to the tasks by selecting one of the multiple-choice options offered in the right-hand panel (Figure 3.8). This was preferable to using two separate systems: one for displaying the stimuli, and one for collecting the participants' responses.

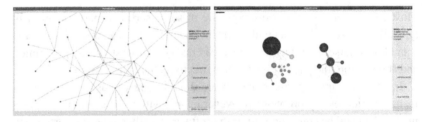

Figure 3.8: Experimental software that allows for exploration of the stimulus as well as submission of the task answer.

3.5 Additional experimental processes

The entire experimental process is more than simply the presentation of the trials and the collection of data. There are several other useful pre- and postexperiment activities that can take place, all of which will assist in ensuring the reliability of the data.

3.5.1 Preexperiment

The participant needs to be adequately prepared for the experiment, and time should be set aside for this preparation. Before starting, the participant should

GRAPH DRAWING EXPERIMENT **TUTORIAL**

Graph drawings are made up of *nodes* (the circles) and these are connected to each other by *edges* (the lines).

A *path between nodes* is made up of the edges that lead from one node to another, through other nodes. This graph shows a *path* between nodes A and E using bold edges. The length of this path is the number of edges it includes, in this case, 3.

However, there is more than one path that connects A and E:

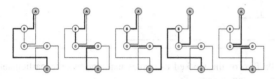

The *shortest path* between two nodes is the path with the minimum length. In this case, the shortest path length between A and E is 2 (shown in the left-most drawing).

Figure 3.9: Extract from the tutorial sheet used in the Orthogonal Corners experiment.

fully understand the experimental process, the relevant concepts, and tasks, and have an opportunity to ask questions.

The experimental process should be described to the participants so that they know what will happen at each stage.[6] This process information may be explained by the experimenter or presented in written form in a "participant information sheet" that is given to the participant to read.

A brief tutorial session can ensure that participants understand the necessary concepts (e.g., for graph drawing experiments such as Examples 1, p 11 Example 4, p 19, and Example 11, p 37 they need to know about graphs, nodes, paths, shortest paths, etc. (Figure 3.9); for a mobile device experiment, participants need to know about different interaction mechanisms and how different gestures can be used).

---

[6] Some experiments deliberately introduce unexpected events (e.g., a simulated power cut, an angry intruder) because it is actually the responses to these events that are of interest. This is rare in HCI experiments.

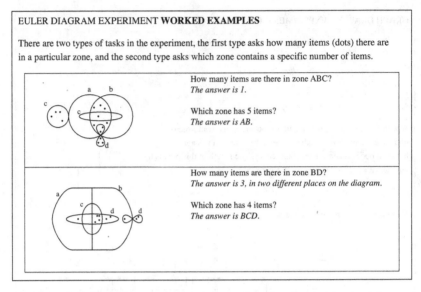

Figure 3.10: Two of the worked examples explained to the participants of the
Euler Diagrams experiment.

Participants need to be told about the tasks they will be asked to perform.
It is a good idea to show them worked examples that illustrate correct answers
so that they know what is expected of them (Figure 3.10). Smaller or simpler
versions of the experimental objects can be used in the tutorial, demonstrations,
and worked examples.

Importantly, the experiment should not proceed until the participant has been
given ample opportunity to ask questions, has no more questions to ask, and
has had their questions answered adequately. Data can be lost (and participant
time wasted) if it is discovered midway through an experimental session that a
participant did not really understand what was required.

Participants should give consent for their data to be used (in accordance
with relevant ethical guidelines) before the experiment starts (see Section 3.7
for more on ethical approval).

3.5.2 Postexperiment

Participant time is a scarce resource, so it is a good idea to make the most of it.
Additional data can be collected once the experimental trials are complete. This
is best done by questionnaire or interview. Participants can be asked questions
about their experience with the stimuli [e.g., which condition they preferred

MENTAL MODEL EXPERIMENT **INTERVIEW**   Participant Identifier____

Age:_____   Female   Male

Occupation: Student/ Other _____

Main subjects studying (or studied): _____

1. Have you ever seen or used node-link diagrams (or anything similar) before, and if so, when?

_____

2. Which features of the diagrams did you focus on when trying to remember them?

_____

3. What aspects of the drawings made them easier to remember?

_____

4. Please indicate on the attached sheet which are the three "easiest" diagrams and the three "hardest" diagrams.

5. Do you have any other comments about this experiment?

Figure 3.11: Extract from the postexperiment structured interview for the Mental Model experiment.

(and why), how conditions should be ranked for ease of comprehension, the process they used to perform the tasks]. Collecting qualitative data (text or verbal responses) is a good idea – free-form comments will help in validating and interpreting the quantitative data. (More information on appropriate data collection methods is provided in Chapter 4.)

This is also a chance to collect demographic data such as age, gender, experience in or knowledge of a topic relevant to the experiment, and education level.

Figure 3.11 shows some examples of questions that may be asked in a postexperiment interview. Although postexperiment questionnaires could be administered using software, participants are more likely to give rich informative answers to questions if they can express them aloud (rather than having to write or type them).

The questionnaire or interview written record should have a participant identifier on it so that it can be related to the data collected from the experimental tasks. This would typically be written by the experimenter rather than the participant.

The participant should have an opportunity to ask questions at the end; indeed, this "debriefing" is often an ethical requirement. It is reasonable to explain to the participant the overall aim of the experiment, but the experimenter should not reveal anything about the experiment that may be passed on to a later participant (prior to his or her own experiment) that may affect his or her behaviour. For example, if a participant found out from a friend before starting the experiment that the experimenter expects performance with condition A to be better than condition B, then they may (consciously or otherwise) not try very hard with condition B.

3.6 Practical issues

The extent of the work required for collecting data from human participants via formal experiments is not always fully appreciated: HCI experiments are difficult and time consuming. The implication of this is that (1) the experimenter must really want to conduct the experiment, and (2) the research question must really be worth answering.

Nothing must go wrong. If things go wrong, then data may need to be thrown away: this is a waste of both experimenter time and participant time. Experiments therefore need to be carefully planned and prepared, with extensive piloting to ensure that the whole process is perfect.

3.6.1 Recruiting and managing participants

Ideally, participants should be people who have no involvement in the research project or with the researchers. If the experiment is associated with a particular knowledge domain, then it may be appropriate to recruit the sample from only one sector of the population (e.g., biologists, geographers); if the experiment is not domain specific, then the wider the range of people in your population, the better, because this allows for greater generalisability (see Section 2.4).

In reality, despite frequent objections, most HCI research experiments will continue to be run on undergraduate or postgraduate students, and usually computer science students. This should be acknowledged as a limitation (see Section 6.3.4). Using friends and family may not be a good idea because they may take the experiment less seriously than strangers recruited anonymously. Demographic information about your participants (age, gender, education level, experience. etc.) should always be collected and reported. This data will be especially useful if there is a wide variability in the nature of the participants because it may help explain any unexpected results (see Section 5.5.3).

The participant experience should be carefully managed: this includes both the recruitment of participants and the conduct of the experiment itself. If signing up for and attending the experiment is not made easy, then some participants will not show up nor will they recommend the experiment to their friends. The process needs to cause the least inconvenience to the participants: this includes careful timetabling, rapid response to any communication, sending a reminder email the day before, choosing a convenient location, being on time, etc. If the experiment is particularly lengthy, then it may be difficult to find people willing to give up their time.

During the experiment itself, there should be nothing that confuses or distracts the participants, or that requires them to think about anything other than the tasks at hand. All participants should be treated exactly the same during their experiment: not doing so may introduce confounding factors into the data.

A small payment (e.g., £6, AUD20, or US$15 per hour in 2012) is often appropriate as an incentive for participation and to compensate participants for their time, and a prize (e.g., a CD voucher) can be offered for the participant with the best performance – a prize can be an incentive for the participants to take the experiment seriously and to perform to their best ability.

3.6.2 Number of participants

There is no easy answer to the question, "How many participants do I need for an experiment?" The commonly cited maxim from Nielsen (2000), that only five participants are needed applies to evaluations, not experiments (as discussed in Section 3.8.3).

There are statistical formulae[7] that can determine how many participants are needed to get a specified "power." "Statistical power" is a number between 0 and 1; conventionally, a power of at least 0.8 is considered adequate.[8] The higher the number of participants, the greater will be the power of the experiment.

Unfortunately, these power formulae are only applicable in specific circumstances, when some information about the data is already available – in effect, you need to know some experimental results before you start! They require that you know (or can make assumptions about) the mean and standard deviation of performance under one of the conditions, as well as the desired difference between the mean performance for this condition and the other conditions. That

---

[7] We've made it so far in this book without mentioning statistics – it had to happen sometime!
[8] A "power of 0.8" means that there is a 20% chance of a Type II error, that is, a 20% chance of not detecting a performance difference between conditions when there is one.

is, they require that you have already collected data from one of the conditions, and that you can speculate in advance about what your results from the other conditions will be. Thus, if a difference in mean accuracy of 0.1 is desired between two conditions (one of which is known to have a mean of 0.5 and a standard deviation of 0.15), then application of the formulae [e.g., in Hinton (1995)] will reveal that fifteen participants are required to ensure a statistical power of 0.8.[9]

Put simply, though, the key points are as follows:

- If there is only a small difference in the performance resulting from different conditions, then a large number of participants will be required to reveal it;
- If there are large performance differences, then a small number of participants will suffice.

In the Graph Aesthetics experiment (Example 11, p 37), it is likely that far fewer than the seventy-two participants would have been needed to demonstrate the poor performance of drawings with several edge crossings; in the Orthogonal Corners experiment (Example 1, p 11), many more than the twenty-five participants who took part might be required to reveal differences in performance between the 90-degree and Smooth bends conditions.[10]

Some experimenters continue testing participants until the results appear to converge, but this is unlikely to occur after only a few participants (except by chance). It also does not help determine in advance how many participants should be recruited and, if an incentive is to be given, the financial resources required. There is also the temptation to stop testing participants if the data collected so far produce statistically significant results; by reapplying the statistical tests after the data have been collected for each participant, the experimenter may want to stop as soon as the data give the desired results, even though further participants had been planned. This is not statistically sound (and also has a hint of deception about it). Every time you apply a statistical test, your chances of finding a result are increased, and, as statistical tests report results with respect to probabilities, successive reapplication of these tests will naturally improve the probability of success.[11] Thus, valid statistical analysis depends on the concept of planning the experiment in advance, collecting all the data, and then performing the analysis.

---

[9] There are several online calculators that will calculate desired sample size based on the input parameters of "minimum expected effect" and "estimated standard deviation."

[10] For a card sorting task, Tullis and Wood (2004) found that having more than twenty-five to thirty participants did not greatly affect the results. Personally, I am never comfortable with less than thirty participants in a within-participants experiment, although I have run experiments with as few as twenty-one, and many people use even less than this. Psychology students are usually told that thirty participants is an acceptable minimum.

[11] The issue of repeatedly analysing data is discussed further in Section 5.2.3.

3.6.3 Experimenter interaction

Experiments can be run with varying levels of interaction between the experimenter and participant, and the extent of essential experimenter interaction needs to be defined. The less essential experimenter interaction the better: leaving the participant alone to do the experiment with no involvement from the experimenter is best. It is difficult for an experimenter to be equally consistent in his or her treatment of participants and to remember everything that needs to be done: the less the experimenter has to do, the less chance of confounding factors (see Section 2.3) being introduced or of an important part of the process being forgotten.

There are therefore three key (and often conflicting) issues to take into account when deciding on the extent of essential experimenter interaction:

- *Participants must know exactly what they are required to do at all times.* If they do not, then the reliability of the data will be affected by misunderstandings. This suggests that extensive personal interaction between participant and experimenter is preferable, so that the former can ask questions, and the latter can ensure that any misunderstandings are resolved.
- *Participants must be treated the same because varying treatment between the participants may affect their performance in the experiment.* This suggests a "hands-off" approach, with little personal interaction, because such interaction may unintentionally vary from participant to participant.
- *Data from participants who do not take the experiment seriously can affect the results.* Although such data can sometimes be identified by computational means, observation by the experimenter of the participants during the experimental process may be useful in identifying participants who do not appear to be taking the experiment seriously or are "cheating."

3.6.4 Web experiments

At one extreme, experiments can be run with no personal experimenter interaction, where all instructions are given in written form. Those conducted over the Internet fall into this category. Becoming more common, these experiments have the advantage of being able to reach a wide range of people remotely and efficiently. However, because there is no personal interaction with the participants, they have several disadvantages:

- It is difficult to see whether the participants are taking the experiment seriously.
- It is not known whether the personal demographic information provided is valid.

- You cannot ensure that the same participant does not do the experiment more than once (and therefore possibly be subject to a learning effect). Similarly, you cannot be sure that the whole experiment from beginning to end has been done by the same person.
- There is no information about pauses in activity: participants may be interrupted, may be seeking help, may stop to get a cup of coffee midexperiment, or may simply be thinking very hard about the experimental task.
- There is no information about the location where the experiment is taking place, and, in particular, whether it might introduce confounding factors: an inappropriate informal environment (e.g., in a bar or a park) could result in unwelcome distractions.
- It is difficult to encourage participants to finish the experiment. Whereas a participant sitting in a room with an experimenter is unlikely to abandon the experiment before finishing it, a participant working alone at a computer is much more likely to give up at the slightest interruption. Partial data sets usually have to be discarded.

This is not to say that online experiments are always flawed, simply that the data collected should be treated with caution. Offering an incentive for completion, or for achieving a specified performance level, may encourage participants at a distance to take the experiment seriously. Showing a progress bar that indicates how much of the experiment has been completed may also encourage completion.

Online participants can be asked to provide comments at the end of the experiment. However, these are unlikely to be as rich and extensive as those elicited by interview or via a paper questionnaire completed in the presence of the experimenter.

So, although online experiments may permit the rapid collection of quantitative data, little useful qualitative data about the conduct of a participant during an experiment or about his or her opinions can be reliably collected. The value of such qualitative data should not be taken lightly. (Chapter 4 provides more on the nature of quantitative and qualitative data.)

Example 19: Lettersets Experiment

Research question: "Can sets of alphabetic letters be generated so that the difficulty in creating English words from each set is the same for all sets?" (Purchase and Hamer, 2010)

In this experiment, John Hamer derived a computational model to create a group of thirty lettersets with nine alphabetic letters in each set. The generation

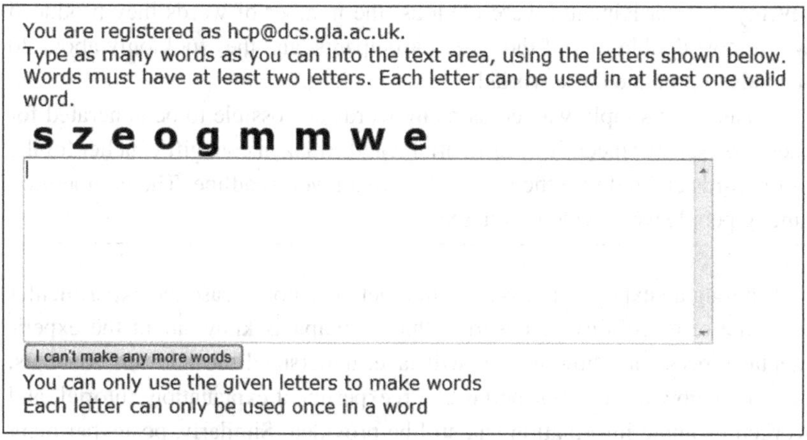

You are registered as hcp@dcs.gla.ac.uk.
Type as many words as you can into the text area, using the letters shown below.
Words must have at least two letters. Each letter can be used in at least one valid word.

s z e o g m m w e

```
I can't make any more words
```
You can only use the given letters to make words
Each letter can only be used once in a word

Figure 3.12: Example of an experimental trial for the online Lettersets experiment.

of these lettersets was based on a corpus of common words from the English language, and we hypothesised that the thirty sets would permit a similar number of English words (with a minimum length of two) to be created.

The data we needed were for as many people as possible to use these lettersets to create as many words as possible, and we used an **online system** for this.

Participants indicated their consent by pressing a button on the introductory web page. The lettersets were then displayed in random order, with the order of the letters scrambled each time they were displayed (Figure 3.12). Participants were asked to create as many English words as they could using each letterset within a 2-minute time limit – they could move on to the next set of words before the 2 minutes were up if they wanted.

The lettersets continued to be presented until the participants indicated that they wanted to stop. Recruitment was done by emailing several mailing lists. Seventy-five people took part on seven continents. Some participants spent as many as 20 hours on the system.

This was a successful way to run this experiment because we were not concerned with the demographics of the participants or whether anyone took part more than once. Because the number of trials was determined by the participant, there was no "end" to the experiment – we simply wanted to collect as many words for each letterset as we could.

The problem in this **online experiment** was in identifying those participants who cheated by using online anagram tools for creating their English words – even though in pressing the "consent" button at the start, the participants were agreeing not to use external resources. The four outliers (out of the seventy-five participants) were obvious: the number of words they produced was almost double that of the other participants, and they took only about 20 seconds to produce these words!

Because we simply wanted as many words as possible to be generated for each letterset, our incentive was to offer a £20 Amazon.com gift voucher for the most words entered into the system before a given deadline. The competition among people worldwide was fierce.[12]

Running an experiment over the Internet does not release the experimenter from the responsibility of ensuring that participants know about the experimental process and how long it will take, understand the relevant concepts, and know how to perform the tasks. Preexperiment explanation, tutorial, and worked example information can still be provided. Similarly, postexperiment questionnaires can be administered online.

Example 20: Visual Complexity Experiment
 Research question: "Can the visual complexity of an image be computed?" (Purchase, Freeman, and Hamer, 2012)

Euan Freeman devised several metrics to quantify the complexity of a digital image. These metrics were based on different measures of the number and variety of colours in the picture, the number and visual strength of edges between objects, and different measures of file size. We needed participants to indicate their judgement of "the complexity" of an image, so we could investigate whether human complexity judgements relate (in a quantifiable way) to any of these measures.

Freeman created an **online system** that presented a row of images and asked participants to move these images (using a drag-and-drop interaction) so that they were sorted, left to right, in order of visual complexity. Each of sixty images were presented twice, with four being randomly selected for each trial (Figure 3.13).

Although it was appropriate to collect a large amount of data this way, what we could not control was the possible effect of the different cultural backgrounds of participants, which may have influenced their judgement of particular images according to their content. We hoped that by clearly asking for judgements on "visual complexity," participants would not focus on the

---

[12] The competition was won by a participant in Zimbabwe who used the £20 prize to donate dictionaries to a local rural school – he did not use an anagram generator!

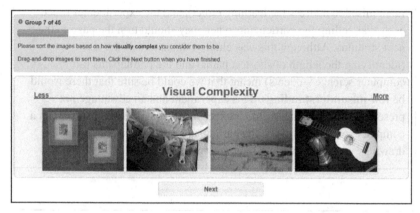

Figure 3.13: Example of an experimental trial for the online Visual Complexity experiment.

content of the images. We were also unable to identify participants who did not take the task seriously, although we removed all trials with a near-zero time. Of the 116 people who started the experiment, only 54 completed it: this was despite clearly telling the participants at the start that the experiment would only take around 15 minutes (the mean completion time of the 54 participants was just a few seconds over 15 minutes) and the inclusion of a progress bar.

3.6.5 Group experiments

Experiments can be run in a group setting, where more than one participant does the experiment concurrently, with instructions given by an experimenter to all participants at the same time. The experimenter has little personal interaction with each participant. This is only appropriate when there is complete confidence that none of the participants will require any detailed individual explanation of the concepts and tasks before commencing the experiment, and, typically when the tasks are simple, and only limited contextual information needs to be provided. It is also important in this case that nothing goes wrong because it will not be possible for the experimenter to address problems experienced by individual participants during the experiment.

The Graph Aesthetics experiment (Example 11, p 37) was conducted as a **group experiment**, with a large class of seventy-two students. Each participant had a paper booklet that contained the stimuli (appropriately randomised to address the learning effect), and the experimenter timed each trial, telling the participants when they should turn the page to the next stimulus. Although this was clumsy, the nature of the task (identifying the length of shortest paths) and the participants (all computer science students) meant that we could be sure that there would be **few misunderstandings**. This experiment had an advantage not present in the subsequent similar experiments that presented stimuli on a computer screen: it allowed the participants to annotate the graph drawings while working out their answer.

Example 21: Metro Maps Experiment
Research question: "Which layout of Metro maps best supports the planning of underground travel?" (Stott, 2011)

Jonathan Stott compared three different layout methods for Metro maps: the published map, a map based on the geographic location of underground train stations, and a map produced by his own layout algorithm. He applied these methods to the underground maps of six cities – Atlanta, Bucharest, Mexico City, Stockholm, Toronto, and Washington, DC (the six experimental objects) – producing eighteen stimuli.

Figure 3.14 shows the three stimuli for Bucharest. Two different types of task were asked of each stimulus (with each task asked more than once as different variants using different station names), up to a total experiment length of 20 minutes:

- "How many changes are required to get from station X to station Y?"
- "How many stations do you go through to get from station X to station Y?"

This was a between-participants experiment that was conducted in three **condition-groups** (approximately fifteen participants per group), with each group using the stimuli for one of the conditions. The participants in each group were seated in a laboratory at their own computers, which presented the experimental trials. Participants indicated their answer by selecting their choice from a given set of possible on-screen answers. Preexperiment training was done as a group, with the experimenter using an overhead projector at the front of the laboratory. This group method of running the experiment was appropriate because it was a reasonable assumption that the undergraduate

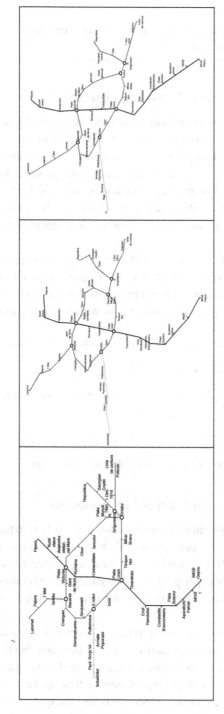

Figure 3.14: Three stimuli for Bucharest: automatically drawn, normalised version of the published map, and geographic map.

students taking part in the experiment would understand the concept of reading and interpreting a train map.

3.6.6 Individual experiments

At the other extreme, the complexity of the tasks may be such that it is necessary for each participant to take part individually, with only one participant and the experimenter present. This gives the experimenter the opportunity to ensure that the participant fully understands the task and has no questions prior to starting the experiment, and that the data will not be affected by the participant's misunderstanding. This method has the obvious disadvantages that much more experimenter time is required, and individual timetabling is needed for each participant.

The Euler Diagrams experiment (Example 6, p 24 required participants to fully understand how to interpret Euler diagrams correctly (Figure 3.15). Because this understanding could not be assumed of any participant, the experiment was conducted on a **one-to-one basis**, with only one participant and the experimenter present.

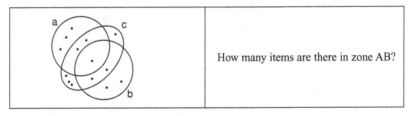

Figure 3.15: An example trial from the Euler Diagrams experiment.

3.6.7 Procedure document

There is a lot for an experimenter to remember to do and say to participants: it is important that the process goes as smoothly as possible and that all participants are treated equally. It is a good idea to write an "experimenter's procedure document" that describes, step by step, everything the experimenter should do and say – this ensures that all participants are treated the same, and that nothing is forgotten.

This document could include important, obvious things such as "ask the participant if he or she has any questions before commencing the experiment" and "change the name of the folder containing the data so that it includes the participant number," as well as trivial things such as "make sure there is a pen available for the participant to use for answering the questionnaire" and "ask the participant to turn off his or her mobile phone." It is useful in ensuring that all experiments are conducted without problems. The document also has added benefits in that it can be annotated by the experimenter during the experiment itself if there are any unusual occurrences, and it can be used by more than one experimenter. The more detailed the procedure document, the better – it is not intended to be a quick reference, rather it is a script that describes every step of the process in detail.

Figure 3.16 shows an extract from the detailed procedure document used in the Mental Model experiment (Example 17, p 62).

3.7 Ethical approval

Most institutions now require that formal ethical approval be given before human participants can be used to collect research data. No matter how much an HCI experimenter may believe that such approval is unnecessary for his or her own project, this is a process that simply needs to be dealt with. Although it may seem unnecessary for participants to give consent for the collection of data when they are simply interacting with software (rather than taking part in a drugs trial, having their brain waves measured, or revealing intimate personal details), ethical approval is still required. Ethical approval ensures that participants are not asked to do anything unreasonable (e.g., perform a series of repetitive tasks for 2.5 hours, stand for long periods of time listening for three-dimensional audio cues by turning their head from side to side, navigate while blindfolded through unfamiliar territory),[13] and that their data are treated with respect.

Ethical requirements vary from country to country and institution to institution. A typical ethics application will ask a researcher to consider the following issues:

1. *The extent of risk that the participants will be exposed to is no greater than that encountered in their normal working life.* Experimenters have a responsibility to protect participants from physical and mental harm during the experiment. Examples where particular care needs to be taken are experiments that occur outside usual laboratory areas; require participant mobility (e.g., walking, running, use of public transport); warrant unusual or repetitive activity or movement; use sensory deprivation (e.g., ear plugs or blindfolds), bright or flashing lights, loud or disorienting noises, or vibration; involve smell or taste or force feedback; or use particularly unusual or uncommon equipment. In these cases, experimenters will need to give particular assurances that participants will be protected from harm.

---

[13] As a member of an ethics committee, I have seen HCI experiment proposals that include all three of these scenarios.

A. When the participant arrives
- Put the "Do not disturb" sign on the door
- Ask them to turn off their mobile phone
- Start the SketchNode logging
- Start the recording (the double-blue 'pause' icon should be showing)
- Make sure SketchNode is in drawing mode

B Paperwork
- Give participant the information sheet and ask them to read it
- Ask them if they have any questions
- Ask them to sign the consent form
- Show the participant the example graph drawing, and explain that these are the graphs (or 'node link' diagrams) that will be used in the experiment
- Ask all the questions on the preexperiment interview sheet

C. Software Demo:
- Demonstrate the drawing features of SketchNode (using own stylus)
- Tell them that the stylus is best used vertically, and they should not press the stylus button

D. .....

E. Experiment Demo:
- Explain the rules
   o   Put down the stylus while looking at the drawing
   o   Point at the screen for the spot-the-difference puzzles if necessary
   o   Press 'New graph' at the start of the spot-the-difference puzzles
- Explain that the demo program is a reduced version of the experiment, just to get them used to the process
- Run the demo program (5 drawings, half-size, 3 seconds, a break after 3 drawings), making sure cursor is in the top right corner
- Ask the participant to draw the graphs on SketchNode, and to do the puzzles, as if it were the real experiment
- Remind the participant that the diagrams will be easier to draw if they do them quickly
   .....

Figure 3.16: Extract from the procedure document used for the Mental Model experiment[14]

---

[14] Here's a tip: it is useful to print the tutorial, worked example, questionnaire, and procedure documents (and any other printed materials) on different coloured paper – this makes them much easier to identify and manage during an experiment than if they are all white.

WEB PAGE EXPERIMENT **CONSENT FORM**

Project title: Aesthetic measures: perception of aesthetic worth and usability of pictures of web pages.

This consent form will be held for a period of at least six years.

I have been given and understood an explanation of this research project. I have had an opportunity to ask questions and have them answered. I am aware that this experiment will take not more than 15 minutes.

I understand that the data collected from the study will be held indefinitely and may be used in future analysis.

I understand that I may withdraw myself and any information traceable to me at any time up to 24th October 2009 without giving a reason, and without any penalty.

I understand that I may withdraw my participation during the session at any time.

I understand that the data I provide will be held in an anonymous form that does not identify me as an individual, but may identify my participant group.

I agree to take part in this research by ranking pictures of web pages according to my perception of their aesthetic worth and their potential usability, and to answer a brief questionnaire.

Signed: _____

Figure 3.17: Consent form used for the Web Page Aesthetics experiment.

2. *Participants should give signed consent, indicating that they are taking part voluntarily, and agree to allow their data to be used.* Signed consent is usually required, and in the interests of privacy, a separate consent form is often signed by each participant (Figure 3.17). In some circumstances, for example, collecting data via brief interview in a public place, an ethics committee might agree that verbal consent is sufficient.

3. *The experiment will not make unreasonable demands on the participant.* In particular, an experiment should not require that participants travel long distances or give a great deal of their personal time. As a rule of thumb, the experiment (including the introductory material, practise tasks, and postexperiment information gathering) should be designed so that it does not take much longer than 1 hour, especially if it entails repetitive tasks

or is cognitively demanding. About 1hour to 75 minutes is reasonable, but a 90-minute experiment really ought to have a good reason for being so long. It is easy to lose the attention and goodwill of the participants if the experiment is too long, and participants will easily become fatigued by performing repetitive and demanding tasks.

4. *Any incentive offered to participants is reasonable.* The payment of participants must not be used to induce them to risk harm beyond that which they would risk without payment in their normal lifestyle. For example, a participant is unlikely to be willing to navigate using an unfamiliar mobile device while crossing a busy road in their normal lives; an experimenter should not expect them to do the same in an experiment, even if offered vast sums to do so.

5. *No information about the evaluation or materials will be intentionally withheld from the participants.* Withholding information or misleading participants is unacceptable if participants are likely to object or show unease when debriefed.[15] In some cases, the nature of the research question might require that some deception be used (e.g., if the participant's reaction to an unexpected event is of interest); however, a case would need to be made for this, and this is rare in HCI experiments.

6. *Participants are capable of understanding the consequences of giving consent.* There is usually a minimum age for participants to give their own consent (which varies from country to country; e.g., in the UK, it is 16). If younger than minimum age participants are to be used in the experiment, signed parental consent is required. Similarly, any participants who have an impairment that may limit their understanding or communication will require signed consent from their caregiver.

7. *Participants will not be coerced into taking part by a person in authority.* Authority or influence must not be allowed to pressurise participants to take part in, or remain in, any experiment because this would violate the condition that the participant is taking part voluntarily. It prevents instructors from using their own students as participants or employers from using their employees.

8. *Participants can withdraw at any time.* All participants should be told before the experiment starts that they have the right to withdraw at any time.

9. *Methods of recruiting participants ensure that the sample is representative.* This especially applies to experiments that target particular categories of people such as the visually impaired, the elderly, or specific cultural groups.

---

[15] Practice tasks, filler tasks, and distracter tasks are, of course, all minor forms of deception – these are unlikely to make participants feel uneasy once they discover the truth about them.

10. *Participants can contact the investigator after the experiment.* Although this requirement is probably more important for experiments in which participants may suffer after effects (e.g., drug trials), all participants must be given the experimenter's contact information. Some ethics committees insist that the participants be given an opportunity to indicate whether they would like to see a summary of the final results of the experiment

11. *Participants will be debriefed.* The experiment should be discussed with the participant at the end, and the participant should have the opportunity to ask questions. Potentially, some information may need to be withheld in this debriefing to ensure that subsequent data collection from other participants is not affected.

12. *The data are stored anonymously and securely.* All participant data (both hard- and soft-copy) should be stored securely and anonymously. Some ethics regulations may also require that data are stored within a particular state or country, with no copies stored outside the area, and that it be destroyed after a specified time limit.

Increasingly, ethics committees are also becoming concerned with whether the research aims of the project are valid, and whether it is appropriate for participant time to be spent on attempting to answer the stated research question. They might consider that if the experiment is not well designed or the question is not appropriate, then it is unethical to ask participants to give their time. This can lead to tension between an experimenter who wants to use participants to address a research question and a committee who believes that the experiment is not sufficiently well designed.

Ethics committees usually ask for copies of the experimental documentation (consent form, instructions, questionnaires, etc.) to be submitted with the ethics application; thus, these will need to be prepared early in the experimental design process. Although it may be inconvenient to formalise these documents at this point, most ethics committees will permit minor amendments after formal approval has been given. The best advice is to determine the requirements and apply well in advance of the experiment's start date because ethics committees tend to sit infrequently and approval can take a long time.

3.8 Evaluations

3.8.1 The experience of the potential user

In the context of an evaluation being conducted as part of the system development cycle, the evaluation procedure does not need to be as rigorously defined as for an experiment.

In the absence of conditions, there is no concept of between-user and within-user evaluations. An evaluator may, however, assign different roles to potential users if the system is to be used by different categories of person. In the evaluation of the Aropä peer assessment system (Example 15, p 49), some potential users assumed the role of instructor, whereas others took on the role of student.

The potential user may require some training before using the system in an evaluation, although in some cases (especially in evaluations near the end of the development cycle) the aim of the evaluation may be to see how well a potential user will perform the tasks without any training. All tasks will typically be performed by the potential users without specified time limits. The overall length of the evaluation needs to be considered, however, because there is still the possibility of fatigue affecting potential users' performance and judgement. It is unlikely that filler or distraction tasks will be required.

Prior to the evaluation, potential users may not need a tutorial or any worked examples; however, they will still need to be informed of the intended evaluation process, and have the tasks and context explained to them. All evaluations should have a focus (as represented by the evaluation question); the better informed the potential users are about the focus, the more likely that useful feedback will be obtained.

Postevaluation feedback collection activities (e.g., interviews, question-naires) are a crucial part of the process: these are not simply supplementary data collection exercises (as they might be in an experiment), but constitute the main means of getting feedback to feed into the next design stage of the cycle. (The nature and method of collecting data from evaluations are discussed in Section 4.5.)

3.8.2 Pilot evaluations

Several evaluations will be conducted before the system is ready for deployment. At the start of the iterative development cycle, system developers themselves are likely to pretend to be potential users as part of initial in-house evaluations. Before testing with external potential users, as with experiments, it is a good idea to pre-pilot the evaluation method within the system development team. These pilots will test the suitability and robustness of the evaluation tasks and the procedures for collecting user data and feedback.

However, the pre-pilots and pilots will not only provide feedback on the evaluation method (thus fulfilling the purpose of piloting), but they will also provide feedback on the system itself. This feedback can and should be fed into the next stage of system design. Indeed, the pilots themselves constitute the first round of evaluation in a repeating development cycle.

Pilot evaluations therefore differ from pilot experiments because, in the latter case, any data collected are thrown away. In addition, because evaluations are less tightly controlled than experiments, it does not matter if the evaluation method is changed between potential users – indeed, it may make sense to do so.

3.8.3 Practical issues

As in experiments, potential users need to be recruited, and it is often difficult to get the desired number and nature of potential users. In particular, if the system is to be used by people with different roles, then having potential users within these roles would be ideal – a system to be used by both bank customers and back office staff is best tested by people who already fulfil these descriptions. Indeed, there may be different categories of bank customer for which different aspects of the system are applicable (e.g., students, company directors, treasurers of charity organisations), and real users who hold these roles will give the most valuable feedback.

In practise, however, many evaluations may need to ask potential users to adopt a given role based on scenarios. For example, "Imagine that you are a school leaver wanting to make an enquiry about a student loan. You are not sure about whether to take a gap year and want to weigh the pros and cons of going to university this year or next."

Like participants, potential users should be managed carefully; their time is precious. The process should be made easy, timetabling should be convenient, they should be treated courteously, and a small financial incentive might be appropriate.

In terms of the number of potential users, Nielsen (2000) suggests that only five are needed for an evaluation: five potential users will reveal most of the problems in a system, and as you run more evaluations with more users after this, you will learn less and less about the system per potential user. In the initial stages of the development cycle, a few users will reveal most problems with the system; however, in the latter stages, a larger number of participants will be required to identify the smaller, more subtle issues.[16]

The extent of interaction between the evaluator and potential users is not as much a concern as with experiments because confounding factors are irrelevant. One-to-one evaluations may be necessary in the first round of evaluations (when the feedback is likely to be rich and extensive), whereas large group, remote evaluations may be more appropriate later (when a larger, more varied set of

---

[16] Note that this balance between "number of potential users" and "number of problems" roughly accords with the discussion in Section 3.6.2 on the number of participants needed for an experiment with respect to the size of the performance difference expected between conditions.

potential users is required). Although a procedure document (as described for experiments in Section 3.6.7) might not be essential for an evaluation, it can do no harm for the evaluator to have such a document to ensure that nothing is forgotten in the process – you do not want to let the potential users leave and then realise that they have not been asked to perform an important feedback task.

With regard to ethical approval, many institutions will require that approval be given before conducting an evaluation with potential users outside the research team, although increasingly such evaluations are considered by institutions as "low risk," with trimmed-down, rapid-turnaround approval processes. Unlike experiments, the ethical concern in evaluations is typically focussed on the experience of the potential user, rather than on the use of the data collected because the assumption is that the feedback will feed into the next design cycle, rather than be published. As always, it is best to check well in advance.

3.9 Summary

This chapter focusses on the actual process of running the experiment and considers the decisions that need to be made in defining the participant experience, that is, decisions that must be made before the experiment is conducted.

Having decided on

- the allocation of participants to conditions,
- the experimental parameters (e.g., practise trials, fillers),
- the supplementary materials (e.g., tutorials, procedure documents), and
- the recruitment of participants,

and then piloted the experiment and obtained ethical approval, you may believe that you are ready to roll!

Not quite! Before the experimental method is finalised, it is important to consider exactly what data are to be collected, and in what form.

This is an easy step to forget at the planning stage, although it probably should be done before piloting and before applying for ethical approval. Deciding on what data to collect (and how it will be analysed) in advance ensures that you will get exactly what you want out of your experiment and that your research question will be answered. Data collection is discussed in Chapter 4.

4

Data collection and qualitative analysis

Designing an experiment is more than creating stimuli and tasks and deciding on the participant experience. Before conducting the experiment, the exact form of data to be collected needs to be decided, and importantly, it needs to be confirmed as sufficient for answering the research question.

This chapter focusses primarily on data collection. It describes the different types of data that can be collected for different purposes and the means of collecting it.

We make the traditional distinction between *quantitative* data (represented by numbers; e.g., the number of errors, a preference ranking) and *qualitative* data (not represented by numbers; e.g., a verbal description of problems encountered in performing the task, a video showing interaction with an interface).[1]

In practise, there are two distinct decisions to be made about data:

- What data to collect (a decision made in advance of the experiment), and
- How to analyse the data (a decision made after the experiment has been run).

These two decisions are inextricably linked because the potential means of analysis will influence the decision on what data to collect. Any discussion about data collection therefore necessarily entails discussion on how it will be analysed.

Data analysis is the process of summarising raw data into a useful form. The outcomes of the analysis may be in a variety of forms (e.g., statistical values, written paragraphs of summary text, tables of emergent themes). What is important is that the data that have been collected from a sample of the

---

[1] Note, however, that qualitative data are often converted (even if only partially) into quantitative form for the purposes of analysis and reported numerically; for example, the number of times participants mention a particular feature of an interaction device during an interview, or the number of times participants hesitate before selecting a particular on-screen option.

population are summarised into a form that represents conclusions about the population as a whole.

Data analysis methods for *qualitative data* are included in this chapter, and analysis of *quantitative data* (however collected) is covered in Chapter 5. These analysis methods are separated so as to confine the detailed statistics discussion to one chapter, and because the statistical methods are applicable to many different forms of data. Qualitative analysis methods are, however, best discussed in the context of the method of data collection.

4.1 The data and the research question

In deciding on the form of data to be collected, and the method of collecting it, it is essential to revisit the research question: the data collected must be sufficient to answer the research question, and must be in an appropriate form for its analysis to clearly lead to an answer to the research question. One way to address this issue is to ask: "How will you know that you have answered your research question?", or "What information will you need to ensure that you can answer the question?"

The Euler Diagrams experiment (Example 6, p 24) had seven example stimuli, as shown in Figure 4.1.

If my **research question** is, "Are Euler diagrams a good way of representing set relationship information?", then asking participants to

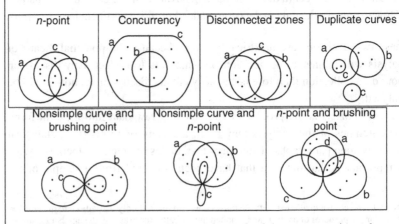

Figure 4.1: Euler diagrams demonstrating each of the seven experimental conditions.

interpret the set relationships in the stimuli will not answer this question. Neither will asking them which of these drawings they prefer. In both cases, there is no alternative representation with which to compare the use of Euler diagrams.

If I ask participants to count the number of dots or colours, or trace around the edge of the sets with a cursor, this does not help in asking the **research question**, "Which well-formedness conditions in the presentation of Euler diagrams are easiest to understand?"

And if I ask them to draw a Euler diagram from given set relationship information, then those data will not be sufficient for answering the **research question**, "Which well-formedness conditions in the presentation of Euler diagrams are easiest to understand?"

The key point is that if the form of the data and the way in which they are to be analysed is not clearly defined *before* the experiment is conducted, there is a chance that a lot of time and effort may be wasted when it is discovered that the data are not sufficient to answer the research question. (Or it may mean changing the research question *after* the experiment to one that *can* be addressed by the data: this is not an advisable course of action, but it is more common than you might think!)

In the Euler Diagrams experiment (Example 6, p 24) we collected preference data at the end of the experiment. Recall that there are six well-formedness properties (BP, CC, DC, DZ, NP, NS); however, because some properties cannot occur without another, these six properties were actually repressed in the experimental objects as seven experimental conditions (CC, NP, DC, DZ, NS&BP, NS&NP, NP&BP). At the end of the experiment, the participants were only asked their preference opinion on the six basic well-formedness properties, rather than on the actual conditions used in the experiment. This meant that **our data were insufficient** for answering a secondary **research question** as to whether there was any relationship between participants' *preferences* for the conditions and their *performance* on those conditions.

One way of ensuring that correct and sufficient data are being collected is to invent some data before running any experiments, and make sure that the analysis of this imaginary data will answer your question. The fabricated data may take any values: they can be randomly generated or invented to take values that could reasonably occur during the experiment. Analysing these data will, of course, produce nonsense, but going through this process before collecting any real data will ensure that the correct form of data are being collected.

In the Visual Complexity experiment (Example 20, p 82), because we had not collected ranking data online before, we wanted to confirm that the data we were about to collect would be sufficient for answering our research question, which was whether we could use computational metrics (colour, etc.) to quantify humans' perception of visual complexity.

Before actually running the experiment, we **fabricated data** from five participants for six images, imagining an experiment where each image was shown twice in a three-way ranking task. We simply made up numbers as to the ranking position these imaginary participants placed each picture for both times they were shown it, as in Table 4.1. We could then relate the total ranking for each image (first presentation ranking plus second presentation ranking) to its computational measure of colour, as in Table 4.2.

We were also able to calculate a correlation coefficient for these data, obtaining the value of 0.35. Although we knew this number was meaningless, we had confirmed that the data we planned to collect would be sufficient to calculate a value that would determine whether there was a relationship between the colour metric and the participants' perception of "visual complexity," and therefore answer our **research question**.

4.2 Some principles of qualitative data collection and analysis

Qualitative data are not represented by numbers, but by text (written or spoken), video, or artefacts. Examples include the following:

- *Text*: an audio recording of a participant describing why he or she preferred one condition over another; a paragraph written by a participant describing how he or she performed the tasks; words written by the experimenter to record the verbal response to a question posed in an interview.
- *Video*: a video of a participant interacting with a tabletop interactive surface, showing the participant's hands and the tabletop display; a screen-cast video capturing the entire screen display and all interactions with it.

Table 4.1: *Fabricated data used to verify the data collection method*

participant	First presentation ranking of six images (1..3)						participant	Second presentation ranking of six images (1..3)					
	i1	i2	i3	i4	i5	i6		i1	i2	i3	i4	i5	i6
p1	3	2	1	3	1	3	**p1**	3	1	1	2	2	2
p2	1	3	1	1	2	2	**p2**	3	3	2	1	2	3
p3	1	2	3	3	3	1	**p3**	1	2	2	1	2	3
p4	3	2	1	3	1	2	**p4**	3	2	1	2	1	3
p5	1	1	3	3	2	2	**p5**	2	2	1	3	1	3
Total	9	10	9	13	9	10	Total	12	10	7	9	8	14

Table 4.2: *Associating fabricated data with the colour metric*

	i1	i2	i3	i4	i5	i6
Rank measure (fabricated)	21	20	16	22	17	24
Colour metric (actual)	94	153	55	32	34	103

- *Artefact*: a screen dump of the status of a system during participant evaluation; an Entity-Relationship diagram drawn by a participant; program pseudocode written by the participant.

Individual qualitative data of the textual variety are typically captured by questionnaire (paper based or online) or interview (informal, semistructured, or structured), or by asking participants to "think aloud" during the experiment. For evaluations, useful feedback can also be elicited using focus groups.[2]

Although interviews are more time consuming than questionnaires, participants are more forthcoming with information when talking rather than writing, so more detailed information is likely to be elicited by interview than by (paper or computer) questionnaire.

Unlike quantitative data, qualitative data cannot be analysed directly; rather, they need to be interpreted before being summarised.

4.2.1 Interpreting textual data

Analysing textual data involves identifying clear themes that emerge from the text and determining those that are most common. Themes are not always identically phrased, so some subjective judgement is required in deciding whether two phrases belong to the same theme. For example, the phrases "too cluttered," "very squidged up," "all on top of each other," and "not very spread out" might be considered to all belong to the theme of "cluttered." It is therefore best if this analysis is independently performed (and subsequently agreed on) by at least two people to ensure that it is valid and unbiased.[3] Note that audio textual

---

[2] Detailed descriptions of these qualitative data collection activities are outside the scope of this book because they are extensively covered elsewhere. I recommend Part IV of Preece et al. (1994) for thorough description of these methods.

[3] It is best if the other person is someone who understands the nature of the research (even if the person is not directly involved in it); otherwise, there may be irrelevant differences of opinion. This may be difficult in a small research team.

data will need to be transcribed (or listened to carefully several times) before themes can be identified.

Once the data from all participants have been analysed and categorised into themes, the number of times clearly identifiable themes were expressed can be counted and summarised in tabular or textual form. For example, "ten of the fifteen participants said that they were unsure about the exact definition of 'visual complexity'; however, of these, eight said that they were confident that they had used an appropriate interpretation."

It is important not to forget the less popular themes – even if only one participant has expressed a view, it should be recorded. For example, "Other negative comments included the colour of the nodes (two participants); the use of the name 'Tim' in the social network (one); the location of the experimental room (two); and the bell warning sound, which was considered 'irritating' (one)."

Good representative direct quotes can be extracted to support the conclusions and to enrich the presentation of the results (e.g., "The landscape pictures were hard to judge – maybe 'cos they are so boring!").

4.2.2 Interpreting video data

Each participant video needs to be watched (usually several times) and described in detail to identify the important actions (or sequences of actions) used, and their timing.[4]

Often, a list of important actions is agreed in advance by the research team.[5] For example, in an experiment that asks participants to rearrange objects in order of size using a drag-and-drop interface, one action category might be "participant moves an object several places to the left and places it between two objects that are not obviously of similar size." This action may indicate that the participant is doing a coarse separation of big objects from small ones, perhaps before doing a later fine-grained separation: this is easier to see from the video screen casts than from a log file that captures all interactions with the system.

---

[4] Special ethical approval and participant consent will be required if the video recording includes participants' faces so that they are identifiable. The same can be said for audio recordings (because people can be identified by their voice), although making a commitment to have the audio recordings completely transcribed before destroying them will appease most ethics committees. It is much more difficult to fully transcribe a video recording, and most experimenters will want to keep the video data.

[5] In the research literature, these categories are often called "codes," and the people who analyse data according to these codes are "coders."

Categorising these actions is a subjective task, and new categories may be revealed during the analysis process. The means of summarising the data may therefore vary between analysts. As with textual data, at least two independent people should perform, and agree on, the interpretation.

An overall account of the activities of all participants can be produced by summarising the extent to which the actions were performed. For example, "Eight of the sixteen participants drew all the nodes first before adding the edges; of these, five drew the nodes in a neat line across the top of the screen, and one drew them in a circle. Of the five that drew the nodes in a line, two labelled them in alphabetic order from left to right: the others labelled the nodes in no discernible order."

4.2.3 Interpreting artefact data

This type of data is less common than text or video data. In this case, the data are artefacts that are not text and have no time dimension. Like videos, these artefacts need to be scrutinised and their properties described and classified, usually by identifying key interesting features (which may be specified in advance or may emerge from the data). For example, pseudocode for an algorithm can be analysed to see whether it uses the most efficient method for storing and accessing variables, whether the choice of variable names is appropriate, whether indentation has been used to indicate nested loops, etc. These are all aspects of the code that are independent of its run-time correctness. As before, such subjective analysis of these artefacts should be performed (and agreed on) by at least two independent people.

The overall summary of the artefacts from all participants will typically be presented in the form of descriptive text or tables. For example, "Twenty-four of the thirty students used appropriate variable names (while one used exactly the same variable name for all variables!); only two students used an indexed array; all the others created ten separate variables. Eleven students used indentation; of these, six used appropriate indentations to show the nested loops. One student wrote the pseudocode for a functional language – this code was discarded."

4.3 Nature of data collected

We can usefully categorise the most common types of data that can be collected as the *five Ps of data collection*:

- *performance*: indicates how well a participant has performed in a task;

- *preference*: records a participant's preferences in comparison tasks;
- *perception*: records a participant's opinions;
- *process*: shows the process that a participant followed when performing the task;
- *product*: collects artefacts created by a participant during the task.

It is important to remember that the data collected are only *indicative* of a perceptual or cognitive activity; it does not represent the activity itself. We can extrapolate from what we discover to speculate about what a participant has seen, thought, or understood, but we can never know exactly. That is, we cannot get into a participant's mind.

4.3.1 Performance data

Performance data measures how well the participant performed the experimental tasks – these data are typically collected quantitatively.

The two most common types of performance data are as follows:

- *Errors*: the correctness of the participant's response, indicating *accuracy*. These are typically easy to count because it would be unusual to use this performance measure without each trial having a unique correct answer.
- *Response time*[6]: the time taken for a participant to complete a task, indicating *efficiency*. This is the time elapsed between the presentation of the stimulus and the participant submitting an answer.

Neither error nor response time data are trivial measures, however (particularly if a time limit has been set for the trials), because decisions need to be made about how to deal with anomalous responses. For example, if a participant has not submitted an answer before the time limit, should the accuracy of this trial count as an error with the response time being set to the time limit, or should it be considered as "missing data"? If the response time for a participant in a particular trial is impossibly short (e.g., microseconds), but the answer is correct, should this data point be discarded as being an example of the participant not taking the experiment seriously or skipping a trial by accident, or should it be recorded as a correct answer?

The length of the time limit also affects the response time. For instance, in the first pilot experimental sessions for the Euler Diagrams experiment

---

[6] Many psychological studies refer to "reaction time" rather than "response time." Reaction time experiments tend to involve fast tasks that focus on perceptual processes (e.g., clicking on a moving object on a screen). Because most HCI experiments involve both cognitive processing and perception, I prefer to use "response time."

(Example 6, p 24) setting a time limit of 45 seconds gave a mean response time of 9.4 seconds over all pilot participants; reducing this time limit to 20 seconds in the second pilot sessions produced a mean time of 7.4 seconds. This reduction in mean time in these two pilots demonstrates the effect of setting a time limit: participants quickly get into a rhythm to ensure that they answer within the time limit.

Intuitively, there ought to be an interaction between response time and errors: answering the questions quickly would mean more errors, whereas taking more time would mean fewer errors. Surprisingly, this is not always the case. Some tasks are so difficult that people will take a long time, and still get the wrong answer. However, if there is a chance that there has been time–error interaction, then this should be investigated once the data have been collected because it may affect the interpretation of the results (this issue is discussed further in Section 5.5.1).

Error data can be collected by a variety of means. In one-to-one experiments, the participant may simply be required to say the answer out aloud, with the experimenter writing it down; participants may be asked to write the answers on an answer sheet; or the answers may be collected by experimental software. Most important is that every answer given by the participant is correctly associated with the appropriate trial: an experimenter who faithfully writes down all the answers given, but does not know (and cannot later find out) the exact random order of the trials for that particular participant, may as well throw the data away! Similarly, experimental software that collects answers in a database, while not also storing the related trial identifier (see Section 2.7), will not prove very useful.

Response time data are only reliably collected by automatic means. Tasks that are expected to take some time [e.g., the class-diagram matching task of the Smalltalk experiment (Example 16, p 53)] may be timed using a watch (or stop watch), but typical HCI experiments will use equipment that will enable time stamp information to be stored whenever a response to a trial is submitted (or when the trial times out). As with error data, the response time data must be correctly associated with a trial identifier, or else it is useless.

As all performance data are quantitative, their analysis is covered in Chapter 5 rather than here.

4.3.2 Preference data

Participants are often asked to indicate their preferences for conditions – indeed, it is advisable to always ask for preference data in a postexperiment questionnaire or interview so as to collect as much data as possible from each participant.

Some experiments collect preference data only, although it is more often used to support other types of data. Preference data can be collected quantitatively or qualitatively.

Preference data are a result of asking participants what they think of the different experimental conditions. Like other forms of data, we cannot get inside participants' heads, but we can ask them what they prefer (and why), and hope that they can express what they think clearly.

In collecting *quantitative preference data*, participants can be asked to rank the experimental conditions or a set of stimuli according to specified criteria (e.g., personal preference, ease of use, aesthetic beauty), or to give a rating to each condition (e.g., a number between 1 and 10 to indicate how attractive an interface is). This quantitative preference data can then be analysed using numerical and statistical methods (see Chapter 5).

For the Web Page Aesthetics experiment (Example 2, p 12), participants were asked to rank all fifteen Web sites according to their perception of (a) how aesthetically pleasing the site was, and (b) how useable the site appeared to be. Thus, for each participant, each web site had two **rank** numbers between 1 and 15 associated with it, one for aesthetic appeal and one for perceived usability.

In the Visual Complexity experiment (Example 20, p 82), as well as asking participants to rank the images, we also asked them to assign a "complexity rating" between 1 and 5 to each image, thus giving us both **rank** and **rating** data for two complexity measures per participant per image.

If sufficient quantitative preference data have been collected, then an interesting additional analysis can be performed to determine whether there is any relationship between the performance data and the preference data: people do not always prefer the conditions that they perform best with. A participant's preference ranking for a condition can be associated with each experimental trial – the correlations between "preference and accuracy" and between "preference and response time" can be calculated over all the trials (see Section 5.4). This will reveal whether participants performed better in the conditions that they preferred.

Qualitative preference data are richer than that obtained from ranking or rating because the participants can express their opinions freely and are not constrained by the form of the data. Even if participants have already performed a ranking or rating preference task, they should still be asked *why* they prefer one condition over another.

The result of the analysis of qualitative preference data would be a textual summary of the views of the participants, focussing on their relative preference judgements. For example, "Nine participants disliked condition A because they thought that it moved too fast, whereas four thought that the speed of condition A was beneficial because it made them think harder about the task," perhaps with accompanying useful quotes if available [e.g., "Graph A was cool: it was so fast it made pretty patterns – it was harder (I think), but more fun!"].

4.3.3 Perception data

Collecting perception data[7] is similar to collecting preference data in that it focuses on eliciting participants' opinions; however, in this case, no explicit comparisons are involved, and the questions asked are broader than asking for relative ranking or rating of conditions or stimuli. Perception data are typically collected qualitatively because quantitative perception tasks are usually a variation of the preference judgements discussed previously.

Qualitative perception data allow for a wide range of issues to be explored and for the participants to express their opinions about the experimental tasks and process freely. For example: What particular aspects of the stimuli did they focus on? Did they notice anything interesting about the stimuli? If so, what features did they notice? Did they devise a particular approach to performing the tasks? Did they start to get tired or lose concentration at any time? If so, when and why?

Even if the participants are not asked specific questions about their experimental experience, simply asking, "Do you have any comments?", at the end of an experiment will elicit a wide range of useful (and often unexpected) information. In the Spring Dynamic Graph experiment (Example 10, p 33) we were surprised when participants said that they believed that some of the dynamic graphs were "too fast," even though the animation speed was the same for all conditions. These comments made us think more about how the different mental map parameters affected not only the movement of the nodes, but also the relative movement of the edges and the relative placement of nodes with respect to edges.

Because perception data do not focus on comparisons (as do preference data), the range of views will be wider and can be guided by the specific

---

[7] Note that the use of "perception" in this context should not be confused with the human perceptual processes of seeing, hearing, etc.; in this context, the term "perception" refers to "opinion" – it has been chosen so as to usefully fit in with the "five P model."

questions asked. For example, "Six participants stated that they focussed on colour when interpreting the chart, whereas four indicated that both colour and shape were important. All the participants said that the tasks were easy and that they were confident that they had performed well. No participants reported feeling fatigued, although one participant said that he was 'a bit bored at the end.'"

4.3.4 Process data

In some cases, it is the process that the participants follow in performing a task that is of interest (i.e., what they actually do to complete the experimental tasks). These data can be collected both quantitatively and qualitatively.

4.3.4.1 Quantitative process data

For stimuli that are highly interactive (as in the Metabolic Pathways experiment, Example 3, p 13) it is useful to collect interaction data because the extent of interaction may relate to the participants' cognitive effort. These process data can include mouse clicks, the use of scrolling, zooming and panning features, eye tracking data, etc., and can be stored automatically in a log file that records everything that the participant did with the system, as well as the time of every action.

Collecting information about the process produces a vast amount of often unwieldy data that can be very time consuming to analyse. It is a good idea to determine in advance, therefore, what use this process data will have, and how it might contribute to answering the research question.

For example,

- If the extent of zoom interaction used by a participant is measured, then this measurement must have some interpretation in terms of the research question. It may be that more zooming is indicative of a difficulty in comprehending the information on the screen, or it may suggest that participants are confused as to where to look for information.
- If eye tracking data are collected, then the fixations (positions on the screen where the participant's eyes pause) and saccades (quick movements between fixations) should have some interpretation with respect to the task. Several saccades in sequence may suggest confusion, or it may indicate that the participant is being diligent in performing a search task. If there is excessive fixation on an area of the screen, then it may indicate difficulty in understanding the object being viewed, or it may relate to a fascination with a particularly interesting object.

- If the number of times a participant replays an animation is counted, this may indicate that the participant was having difficulty finding the answer to the task in the animation, or simply that the participant liked it and wanted to see it again.
- If the participant chooses to speed up the animations in the experiment, it may indicate confidence in being able to find the answer in a fast animation, or simply that the participant is in a hurry.

The key point is that these process data are meaningless unless they are explicitly associated with an interpretation of the participant's experience that is relevant to the experimental research question.

Process data (e.g., log files or eye tracking data) can be analysed computationally using a program that will identify the significant events. Typically, the more high level these events are, the easier to analyse the process. For example, knowing the exact position on the screen of each mouse click is not as useful as knowing which buttons on the screen were selected, and knowing that a participant's eyes moved rapidly from one side of the screen to the other is not as useful as knowing which two objects were being looked at. Quantitative process data collected by computational analysis of process data can be analysed using the methods described in Chapter 5.

4.3.4.2 Qualitative process data

Although in most cases, interactions and the submissions of responses to trials can be logged using an experimental software system, process data can also be collected via video and audio tracks. These data may be collected by screencast software that records a screen and all changes made to it, or by an external video recorder that captures the image of the participants and their experimental actions. An audio track is usually also captured.

Videos and screen casts are more concrete than log files, and will show more clearly what actually happened. They are useful for observing the participant's process of doing a task while seeing exactly what they see. For example, observational analysis of a video screen cast showing the process of a participant rearranging nodes in a graph drawing can reveal the order in which nodes are moved, and whether nodes are moved together or separately. Although this information may be available in a log file, looking at it in a video means that the experimenter can see exactly what the participant could see at the time the adjustments to the graph layout were made.[8]

---

[8] Videos have the additional advantage of being a convenient way to demonstrate the experimental process to other people when presenting your research: 30 seconds of video will

Audio tracks can often indicate what participants are thinking, especially if they have been encouraged to "think aloud"; this is most useful in identifying when they are confused, frustrated, or tired.

The final summary of the video and audio analysis will be a textual or tabulated description of the actions and spoken thoughts of the participants. Taking the (imaginary) example of asking participants to rearrange twenty objects in order of size using a drag-and-drop interface (where the conditions are the different shapes of the objects), the video and audio analysis of the process for one condition might be partially summarised as in Table 4.3.[9] Note that although actions 1 to 5 could have been identified from a log file, actions 2, 4, and 5 relate specifically to what the participant sees on the screen at the time of the action. Note also that this is an example of qualitative data being reduced to a quantitative form (which may be subject to further analysis using quantitative methods).

In the Mental Model experiment (Example 17, p 62) we collected both **log data** and **video screen-cast** data. The **log data** allowed us to identify the number of drawing and editing actions used to create the drawing (an indication of the ease with which the drawings were created), and the number of times the "undo" feature was used (an indication of the confidence with which the participant remembered the diagram). The **screen-cast videos** were visually analysed to determine the process of creating the drawings; that is, whether nodes were typically drawn before edges, or whether edges were moved to better positions. Knowing this process helped us determine which features the participant focussed on when creating the drawings from memory.

4.3.5 Product data

For some experiments, the data collected are artefacts created by the participants (e.g., a diagram, a set of words, a pseudocode algorithm). In these cases, it may still be the case that the response can be judged as "correct" or "incorrect" (giving quantitative performance data), but it is also usual for these artefacts to

---

reveal a great deal more about what actually happened in the experiment than a textual description of the experimental design and stimuli.

[9] The categories in this table are only indicative; several more could be added (e.g., "moved small objects ten or more places from right to left").

Table 4.3: *Example tabulated summary of video data showing number of participants performing each action*

Circular shapes (*n* = 20 participants)	At start (first ten moves)	In middle	At end (last ten moves)
Moved large objects ten or more places from left to right	18	12	2
Moved large objects ten or more places from left to right, to lie between two objects obviously not of similar size	16	8	0
Moved large objects fewer than ten places from left to right	8	20	10
Moved large objects fewer than ten places from left to right, to lie between two objects obviously not of similar size	4	10	0
Swopped two objects not of similar size within the first ten places on the left	5	18	4
Expressed confusion over the comparative size of two objects	0	0	12
Expressed confusion over the comparative size of three objects	1	2	4

These data are for an imaginary experiment that asks participants to rearrange twenty objects in order of size using a drag-and-drop interface. Fabricated data for the "circular shape" condition are shown here.

be analysed for other features of interest. These data are typically qualitative, but may be reduced into some quantitative measures.

For example, an experiment may ask participants to draw some Entity-Relationship diagrams based on a given set of relational tables, the experimental condition being the number and nature of the tables. The data collected would be the diagrams themselves, although supplementary timing data may also be recorded. Note that in this case, creating each artefact may take a long time, and, depending on the number of conditions, a between-participants approach might be preferable (see Section 3.1.1 for a discussion on the between-participants approach and associated timing issues).

The nature of the artefact will determine the best way for it to be analysed. If interesting aspects of the artefact can be measured, then these measurements can represent the artefact as *quantitative data*. For example, if the participant's task was to design interfaces created under different conditions (e.g., with different software resources), and the design of these interfaces can be characterised in terms of interesting quantitative measures (e.g., number of input and output objects, the size, the number of colours used), then quantitative statistical methods analysis (covered in Chapter 5) can indicate whether there is any significant difference in these measures with respect to condition.

In the Mental Model experiment (Example 17, p 62) we collected data on the correctness of the **graph structure** and its **topology**, and the time taken to draw the graphs. However, of most importance was the product: the graph drawing itself. These drawings were quantitatively analysed (using a statistical method that compared them to pseudorandom drawings) to determine whether the presence of the six visual features in the drawings was chance occurrence, or a probable consequence of their having been in the stimuli, and therefore having been internalised in visual memory.

If the artefact cannot be quantitatively measured, then a *qualitative analysis* would need to be performed. For example, observation of a sketched interface may reveal an attempt to place objects symmetrically (even if geometric symmetry is not enforced), a clear direction of interaction flow in a particular direction across the screen (which is difficult to describe quantitatively), and an aesthetically pleasing combination of colours. The output of the analysis will typically be presented in the form of descriptive text or tables. As with process data, these qualitative data may be reduced to a quantitative form and subsequently analysed using numerical methods.

4.4 Collecting a variety of data

It can be tempting to collect all five types of P data – performance, preference, perception, process, and product – to get as wide a view as possible of the effects of the different conditions. However, this approach has its pitfalls: experiments that collect everything require careful planning and administration, may take a long time to conduct (longer than is acceptable for a participant to spend on an experiment), and require extensive analysis and cross-referencing.

The most important data to collect is that which is meaningful to the research question, can be analysed to answer the research question, and can be collected in a reasonable manner – doing otherwise can lead to wasting both the experimenter's and participants' time, and may lead to ethical concerns.

However, as mentioned in Section 2.3, no experiment can ever be perfect, and all experiments are limited by their parameters, so anything we can do to overcome the limitations is a good thing. If only one type of data is collected, then the worth of the conclusions arising from this single data set may be questionable. Analysing a combination of data types will give a more comprehensive overall picture of results, and will therefore lead to firmer conclusions. A "mixed methods approach" is often advocated, whereby the experimenter deliberately collects both qualitative and quantitative data in the investigation of a single research question.

In social science studies, "triangulation" is often used to verify results collected by different methods. If data are collected using two methods, and the results support each other, then the overall conclusions are much more likely to be accepted. If the results are contradictory, then you cannot be sure which is more likely to be correct. A third form of data (the third point of the "triangle") will confirm which data to have more confidence in (or, if all three are contradictory, will indicate that there are some serious problems with the research question, the experiment, or the data collection).

At the least, a typical comparative experiment should collect both performance and preference/perception data for the conditions and should include an "any other comments?" question at the end. Experiments with more complex research questions might also collect process and product data.

4.5 Evaluations

The fact that evaluations take place as part of an iterative development cycle does not release the evaluator from thinking carefully about what data should be collected, how they should be collected, and whether they will be sufficient for answering the evaluation question. As in experiments, if these issues are not considered in advance, then valuable potential user time will be wasted.

The difference between experiments and evaluations comes in the purposes for which the data are being collected: although experimenters aim to collect data that will demonstrate the relative worth of different HCI ideas (and to publish the findings in the literature), evaluators want to prepare a report that can be passed to the design team to inform subsequent design and implementation decisions. Therefore, the evaluation data should always be collected in a manner that focuses on identifying how the system can be improved.

The most important data Ps are likely to be *perception* (getting participants' opinions on the system) and *process* (finding out what potential users actually did when using the system). *Preference* data might help a design team find out which of several design options to take, but *performance* and *product* data are less likely to be useful.

Data for evaluations may be quantitative or qualitative, but qualitative data are more likely to be useful. If quantitative data are collected, then they could be summarised in simple charts and mean values, and would probably not need to be subject to the detailed statistical analyses described in Chapter 5.

The qualitative data need to be summarised in a useful form for the design team. This would typically be done in terms of a list of the most common issues arising from the evaluation, supplemented by any suggestions for improvement made by the participants themselves. In this case, the perception data collected would not simply seek to collect potential users' opinions, but also their recommendations as well.

As with the analysis of qualitative data, having more than one person categorise the data according to theme before preparing the report is a good idea (especially if there is a large number of potential users). Similarly, even those issues mentioned by only a few participants should be included.

In the Aropä evaluation (Example 15, p 49), potential users were asked to perform a series of scenarios, taking the roles of both lecturer and student.

Most of the useful information came from the **summary of the qualitative data**. This included, for example,

- "Registering users and allocating reviews proved to be . . . the task where most errors occurred, and some backtracking was involved."
- "Setting up the grading rubric . . . there was some confusion while navigating to the required page, and errors were involved where participants created a blank rubric instead of using the provided template."
- "There seemed to be a dislike of certain features of Aropä such as the unintuitive buttons, the allocating reviews section, and the layout of the web site as a whole."
- "The focus of the feedback was on improving the navigation of the web site and making the functionality of buttons more clear. Addition of a

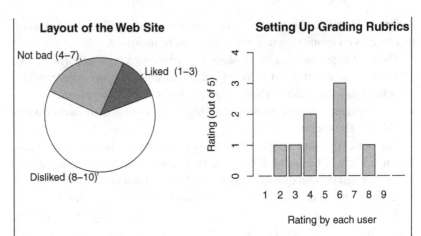

Figure 4.2: Example of quantitative data provided on "the ease with which grading rubrics can be created in Aropä" and "the layout of the Web site."[10]

calendar, creating a sort of a visual progression line; changing the view of the reviews section; and creating a new layout design were some of the other suggestions provided by participants."

Some **quantitative data** were also provided in the report (Figure 4.2), but these were less useful.

4.6 Summary

This chapter describes five different types of data that can be collected, and the means of analysing them (as summarised in Table 4.4).

As mentioned in the introduction to this chapter, defining the data to be collected and determining the means of analysing the data, are important and closely entwined stages of the initial experimental design. The process of planning the data collection and analysis before actually running the experiment is an important and easily forgotten step. Taking care with these stages will ensure that valuable participants' time will be used effectively in addressing your specific research question.

The next chapter focuses on statistical methods for analysing quantitative data, which apply to all quantitative data collected under any of the five P data

---

[10] These charts have been lifted directly from the Aropä evaluation report: it is not usually considered a good idea to use pie charts for presenting numerical data.

Table 4.4: *Summary of five P data categories: collection and analysis*

		Collection	Analysis
Performance	Quantitative	Time, errors	Statistical
	Qualitative	Not applicable	
Preference	Quantitative	Ranking, ratings	Statistical
	Qualitative	Interviews, questionnaires	Textual analysis, resulting in summary of preferential opinions
Perception	Quantitative	Rare: usually reduces to preference data	
	Qualitative	Interviews, questionnaires	Textual analysis, resulting in summary of general opinions
Process	Quantitative	Logging, eye tracking	Statistical analysis of important identifiable events
	Qualitative	Video, audio	Observation and listening analysis, resulting in summary of processes
Product	Quantitative	Artefact creation	Statistical analysis of feature counts
	Qualitative	Artefact creation	Artefact analysis, looking for nonquantifiable features

categories. As such, it is somewhat tangential to the sequential flow of the chapters of this book, and can be ignored for evaluations, or if only qualitative data are to be collected in an experiment.[11]

---

[11] Even though some qualitative data may be summarised quantitatively, it is rare that these derived numerical data are complex enough to warrant statistical analysis. Instead, they are typically summarised in simple bar charts and averages.

5

Statistics

As mentioned previously, experimental methods can be a matter of dispute: there can be as many views of the "correct" way to run an experiment as there are experimenters. Such disagreements are most obvious in the approach taken to statistical analysis of data: everyone has their own favourite method, there can be many different valid ways to analyse data, and even statisticians do not always agree on the best approach.

This chapter is not intended to be a statistics primer: it simply describes the statistics tests that I find most useful in analysing data and shows examples of their application. It does not discuss any theoretical aspects of these tests or why they "work." Rather, it is a practical guide that will enable an experimenter to make considerable headway with some simple analyses, and to be able to consult a statistics text for more information with confidence.[1]

In most cases, these tests will be sufficient for answering the type of research questions discussed so far. Other analyses may require reference to a good statistics book or guidance from a statistics consultant.

5.1 Statistical analysis

5.1.1 Aim of the analysis

As discussed in Section 4.3, quantitative data can be collected within all "five P" data categories: they may be collected directly (e.g., as errors or preference rankings), or they may be derived from more complex data (e.g., interaction events derived from logging or eye tracking data, or features of artefacts).

---

[1] Reference to a good statistics book is advised – I recommend *Statistics Explained: A Guide for Social Science Students* (Hinton, 2004) and *Using Statistics to Understand the Environment* (Cook, Wheater, and Wright, 2000) as easy-to-read introductions.

Quantitative data provide values for the *dependent variables*; the experimenter has control of the form and meaning of these variables, but not of what values they will take. Examples of dependent variables are as follows:

- *response time:* a number greater than zero, expressed to two decimal places, representing the number of seconds elapsed between a task being shown on a screen and the Next button being pressed (indicating that the participant is ready for the next trial);
- *usability rating:* an integer between one and ten, representing the extent to which the participant considers a device "easy to use";
- *crossing ratio:* a number between zero and one, expressed to two decimal places, representing the ratio of the number of crossed edges in the graph drawn by the participant to the total number of edges in the graph.

The *independent variable* is the set of conditions (see Section 2.2) that the experimenter has defined and has control over. Examples of independent variables that might have been associated with experiments producing the dependent variables listed previously are as follows:

- *the language in which the task was worded*: English, Spanish, Swedish;
- *different devices with different interaction*: a touch-screen mobile device, a desktop device, a multitouch tabletop surface device;
- *the manner in which relational information was presented to the participant as the basis for drawing the graph*: list or matrix.

The aim of the analysis is to determine what effect (if any) the values of the independent variables have had on the values of the dependent variables. Put another way, we want to find out if different values of the dependent variables can be attributed to the different values of the independent variable.

5.1.2 Getting an overview of the data

The most common numeric data collected are performance data, typically represented as response time and errors, and much of this chapter assumes this form of data. However, the methods of analysis introduced here can be used for any form of quantitative data (i.e., any data represented by numbers).

Note that it is useful to present and analyse "errors" (i.e., trials that have an incorrect answer) rather than "accuracy" (i.e., trials that have a correct answer). Doing so means that a "high" measure in either type of performance data (high response time, high errors) implies poor performance and a "low" measure implies good performance. This consistency in interpretation makes performance bar charts easier to read and compare.

Table 5.1: *Typical form of performance data*

	Trial 1		Trial 2		Trial 3		...		Trial S	
participant	Time	Error	Time	Error	Time	Error	Time	Error	Time	Error
p1										
p2										
p3										
p4										
...										
pn										

Typically, the dependent variable data will be of the following form: there is one row per participant, and, for each trial, there are as many columns as there are dependent data measures. Table 5.1 shows the form for error and response time data because these are the most common.[2]

Large tables of numbers are not very useful for forming conclusions; they need to be summarised into meaningful *statistics*. A *statistic* is a number that is calculated from a set of numbers and that characterises an aspect of that set of numbers (e.g., mean, standard deviation, sum of the squares).

The first step in creating useful statistics is to condense the raw data into a form that is meaningful to the research question – we do this using *aggregation*, the process of taking a set of numbers and representing it as one summary statistic, usually by taking the mean.[3]

Recall that each trial is a combination of *condition, experimental object*, and *task* (see Section 2.7). The conditions are the most important of these because they comprise the independent variable whose effect is being investigated and which forms the core of the research question. We therefore need a summary statistic that represents each participant's performance for each condition. The data for all trials that are associated with each condition are aggregated to create a single value for that condition. This is termed "aggregating over experimental objects and tasks" or "aggregating according to condition." Separate aggregations are made for the different dependent data measures of time and errors. Table 5.2 shows the form of these data after this aggregation.

---

[2] Note that S trials are represented here, but recall (see Section 3.2) that each trial may have been presented more than once (i.e., **m** times, giving **mS** trials presented to participants). In this table, the values will be the mean of the **m** instances of each trial.

[3] In general, aggregation can also use the sum of the numbers, and less frequently, the median or mode.

Table 5.2: *Form of data after aggregating over tasks and experimental objects according to condition*

Mean time	cond1	cond2	cond3	cond4	Mean errors	cond1	cond2	cond3	cond4
p1					**p1**				
p2					**p2**				
p3					**p3**				
p4					**p4**				
...					...				
pn					**pn**				
Mean for each condition					Mean for each condition				

The number in the highlighted cell represents the mean response time for the second participant over all trials related to condition 2. The final row is the mean of the means, giving summary performance measures for each condition

119

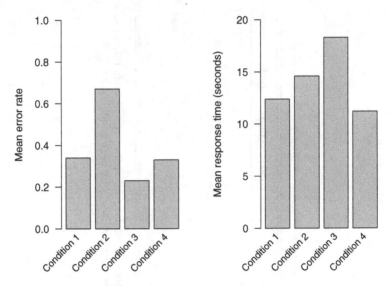

Figure 5.1: Form of the overview bar charts, showing relative performance differences according to condition.

The data in this form allow for useful overview bar charts to be produced, plotting the mean performance for each condition (the final row of the table in Table 5.2). It is a good idea to draw these charts as a first step to determine which conditions may have had an effect on performance: it will help identify what needs to be investigated, what conclusions may be revealed by the analysis, and whether ceiling or floor effects may have occurred (see Section 2.6).

Figure 5.1 shows the form of the overview bar charts. Recall that because the data collected are "errors" rather than "accuracy," tall bars always represent worse performance, and short bars always indicate better performance.

In fact, it is useful to explore the data visually as much as possible before doing any statistical analysis by producing box plots, error bars, histograms, or scatter plots, indeed anything that provides a visual representation of the data:

- Box plots show the distribution of the values associated with a condition with respect to quartiles. They show the minimum value, the lower quartile (the value below which 25% of the values lie), the median (the value below which 50% of the values lie), the upper quartile (the value below which 75% of the values lie), and the maximum. Box plots are useful for seeing the distribution and spread of values within a condition, and for identifying outliers.
- Error bars can be added to bar charts to show the accuracy of the measurements for each condition. They indicate uncertainty in the measurement by

showing the "standard error" on either side of the mean. If the standard error bars between the performance measures for two conditions do not overlap, then it is likely that the difference in performance will be statistically significant.

- Histograms show frequency. They indicate how many instances of each value (or values within a range) have occurred. This is useful for seeing whether the data are skewed or can be considered "normally distributed" (see Section 5.1.5).

- Scatter plots plot each value against another value with which it is paired. They can be used to determine whether there is any relationship between two dependent variables.

For the DAGMap experiment (Example 5, p 23) Koenig produced the **bar charts** in Figure 5.2 after conducting the experiment on twenty-two participants, showing mean errors and mean response times for each of three experimental conditions.

Other **exploratory charts** can also be created from these data (Figure 5.3). Note that the scatterplot is not very useful because of the limited number of values that mean error can take in this experiment (0, 0.33 and 0.67, 1).

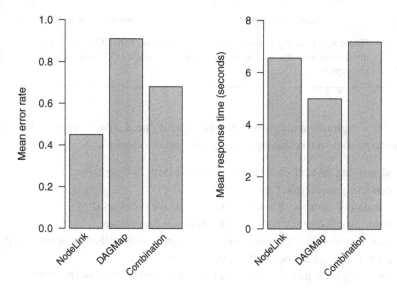

Figure 5.2: Bar charts representing performance for each condition in the DAGMap experiment.

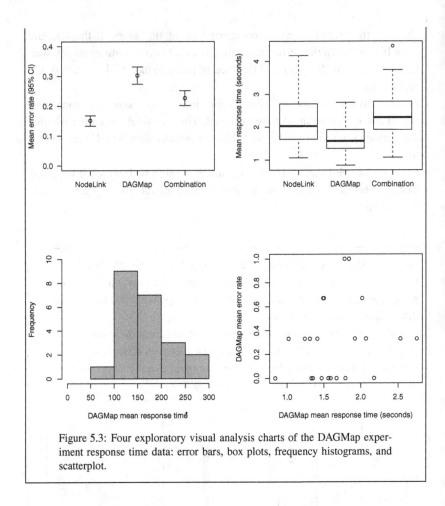

Figure 5.3: Four exploratory visual analysis charts of the DAGMap experiment response time data: error bars, box plots, frequency histograms, and scatterplot.

Such exploration may reveal that the data may need some "cleaning" before analysis; some data cleaning activities include, for example:

- identifying missing data values and filling them in if possible;
- correcting mislabelled data;
- translating numeric data to categorical data (or vice versa);
- ensuring consistency between the formats of data values;
- removing the data from obvious outliers (especially if their removal is supported by related qualitative data);
- removing the data for a participant who admitted to not concentrating;
- removing the data for an experimental session during which there was a serious interruption (e.g., software failure, fire drill, phone call).

Doing a data cleaning process at this stage will prevent analyses having to be repeated later when problems or omissions are found in the data.

5.3.1 Summary of the analysis process

The aim of the analysis is to determine what effect (if any) the different values of the independent variables have had on the dependent variables. The overall process can be briefly described as follows:

STEP 1: Analyse the data to determine whether the different conditions had any effect on the dependent variables when there are
- only two conditions, or
- more than two conditions.

STEP 2: In the case of there being more than two conditions, determine which conditions performed better or worse than other conditions by comparing pairs of conditions.

STEP 3: In the case of there being more than one dependent variable, investigate any relationship between them.

STEP 4: If appropriate, split the data to investigate more specific research questions.

Existing statistics tools (e.g., SPSS, the Analytic Tools add-in for Excel, R) will perform many of the calculations required for these analyses. This chapter describes the formulaic process of performing the analysis, with reference to the mechanisms of executing them in SPSS.[4]

5.1.4 Basis of statistical analysis

To answer the research question, the data need to be analysed to determine whether there is evidence that the conditions have had an effect on the performance data. Because we are using a comparative approach, we want to identify pairs of conditions for which the performance of the participants varied (with one being either better or worse than the other).

By looking at the summary bar charts, it may seem obvious that one condition has produced better or worse performance than another condition. However, clear conclusions cannot be made without the data being analysed statistically. For example, in Figure 5.2, although it looks as if the DAGMap condition produced more errors than the other two conditions, the difference in the error

---

[4] I recommend Hinton, Brownlow, and McMurray (2004) as a useful introductory guide to SPSS; this resource corresponds to Hinton's *Statistics Explained* (2004).

means could have occurred simply by chance, rather than as a consequence of the differing nature of the conditions.

This is what statistical analysis determines:

- Whether the performance differences are simply a matter of chance (i.e., they just happened that way), or
- Whether performance differences really can be attributed to the different conditions (i.e., the conditions caused the differences).

Recall that the data only represent the performance from a *sample* of the whole *population* (see Section 2.4) and that the final experimental conclusions are extrapolations from the performance of these participants to the population as a whole. Conclusions can only be stated with absolute certainty if the sample participants are the same as the whole population. This is extremely rare in practise, and, in any case, there are likely to be other factors that prevent 100% certainty. Thus, conclusions can only be stated in terms of probabilities, that is, the likelihood of them being valid. A result is never actually "proven," it can only be "highly likely."

Our experimental conclusions are therefore expressed in terms of probabilities. Statistical analysis enables us to calculate these probabilities, usually expressed as a *p-value*.

If we say, for example, that "the performance for the Green condition is significantly worse than for the Blue condition, with $p < .01$," this means that there is a less than 1% chance that this statement is incorrect. That is, there is a less than 1% chance that the Green condition would be better than or equivalent to the Blue condition if the experiment were to be conducted with the whole population, rather than just a sample. The lower the p-value, the higher confidence there can be in the truth of the conclusion when applied to the whole population.

Another way of looking at this is in terms of "chance happening." If we again say that "the performance for the Green condition is significantly worse than for the Blue condition, with $p < .01$," we also mean that the probability of this difference having occurred by chance (rather than because of the difference between the conditions) is less than .01.

The acceptable p-value for an experiment is set in advance of the data analysis, typically at .05, which Hinton (2004), describes as "conservative", indicating that there is a one-in-twenty chance (i.e., 5% chance) that the conclusion does not hold for the whole population. It is rare for .1 to be used, but not uncommon for the more conservative .01 value to be used. A researcher will often state conclusions based on a .05 level of significance; however, if the data reveal significance at $p < .01$, then this will also be reported to demonstrate the greater strength of this particular conclusion.

It is important to note that if no significant differences are found between the performances of experimental conditions, then *no conclusions can be made*. If it is discovered that the performance for the Green condition is *not* significantly worse than for the Blue condition at $p < .05$, then this does not mean that the Green performance is better or equivalent than Blue – it simply means that no conclusions can be made based on the data collected from the sample of the population who took part in the experiment.

This, then, is the definition of *statistically significant*. If there is a p-value statistically significant difference between the performance data obtained from two conditions, then the probability of this difference being attributed to chance is p-value.

5.1.5 Importance of normal distribution

Different statistical methods need to be used depending on whether the data are normally distributed. "Normally distributed" means that the frequency of the data values for each condition follows a normal distribution curve.

If we can make the assumption that the data are normally distributed, then we can use *parametric statistical methods*. If we cannot make this assumption, then we will need to use *nonparametric statistical methods*.

Often, visual inspection of the histogram and some simple distribution calculations will be sufficient to see whether the data are likely to be normal. For large sample sizes (greater than 50), the "68-95-99.7 rule" may be used: roughly, 50% of the data points should lie on either side of the mean, 68% of the values should lie within one standard deviation on either side of the mean, 95% within two standard deviations of the mean, and nearly all (99.7%) within three standard deviations of the mean.

Many statistical tools have inbuilt functions to determine whether data are normally distributed. For example, SPSS will calculate two useful statistics: Kurtosis and Skewness.[5] The general rule is that if these are not both between −2 and +2, then the data are not considered to be normally distributed.

There were seven conditions in the Euler Diagrams experiment (Example 6, p 24), and two dependent variables (response time and errors). To determine whether parametric analysis could be used, these variables were tested to see if they followed a **normal distribution**.

For parametric analysis to be appropriate, the data within *all* conditions need to be **normally distributed**. This was the case for the

---

[5] The SPSS "Explore" feature will produce these values.

response time data for the Concurrency condition. The response time data were aggregated over all experimental objects and tasks to produce the mean response times for the Concurrency condition for each of the twenty-two participants (as shown in Table 5.3).

Table 5.3: *Mean response time data for Concurrency condition in the Euler Diagrams experiment for all 22 participants*

p1	11.86	p5	11.96	p9	13.16	p13	15.06	p17	15.56	p21	23.87
p2	19.83	p6	16.82	p10	17.01	p14	11.84	p18	17.24	p22	20.60
p3	13.40	p7	12.30	p11	9.55	p15	26.66	p19	9.24		
p4	21.59	p8	16.44	p12	14.09	p16	20.10	p20	18.99		

When these values are plotted in a histogram, they roughly follow a normal distribution (Figure 5.4). The Skewness value for these data are 0.504, the Kurtosis value is –0.227, and both values lie between –2 and +2.

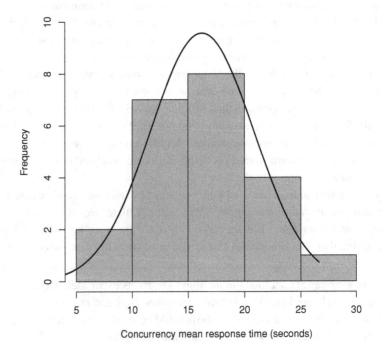

Concurrency mean response time (seconds)

Figure 5.4: Distribution of the data shown in Table 5.3, together with a normal distribution curve. The mean of all data points is 16.24, and the standard deviation is 4.59.

Table 5.4: *Mean response time data for Duplicated Curve label condition in the Euler Diagrams experiment for all 22 participants*

p1	14.39	p5	16.60	p9	19.51	p13	17.58	p17	18.88	p21	46.57
p2	22.79	p6	22.97	p10	21.41	p14	17.66	p18	19.94	p22	19.39
p3	17.87	p7	13.94	p11	11.40	p15	38.91	p19	15.44		
p4	21.94	p8	19.73	p12	19.95	p16	22.14	p20	32.81		

In contrast, the Duplicated Curve Label condition response time data for the same experiment were **not normally distributed** (Table 5.4 and Figure 5.5).

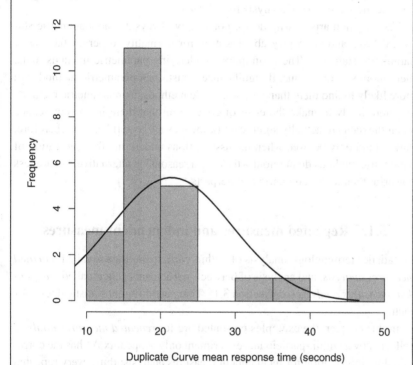

Figure 5.5: Distribution of the data from Table 5.4, together with a normal distribution curve. The mean of all data points is 21.45, and the standard deviation is 8.17.

The Skewness value for these data is 1.955, and the Kurtosis value is 4.020. Because one of these values is outside the −2 to +2 range, the data cannot be considered normally distributed. With only twenty-two data points for each condition, we could not use the 68-95-99.7 rule.

In analysing this response time data for all seven conditions in the experiment, we therefore used a **nonparametric analysis** method (see Section 5.3) because the data for at least one of the conditions were not normally distributed.[6]

Note that the requirements for normality of the data in all conditions relate to different dependent variables separately. Thus, it may be possible to use parametric methods for error data if they are normally distributed for all conditions, even though the response time data are not normally distributed (requiring nonparametric analysis). Despite this, it may be expedient (and easier to report) if you use the same type of analysis for all data.

The question arises: why do we not simply always use nonparametric statistical tests, and not worry about testing for normality to permit the use of parametric statistics? The assumptions underlying parametric methods make them more sensitive; thus, if significances exist, then parametric methods are more likely to find them than nonparametric methods. Nonparametric methods are more likely to make the error of concluding that there is no significance when the data are actually significant (known as a "Type II" error). Therefore, they should only be used when the assumptions underlying the application of parametric methods do not hold – they are a reasonable alternative, but are less powerful than their parametric counterparts.[7]

5.1.6 Repeated measures and independent measures

In statistics terminology, analysis of within-participants data is called *repeated measures analysis*, and analysis of between-participants data is called *independent measures analysis* (see Section 3.1). There are different statistical tests for each.

In this chapter, the examples presented are for *repeated measures analysis* collected by a within-participants experiment only. Appendix A1 has the corresponding information for independent measures analysis: thus, every repeated measures example and description in this chapter has a direct association with an independent measures counterpart in Appendix A1.

---

[6] In this experiment, the error data from only four of the seven conditions were normally distributed, so we used nonparametric methods for analysing both error and response time data.

[7] It may be possible to use parametric tests on nonparametric data if the data are transformed first (e.g., using a log function) so as to make them normal, but (arguably) also making it more difficult to interpret and report.

5.2 Parametric analysis (for normally distributed data)

The first step is to establish whether the independent variable (as represented by the conditions) has had any effect on the data:

STEP 1: Analyse the data to determine whether the different conditions had any effect on the data:
- when there are only two conditions, or
- when there are more than two conditions.

The subsequent analysis process can be followed for both time and error data (and any other form of normally distributed data). However, let us consider first the case where there are only two conditions before looking at the more complex analysis involving more than two conditions.

5.2.1 Two conditions (*t*-test)

A *t-test* can be used to determine whether two different conditions have had any effect on performance data. It can be used in one of two ways: *one-tailed* or *two-tailed*.

One-tailed tests are used when a one-way difference is of interest; that is, when the experimenter is only interested in whether one specified condition produces "better" (or "worse") performance than another (rather than "different" performance). For example, if the research question were "Is performance using Green *better than* performance using Blue?", then a one-tailed *t*-test will answer this question, but it will not answer the question as to whether performance using Green is *worse than* performance using Blue.

Two-tailed tests are used when *any* difference is of interest, regardless of the direction in which the difference lies. In this case, the research question is more likely to be "Is performance using Green *different from* performance using Blue?", and the test will reveal either that Blue is better than Green or that Green is better than Blue (or be inconclusive if there is no significance).

One-tailed tests are rare in HCI experiments, and it seems somewhat perverse to be only interested in one-way differences. If there is any doubt, a two-tailed test should always be used. The following discussion assumes a two-tailed test.

For a *t*-test, the data points are tabulated as shown in Table 5.5.

The repeated measures *t*-test (also called a *paired t-test* or a *matched t-test*) calculates a variety of statistics from the data such as the sums of the square of all data points, the square of the sum of all data for each condition, and

Table 5.5: *Form of data for t-test (repeated measures), with example data: all participants have used both conditions*

Participant	Mean error for each condition	
	Condition 1	Condition 2
p1	0.32	0.34
p2	0.50	0.62
p3	0.54	0.47
p4	0.32	0.32
...		
pn	0.44	0.56
Mean (over all participants)	0.39	0.43

the "degrees of freedom."[8] It also calculates a final *t-value* statistic, which is usually expressed to three decimal points.[9]

A *critical t-value* can then be read off a statistical table[10] showing the values of the *t* distribution. The degrees of freedom used is the total number of participants less one, the *p*-value is usually .05, and a choice between a one-tailed or two-tailed test will need to be made. Statistical significance can then be determined as follows:

- If the calculated *t*-value $\geq$ critical *t*-value, then the result is statistically significant, with a confidence of *p*-value. This means that the conditions have had an effect on performance.
- If the calculated *t*-value < critical *t*-value, then no conclusions can be drawn.

If significance has been found, then looking at the means for each of the two conditions will indicate which condition produced "better" performance than the other.

It is obviously better to use statistical software, rather than having to calculate the *t*-value manually. A statistical package will typically return the *t*-value statistic, as well as a *p*-value, the probability of the differences being due to chance. If *p*-value < .05, then the difference between the data associated with

---

[8] The "degrees of freedom" of a statistic is the number of values in its calculation that are free to vary. Its value varies for different statistical tests, and is typically based on formulae using the number of participants and the number of conditions.

[9] The formulae for calculating the *t*-value statistics are given in Appendix A2, Tables A2.1 (repeated measures) and A2.2 (independent measures).

[10] Statistics tables appear at the back of most statistics books and online.

the two conditions is statistically significant. No reference need be made to statistical tables.

The Aural Tables experiment (Example 8, p 31) had two conditions (Sonification and Speech). Example data for this **two-condition** within-participant experiment are presented in Table 5.6 and Figure 5.6.[11]

Table 5.6: *Example data from the Aural tables experiment for 30 participants*

participant	Mean time: sonification	Mean time: speech	participant	Mean time: sonification	Mean time: speech
p1	7.58	6.97	p16	6.93	7.11
p2	7.27	7.45	p17	7.28	7.02
p3	7.11	7.43	p18	6.91	7.24
p4	7.50	7.59	p19	6.85	7.33
p5	7.35	7.37	p20	6.99	7.21
p6	7.06	7.63	p21	7.05	7.69
p7	6.89	7.40	p22	6.78	7.34
p8	7.23	7.29	p23	6.75	7.48
p9	7.44	7.04	p24	7.72	7.13
p10	7.05	7.44	p25	6.86	7.29
p11	7.47	7.25	p26	7.07	7.26
p12	7.27	7.50	p27	7.29	7.47
p13	7.45	7.23	p28	7.14	7.74
p14	7.30	7.18	p29	7.34	7.98
p15	7.35	7.38	p30	7.50	7.32

Each data point is the mean response time (in seconds) for all trials relating to the specified condition.[12]

A **paired-samples *t*-test** in SPSS gives the following information:

$t = 2.479$, two-tailed significance $p = .019$,

using degrees of freedom $= 29$.

Because $.019 < .05$, we can say that there is a significant difference between the performance from the Sonification condition and the Speech condition (with a significance level of $p < .05$).

---

[11] An independent measures *t*-test example is given in Section A.1.1.1 of Appendix A1.
[12] These data were fabricated for the purposes of illustration.

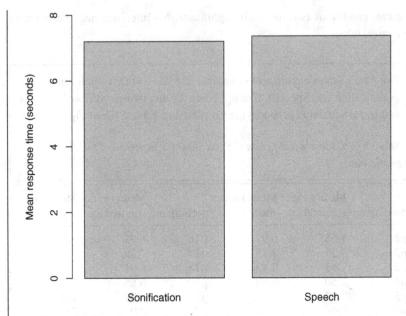

Figure 5.6: Bar chart showing the overall response time means for each condition: the mean for the Sonification condition is 7.19 seconds, and the mean for Speech is 7.36.

Observation of the bar chart showing the means for each condition confirms that the Speech condition took a longer time than the Sonification condition. This can be reported as a result in the following manner:

> There were significant differences in performance as represented by the response time data according to condition under a two-tailed repeated measures t-test, with the Sonification condition taking less time than the Speech condition: $t(29) = 2.479, p = .019$.

5.2.2 More than two conditions (analysis of variance)

If there are more than two conditions, then the analysis has to be done in two parts:

STEP 1: We need to determine whether the values of the independent variable have had any effect on performance over *all* conditions.

STEP 2: Once we have established this, we can determine which conditions performed better or worse than other conditions by comparing pairs of conditions.

Table 5.7: *Form of data for ANOVA test (repeated measures), with example data: all participants have used k conditions*[13]

Participant	Mean error for each condition					Mean (over all conditions)
	Condition 1	Condition 2	Condition 3	...	Condition k	
p1	0.34	0.39	0.45		0.32	0.38
p2	0.23	0.61	0.26		0.64	0.52
p3	0.64	0.50	0.48		0.71	0.55
p4	0.55	0.29	0.48		0.46	0.46
...						
pn	0.35	0.57	0.61		0.32	0.42
Mean (over all participants)	0.43	0.44	0.52		0.39	

For Step 1, an *analysis of variance (ANOVA)* statistical test can be used to determine whether the different conditions have had any effect on performance. As with *t*-tests, there are different ANOVAs for repeated measures and independent measures data. Unlike the *t*-test, there is no distinction between a one-tailed or two-tailed test for ANOVA calculations because the test indicates overall effect of all conditions, rather than whether some conditions are better or worse than others (see later in this section).

For Step 2, a *post-hoc pairwise comparison test* will show where the differences between the conditions lie. Post-hoc tests are done after an initial *successful* ANOVA test, as a means of finding out more about the data. If the ANOVA does not indicate any significance in the data, then there is no point in performing a post-hoc test. If there are overall differences in the data, then a post-hoc test will indicate where the differences lie (see Section 5.2.3).

For the ANOVA test, the data points are tabulated as shown in Table 5.7.

The ANOVA repeated measures test calculates a variety of statistics from the data such as the sums of the square of all data points, the square of the sum of all data for each condition, and various types of degrees of freedom. It calculates a final *F-value* statistic, usually expressed to three decimal points.[14]

A *critical F-value* can then be read off a statistical table showing the values of the *F* distribution. Two degrees of freedom are needed (*dfBetweenConditions* = the number of conditions less one; *dfError* = the number of participants less one multiplied by the number of conditions less one). The *p*-value is usually .05.

---

[13] The corresponding independent measures table appears in Appendix A1 as Table A1.3.
[14] The formulae for calculating the *F*-statistic are given in Appendix A2, Tables A2.3 (repeated measures) and A2.4 (independent measures).

- If the calculated F-value $\geq$ critical F-value, then the result is statistically significant, with a confidence of p-value. This means that the conditions have had an effect on performance.
- If the calculated F-value $<$ critical F-value, then no conclusions can be drawn.

Statistical software will calculate the F-value, as well as a p-value (the probability of the differences being due to chance). If the p-value $< .05$, then the values of the independent variable have affected performance as measured by the dependent variable in a statistically significant manner.

We can look at the means of the performance associated with the conditions and speculate which conditions produced "better" or "worse" performance. However, the ANOVA test does not tell us this pairwise comparison information.

The DAGMap experiment (Example 5, p 23) was a repeated-measures experiment with **three conditions**. The data for this experiment is presented in Table 5.8 and Figure 5.7.[15]

A **repeated measures ANOVA** test in SPSS gives the following information:

$F = 4.632$, Within-Subjects Effects significance, $p = .015$.

The degrees of freedom values are 2 and 42.

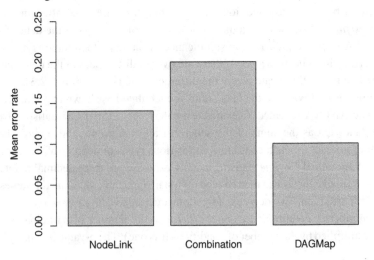

Figure 5.7: Bar chart showing the overall error means for each condition.

---

[15] An example of an independent measures ANOVA analysis is given in Section A1.1.2 of Appendix A1.

Table 5.8: *Data for the DAGMap experiment*

Participant	NodeLink	Combination	DAGMap
p1	0.11	0.22	0.00
p2	0.33	0.00	0.22
p3	0.00	0.11	0.11
p4	0.22	0.22	0.11
p5	0.11	0.33	0.11
p6	0.00	0.22	0.11
p7	0.00	0.22	0.11
p8	0.33	0.33	0.00
p9	0.11	0.33	0.00
p10	0.00	0.11	0.00
p11	0.22	0.33	0.11
p12	0.11	0.11	0.11
p13	0.11	0.22	0.33
p14	0.00	0.11	0.11
p15	0.00	0.22	0.22
p16	0.11	0.00	0.00
p17	0.11	0.33	0.11
p18	0.22	0.00	0.11
p19	0.45	0.33	0.11
p20	0.33	0.33	0.00
p21	0.11	0.11	0.00
p22	0.11	0.22	0.22

Each data point is the mean number of errors made over the nine trials for each condition: there were three tasks and three experimental objects per condition.[16]

Because .015 < .05, the results are significant. This means that the type of visualisation method used for presenting directed acyclic graph information significantly affected the number of errors, and the probability of the differences in performance being due to chance is less than .05.

This can be reported as a result in the following manner:

There were significant differences in performance, as represented by the error data according to condition, under a repeated measures ANOVA test: $F(2,42) = 4.632, p = .015$.

---

[16] Note that these data are based on the data of the DAGMap experiment, although some of the numbers were altered for the purposes of effective illustration.

Table 5.9: *Matrix of pairwise condition differences*

	Condition 1	Condition 2	Condition 3	Condition 4
Condition 1		5.23	2.45	2.21
Condition 2			3.34	5.11
Condition 3				4.89
Condition 4				

Each unshaded cell represents the absolute difference in the performance means between the two conditions.[17]

5.2.3 Post-Hoc Pairwise Comparisons (Tukey)

An ANOVA test may reveal that the conditions have significantly affected performance (Step 1), but it will not indicate where the differences lie; that is, it will not say which of the conditions produced better or worse performance. An ANOVA result is seldom sufficient information, so pairwise comparison analyses need to be made (Step 2).[18]

> **STEP 2:** In the case of there being more than two conditions, determine which conditions performed better or worse than other conditions by comparing pairs of conditions.

Post-hoc tests calculate the differences between the means of all pairs of conditions and compare each of them with a *critical difference*, which, like the critical t-value and the critical F-value, is based on statistical tables.

First, the absolute value of the difference between the means of all pairs of conditions needs to be calculated, producing a pairwise diagonal matrix of the form shown in Table 5.9. Note that we are not interested in the direction of the difference (because that can easily be determined from looking at the data or the overview bar charts), rather it is the size of the difference that matters. We therefore ignore any minus signs and take the absolute value of the differences.

After creating this table of pairwise differences, a *critical difference* statistic can be calculated from the data, and any pairwise difference that is greater than this *critical difference* indicates a significant difference between the two conditions.

---

[17] This table uses fabricated data for the purposes of illustration.
[18] Note that if there are only two conditions, then an ANOVA test is equivalent to a t-test, and no further pairwise analysis is necessary.

There are several post-hoc statistics that can be used to determine the *critical difference* and a variety of views on when they are most appropriate. The formulae for the Tukey's Honestly Significant Difference (HSD) statistic, as recommended by Hinton (2004), appears in Appendix A2, Tables A2.5 (repeated measures) and A2.6 (independent measures).[19]

The calculation of the *critical difference* is based on both the actual data (using some of the numbers calculated from the ANOVA test) and the *q-value*. The *q*-value can be read directly from a "Studentized range statistic" table using the *p*-value, the number of conditions, and the *dfError* (i.e., the number of participants less one multiplied by the number of conditions less one). The *critical difference* is then compared with all cells in the pairwise matrix. Any cell that has a value greater than the *critical difference* indicates a pairwise significant difference. A significant difference between the two conditions represented by the cell can then be stated as a conclusion (with confidence less than the *p*-value).

Statistics packages will calculate a *p*-value for each pairwise difference, and may also return the *critical difference*. If the calculated *p*-value is less than the required *p*-value (usually .05), then the pairwise difference is significant.

There is an important caveat to the process of performing pairwise comparisons. The Tukey HSD test is a *single-step* pairwise comparison method for which the *p*-value used is usually the typical .05. The alternative to doing a single-step comparison method is to perform a series of *t*-tests between each pair of conditions. Because this entails repeated analysis of the same data, the required *p*-value for significance needs to be reduced by the number of *t*-tests performed:

- For three conditions, there will be three pairwise *t*-tests, and so the *p*-value for each pairwise comparison must be less than $.05/3 = .0167$ for significance.
- For four conditions, there will be six pairwise *t*-tests, and the *p*-value must be less than $.05/6 = .008$.

The rationale for this reduction in the *p*-value is as follows: when the same set of data is analysed multiple times, the chances of finding significance are

---

[19] As mentioned previously, statistics is a battleground, and there is not always consensus on the best approach to use. People will give different opinions as to whether the Tukey HSD is appropriate for repeated measures analysis; even Hinton changed his recommendation on this from "generally agreed" to "whilst not universally agreed on, it is reasonable to" between the two editions of his book. That's good enough for me! If you are concerned, then you should consult a statistics expert for his or her opinion.

naturally increased, and so the *p*-value for subsequent analyses needs to be reduced. Recall that using *p*-value = .05 means that there is a less than 5% chance that the significant results we find have arisen by chance (i.e., are not really significant at all).

Because statistical methods are based on probabilities, if we analyse the data twenty times, then we are likely to find significant results with a *p*-value =.05, even if the conditions have had no effect on the data. Simply by doing the analysis repeatedly, the .05 probability will eventually work in our favour and produce a statistically significant result. To mitigate against this, the "Bonferroni adjustment" states that for each subsequent pairwise analysis in post-hoc comparison tests, the required *p*-value should be reduced.

However, because single-step post-hoc tests like Tukey automatically take the Bonferroni adjustment into account, .05 can be used per usual. It is thus preferable to use a single-step method because *p*-value adjustments do not need to be made. In contrast, if a statistical package does not perform a single-step test like Tukey HSD, then the experimenter must make sure that appropriate adjustment is made to the *p*-value in pairwise *t*-test comparisons.

Fortunately, SPSS does these adjustments automatically: the independent measures One-Way ANOVA includes an option for a Tukey post-hoc analysis, and the repeated measures ANOVA includes a Bonferroni Confidence Interval Adjustment that will do the adjustments. In both cases, a *p*-value of .05 can be used because the adjustments have already been made in the internal statistical calculations.

We revisit the repeated measures ANOVA calculation for the DAGMap experiment (Example 5, p 23).[20] Having determined that the presentation method (DAGMap, NodeLink, or Combination) had a significant effect on the errors, we now try to determine which pairs of conditions produced significantly different performances.

The **absolute differences** between the mean values for each pair of conditions can be calculated and represented in a diagonal matrix (Table 5.10).

The first method uses the manual **single-step Tukey** calculation (using the formula in Table A2.5) and returns a HSD of 0.0804, having used a *q*-value from the Studentized range statistic table ($k = 3$, *dfError* = 42,

---

[20] An example of independent measures post-hoc pairwise comparison is given in Section A1.1.3 of Appendix A1.

Table 5.10: *Absolute values between mean values for each pair of conditions for data in Table 5.8*

	NodeLink	Combination	DAGMap
NodeLink		0.06	0.04
Combination			0.10
DAGMap			

$p = .05$) of 3.44. Looking at the matrix of pairwise differences, we can conclude that there is a significant difference between the mean error rate for the DAGMap presentation and the Combined presentation because $0.10 > 0.0804$. However, we cannot conclude anything about the performance associated with the NodeLink presentation.

The second method uses the **Bonferroni confidence interval adjustment** when comparing main effects under a repeated measures ANOVA in SPSS, which gives $F = 4.632, p = .015$ (as previously). SPSS also gives the p-values for the pairwise comparisons in a diagonal matrix (Table 5.11). Having chosen the **Bonferroni adjustment** in this SPSS analysis, we can use $p = .05$ in determining where the significant **pairwise differences** lie. In Table 5.11, there is a significant difference between the mean error rate for the DAGMap presentation and the Combined presentation because $0.016 < .05$; there are no other pairwise differences.

Table 5.11: *p-values for each pair of conditions for data in Table 5.8 using Bonferroni confidence interval adjustment in SPSS*

	NodeLink	Combination	DAGMap
NodeLink		.237	.764
Combination			.016
DAGMap			

The third method uses **repeated *t*-tests** (using an adjusted p-value $= .05/3 = .0167$), which gives the same result; the p-values for the pairwise combinations using t-tests are shown in a diagonal matrix

(Table 5.12). In this case, even if the p-value between the NodeLink and Combination presentations had been, for example, .029, this would not have indicated a significant result because it needs to be less than .0167 for significance.

Table 5.12: *p-values using repeated t-tests on each pair of conditions for data in Table 5.8*

	NodeLink	Combination	DAGMap
NodeLink		.079	.255
Combination			.005
DAGMap			

Observation of the bar chart (Figure 5.7) shows that the mean errors were greater for the Combination presentation than for the DAGMap. This can be reported as follows:

There were significant differences in performance as represented by the error data according to condition: $F(2,42) = 4.632$, $p = .015$. Bonferroni adjusted pairwise comparisons revealed where the differences lie: the DAGMap presentation produced better performance than the Combination presentation ($p = .016$). There were no other significant pairwise differences.

There are therefore three ways that pairwise differences can be investigated following an ANOVA that indicates significant differences between the data from a set of conditions[21]:

- Do the Tukey calculations by hand (the formulae in Tables A2.5 and A2.6) using $p = .05$. Reading from the Studentized range statistic table, determine a *critical difference*, and see which of the pairwise differences in means are greater than this critical difference.
- Use a one-step pairwise comparison method in a statistical package (in SPSS: the Bonferroni Confidence Interval Adjustment for repeated measures; the Tukey post-hoc test for independent measures), and identify those pairwise p-values that are less than .05.

[21] These three methods may not always give exactly the same results, especially if there are borderline cases: the Tukey test is known to be conservative and may be more sensitive to highly skewed data.

- Perform a series of *numTests* *t*-tests, identifying those pairwise *t*-tests for which the *p*-value is less than .05/*numTests*. If all pairwise comparisons are tested, then *numTests* = $k(k + 1)/2$, where *k* is the number of conditions.

At this point, if your data are normally distributed and you have been able to use parametric methods, then you would have answered your research question – you would be able to say whether the independent variable has had an effect on performance, and where the significant pairwise differences lie. In contrast, if the data are not normally distributed, then nonparametric methods should be used.

5.3 Nonparametric analysis (for nonnormally distributed data)

The *t*-test, ANOVA, and pairwise analysis methods assume that the data are normally distributed (i.e., the data points within the conditions have a frequency distribution that follows a normal curve). For data that is not normally distributed, nonparametric methods should be used. These methods transform the data into ranks and calculate statistics using the rank values rather than the actual data points collected.

For example, in a within-participants experiment, the performance data points associated with one participant will be sorted in numeric order, and each one replaced with an integer indicating its rank order within the set of data. Thus, if there are three conditions, then the condition that the participant took the longest time on would have the time represented as a 3, the least time as a 1, and the one in the middle as a 2.

Table 5.13 demonstrates this ranking process for repeated measures data, using four conditions (c1–c4). On the left is the original (fabricated) response

Table 5.13: *Example of transformation of data into ranks for repeated measures data: data on the left, ranks on the right*

	c1	c2	c3	c4		c1	c2	c3	c4
p1	14.7	21.5	19.0	22.5	p1	1	3	2	4
p2	23.0	25.3	20.5	19.9	p2	3	4	2	1
p3	15.7	20.4	18.3	20.4	p3	1	3.5	2	3.5
p4	27.4	27.4	29.1	27.4	p4	2	2	4	2
p5	30.1	25.9	22.2	22.4	p5	4	3	1	2

Table 5.14: *Correspondence between parametric and nonparametric analysis methods*

Parametric test	Nonparametric test
Repeated measures *t*-test	Wilcoxon
Independent measures *t*-test	Mann-Whitney
Repeated measures ANOVA	Friedman
Independent measures ANOVA	Kruskal-Wallis
Post-hoc Tukey HSD (after RM ANOVA)	Nemenyi (after Friedman)
Post-hoc Tukey HSD (after IM ANOVA)	Dunn or Nemenyi (after Kruskal-Wallis)

time data; on the right is the same data transformed into ranks. Note how the tied values for p3 and p4 are treated (shaded): all rank rows must add up to the same number (in this case, 10).[22] This rank transformation is the basis of nonparametric statistical analysis.

There is a clear mapping between the parametric methods described in Section 5.2 and the nonparametric methods (Table 5.14). Nonparametric methods tend to be named after the people who devised them.

5.3.1 Two Conditions (Wilcoxon)

Recall that the principle of the *t*-test is to calculate a *t*-value, read a critical *t*-value from a statistical table, and compare these two values (see Section 5.2.1). The nonparametric version is similar except that the analysis is performed on ranks derived from the original data, rather than from the data itself.

The repeated measures two-condition nonparametric test is the Wilcoxon test, for which a *T-value* is derived. The independent measures counterpart is the Mann-Whitney test, for which a *U-value* is derived. Different statistical tables are used to determine a *critical T-value* and a *critical U-value*.

Like the parametric versions, there are one- and two-tailed versions of these tests, and a two-tailed approach is assumed here.

[22] The corresponding independent measures rank transformation is given in Appendix A1, Table A1.7.

Table 5.15: *Form of ranking data required for Wilcoxon test*[23]

	Condition 1 performance	Condition 2 performance	Sign of difference	Size of difference	Rank of difference
p1	14	4	+	10	9
p2	9	15	−	6	3.5
p3	10	10			
p4	17	10	+	7	5
p5	13	5	+	8	6.5
p6	14	8	+	6	3.5
p7	9	13	−	4	2
p8	5	14	−	9	8
p9	15	7	+	8	6.5
p10	17	20	+	3	1

For repeated measures two-conditions analysis (the Wilcoxon test), the sign and size of the difference between the two data points for each participant is determined, and the size of the difference is ranked (Table 5.15). Note that participant 3 is excluded from any further analysis (showing no difference in performance between the two conditions), that the ranks for the two tied values (i.e., P2 and P6) are halved, and that the shading distinguishes between differences that are positive or negative.

The formula for the Wilcoxon test statistic is given in Appendix A2, Table A2.7.[24] If the calculated T-value $<$ critical T-value (which can be read from the Wilcoxon statistical table of critical values, based on the number of participants who do not have tied data), the difference between the two conditions is significant.[25]

Statistics packages will produce a p-value for the Wilcoxon test, indicating the probability that the difference in the two conditions is due to chance; if this value is $< .05$, the differences are significant. The SPSS Related Samples tool produces the value of the Wilcoxon statistic.

---

[23] The corresponding independent measures ranking table for the Mann-Whitney test appears in Appendix A1 as Table A1.8.

[24] The formula for the independent measures Mann-Whitney test is given in Appendix A2, Table A2.8.

[25] Note that the two nonparametric two-sample tests (Wilcoxon and Mann-Whitney) differ from all other tests in that they both require that the calculated value be *less than* the value read off the statistical table; all other tests require that the calculated value be *greater than* the table value.

In the Clustering experiment (Example 18, p 72) there were **two conditions:** No Cluster (NC) and Path-preserving Cluster (PPC), Figure 5.8. There were four experimental objects, and four tasks. Both the error and response time data were **not normally distributed**, so nonparametric analysis methods were used.[26]

Table 5.16: *Mean error data for the Clustering experiment, aggregated over all four tasks and all four experimental objects*

	Mean error		Sign of difference PPC-NC	Size of difference PCC-NC	Rank of difference
	PPC	NC			
p1	0.08	0.13	−	0.05	4.5
p2	0.25	0.13	+	0.12	13
p3	0.17	0.17			
p4	0.29	0.29			
p5	0.17	0.25	−	0.08	8
p6	0.08	0.17	−	0.09	11
p7	0.21	0.13	+	0.08	8
p8	0.25	0.04	+	0.21	20.5
p9	0.25	0.04	+	0.21	20.5
p10	0.25	0.25			
p11	0.21	0.08	+	0.13	15.5
p12	0.25	0.04	+	0.21	20.5
p13	0.29	0.29			
p14	0.17	0.25	−	0.08	8
p15	0.08	0.08			
p16	0.29	0.08	+	0.21	20.5
p17	0.29	0.17	+	0.12	13
p18	0.04	0.08	−	0.04	2
p19	0.29	0.21	+	0.08	8
p20	0.08	0.04	+	0.04	2
p21	0.04	0.21	−	0.17	17.5
p22	0.33	0.04	+	0.29	23
p23	0.29	0.46	−	0.17	17.5
p24	0.21	0.29	−	0.08	8
p25	0.08	0.13	−	0.05	4.5
p26	0.04	0.08	−	0.04	2
p27	0.25	0.13	+	0.12	13
p28	0.17	0.04	+	0.13	15.5

[26] An example of a Mann-Whitney test is given in Section A1.2.1 of Appendix A1.

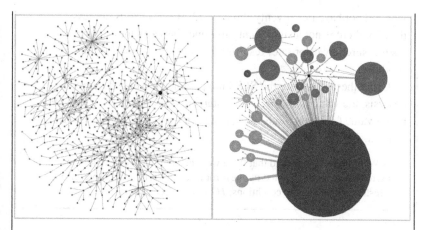

Figure 5.8: Two conditions in the Clustering experiment: on the left, NC (No
Cluster); on the right, PPC (Path-preserving Cluster).

Because there were only two conditions and the experiment was a
within-participant design, the **Wilcoxon** test was used. Table 5.16 and
Figure 5.9 show the error data for the twenty-eight participants and the
two conditions, together with the relevant ranking information.

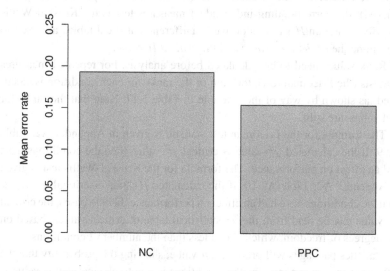

Figure 5.9: Bar chart showing the difference in the overall means.

Using the **Wilcoxon** formulae (Appendix A2, Table A2.7), the
Wilcoxon statistic calculated from this data is 83. The value read from the
two-tailed Wilcoxon table using $p = .05$ and the number of participants

who did not have ties (twenty-three) is 73. Because 83 is not less than 73, there is not a significant difference between the performance (as measured by error rate) resulting from the use of the PPC and the NC condition.

Using these data with the SPSS nonparametric Related Samples analysis, the value of the Wilcoxon statistic is presented (83), as well as a *p*-value (.094) that indicates no significance. This can be reported as follows:

> A Wilcoxon test indicated that there were no significant differences in performance as represented by the error data between the Path-preserving Cluster and No Cluster conditions: $T(23) = 83, p = .094$.

5.3.2 More than two conditions (Friedman)

Recall that the principle of the ANOVA test is to calculate an F-value, read a critical F-value from a statistical table, and compare the two values (see Section 5.2.2). The nonparametric version is similar except that it applies to ranked data. The nonparametric more-than-two-condition comparison test for repeated measures is the Friedman test (for which a *Chi-square value* (χ^2) is derived); the corresponding independent measures test is the Kruskal-Wallis test (for which an *H-value* is derived). Different statistical tables are used to determine the *critical χ^2-value* and the *critical H-value*.

Rank values need to be calculated before analysis. For repeated measures analysis (the Friedman test), the sum of the ranks for each condition is calculated, as shown by way of the example in Table 5.17. Note that the ranks for tied values are split.

The formula for the Friedman test statistic is given in Appendix A2, Table A2.9. If the calculated χ^2-value > critical χ^2-value, then the conditions have had an effect on performance. The formula for the Kruskal-Wallis test is given in Appendix A2, Table A2.10. If the calculated H-value > critical χ^2-value, then the conditions have had an effect on performance. In both cases, the critical χ^2-value can be read from the χ^2 statistical table of critical values, based on the degrees of freedom, which is one less than the number of conditions.

Statistics packages will produce a *p*-value, showing the probability that the difference in performance for the conditions is due to chance; if this value is < .05, then the independent variable has had a significant effect on the performance data. The SPSS Related Samples tool (Friedman's Two-way ANOVA by ranks) will also produce the value of the Friedman statistic.

Table 5.17: *Form of ranking data required for Friedman test: data on the left, ranks on the right*[27]

	Condition 1	Condition 2	Condition 3		Condition 1 Rank	Condition 2 Rank	Condition 3 Rank
p1	2.26	1.20	4.19	**p1**	2	1	3
p2	1.49	3.78	3.78	**p2**	1	2.5	2.5
p3	2.89	4.03	1.67	**p3**	2	3	1
p4	0.88	5.84	0.88	**p4**	1.5	3	1.5
p5	2.07	3.13	2.81	**p5**	1	3	2
p6	1.53	0.71	0.84	**p6**	3	1	2
				Condition Rank total (T)	10.5	13.5	12

[27] The corresponding independent measures ranking table appears in Appendix A1 as Table A1.10.

In the second version of the Euler Diagrams experiment (Example 6, p 24), there were **seven conditions** (six based on the six well-formedness principles, and one Well Formed condition), three experimental objects, and three tasks.[28] The research question was "which well-formedness principles in the presentation of Euler diagrams, when broken, are easiest to understand?" Response time and error data were collected.

For the error data, of the 1,386 data points, 82 were incorrect, a mean error rate of 0.06. This represents a "floor" effect (see Section 2.6), where the tasks were so easy that most participants got them all right, and so there was no variability in the error data between the seven conditions.

The time data was **not normally distributed** for at least one of the conditions (the Well Formed condition, as indicated by the histogram in Figure 5.10), and so a nonparametric analysis method was used.

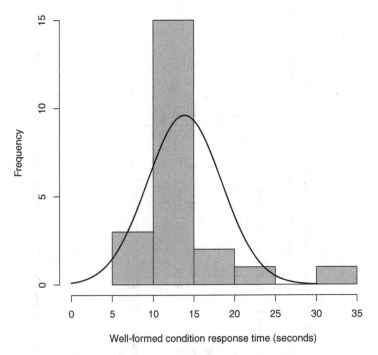

Well-formed condition response time (seconds)

Figure 5.10: Frequency distribution of the response time data for the Well Formed condition in the second Euler Diagrams experiment.

[28] A Kruskal-Wallis independent measures example is given in Section A1.2.2 of Appendix A1.

The response time data for this experiment is as shown in Table 5.18.

Table 5.18: *Response time data (in seconds) for the second version of the Euler Diagrams experiment*

Participant	BP	CC	DC	DZ	NS	NP	WF
p1	12.19	11.86	14.39	9.99	12.71	13.34	12.04
p2	25.70	19.83	22.80	27.30	16.46	27.46	13.17
p3	11.70	13.40	17.87	12.77	10.20	16.43	12.27
p4	17.98	21.59	21.94	20.78	20.10	15.88	17.69
p5	9.67	11.96	16.61	11.99	10.04	13.38	13.00
p6	14.81	16.82	22.97	16.10	13.77	18.83	13.21
p7	13.94	12.30	13.90	13.69	13.47	11.78	9.82
p8	9.64	16.44	19.73	13.51	14.15	15.38	12.79
p9	12.57	13.16	19.51	13.53	15.43	15.44	12.15
p10	13.14	17.01	21.41	15.92	17.77	18.51	12.84
p11	8.99	9.55	11.40	13.29	8.98	11.72	8.35
p12	16.63	14.09	19.95	14.52	13.97	15.03	13.63
p13	14.39	15.06	17.58	16.97	14.31	14.00	12.86
p14	11.83	11.84	17.66	15.81	15.42	13.68	13.60
p15	29.93	26.66	38.91	25.42	18.80	22.63	12.10
p16	15.01	20.10	22.14	14.38	18.05	16.34	13.43
p17	15.88	15.56	18.88	15.48	15.71	15.34	16.34
p18	17.80	17.24	19.94	17.75	13.08	15.45	12.05
p19	10.70	9.24	15.44	9.84	10.56	10.33	7.86
p20	20.64	18.99	32.81	21.77	19.48	25.86	20.86
p21	24.02	23.87	46.57	25.50	25.69	25.22	30.15
p22	16.39	20.60	19.39	18.45	18.15	21.95	14.77

Table 5.19 shows the table of ranks when the data points are ranked within-participant. Note that there are no tied ranks, which is not unexpected for timing data.

Using the **Friedman** formula of Appendix A2, Table A2.9, the Friedman statistic can be calculated as 53.844. The critical χ^2-value from the statistical table for the χ^2 distribution ($df = 6, p = .05$) is 12.59. Because the calculated χ^2-value (53.844) is greater than the critical χ^2-value, there are significant differences between the performances relating to the seven conditions. The degrees of freedom $= 6$, which is one less than the number of conditions.

Using the Friedman Related Samples option in SPSS, the Friedman statistic is produced (53.844) with a p-value of .000.

Table 5.19: *Table of ranks for response time data for the second version of the Euler Diagrams experiment*

Participant	BP	CC	DC	DZ	NS	NP	WF
p1	4	2	7	1	5	6	3
p2	5	3	4	6	2	7	1
p3	2	5	7	4	1	6	3
p4	3	6	7	5	4	1	2
p5	1	3	7	4	2	6	5
p6	3	5	7	4	2	6	1
p7	7	3	6	5	4	2	1
p8	1	6	7	3	4	5	2
p9	2	3	7	4	5	6	1
p10	2	4	7	3	5	6	1
p11	3	4	5	7	2	6	1
p12	6	3	7	4	2	5	1
p13	4	5	7	6	3	2	1
p14	1	2	7	6	5	4	3
p15	6	5	7	4	2	3	1
p16	3	6	7	2	5	4	1
p17	5	3	7	2	4	1	6
p18	6	4	7	5	2	3	1
p19	6	2	7	3	5	4	1
p20	3	1	7	5	2	6	4
p21	2	1	7	4	5	3	6
p22	2	6	5	4	3	7	1
Mean rank	3.50	3.73	6.64	4.14	3.36	4.50	2.14

This result can be reported as follows:

There were significant differences in performance as represented by the response time data according to condition under a Friedman test: $\chi^2(6) = 53.844 > \chi^2 (6, p = .05) = 12.59$.

Or:

There were significant differences in performance as represented by the response time data according to condition under a Friedman test: $\chi^2(6) = 53.844, p < .001$.[29]

---

[29] It is common practise to quote a probability as being <.001 when a statistical package presents it as .000.

5.3.3 Post-hoc pairwise comparisons (Nemenyi and Dunn)

As with the ANOVA tests, the Friedman and Kruskal-Wallis tests only indicate whether the conditions have had any significant effect on the results, they do not indicate where the differences lie. So, as with ANOVA tests, we need to perform a post-hoc test that will indicate any significant pairwise differences.

The Nemenyi test is a one-step nonparametric version of the Tukey test for nonparametric analyses, and, like the Tukey test, it allows us to investigate pairwise differences without having to apply statistical corrections.[30] Instead of calculating the absolute value of the difference between the *means* of all pairs of conditions to produce our pairwise diagonal matrix, we calculate the absolute value between the *mean of the ranks* of all pairs of conditions, as shown in Tables 5.20 and 5.21.

After creating this table of pairwise mean rank differences, the next step is to calculate the *critical difference* statistic. The *critical difference* is then compared with all the cells in the pairwise matrix. Any cell which has a value greater than the *critical difference* indicates a pairwise significant difference. A significant difference between the two conditions represented by the cell can then be stated as a conclusion (with confidence < *p*-value).

The Nemenyi formula calculates the *critical difference*, as shown in Appendix A2, Table A2.11. Like the Tukey test, it relies on obtaining the value of q from the Studentized range statistic table, and like Tukey, because it is a single-step pairwise comparison method, the *p*-value is .05.[31]

Statistics packages will calculate a *p*-value for each pairwise difference, and may also return a *critical difference*. If the *p*-value is less than the required *p*-value (usually .05), then the pairwise difference is significant. Recent versions of SPSS return the pairwise difference of mean ranks and an adjusted significance level for each pair of conditions when the All Pairwise option is chosen for a Related Samples nonparametric test – if the adjusted significance level is <.05, then the pairwise difference is significant.

---

[30] There are two versions of the Nemenyi test, one for repeated measures and one for independent measures, and the Dunn test is an alternative for independent measures when there are different sample sizes for the conditions.

[31] The formulae for the independent measures Nemenyi and Dunn tests are given in Appendix A2, Tables A2.12 and A2.13.

Table 5.20: *Ranks for repeated measures data, using fabricated data for purposes of illustration: data on the left, ranks on the right*

	Condition 1	Condition 2	Condition 3	Condition 1 Rank	Condition 2 Rank	Condition 3 Rank
p1	8	10	6	2	3	1
p2	7	5	7	2.5	1	2.5
p3	5	8	9	1	2	3
p4	10	9	1	3	2	1
p5	3	7	3	1.5	3	1.5
p6	2	4	3	1	3	2
p7	5	9	6	1	3	2
p8	5	8	6	1	3	2
p9	2	9	1	2	3	1
p10	5	10	8	1	3	2
Condition mean rank				1.6	2.6	1.8

Table 5.21: *Pairwise mean rank differences for data in Table 5.20*[32]

	Condition 1	Condition 2	Condition 3
Condition 1		1.0	0.2
Condition 2			0.8
Condition 3			

Following on from the Friedman analysis of the Euler Diagrams experiment, we can perform a **Nemenyi** analysis to find out which pairwise differences are significant.[33] The **absolute differences** between the **mean rank values** for each pair of conditions is calculated and represented in a diagonal matrix (Table 5.22).

Table 5.22: *Absolute values between mean rank values for each pair of conditions for data in Table 5.18*

	BP	CC	DC	DZ	NS	NP	WF
BP		0.23	**3.14**	0.64	0.14	1.00	1.36
CC			**2.91**	0.41	0.36	0.77	1.59
DC				**2.50**	**3.27**	**2.14**	**4.50**
DZ					0.77	0.36	**2.00**
NS						1.14	1.23
NP							**2.36**
WF							

The manual repeated measures **Nemenyi** calculation (using the formula in Appendix A2, Table A2.11) returns a *critical difference* of 1.920, having used a *q*-value from the Studentized range statistic ($k = 7$, *dfError* = infinity, $p = .05$) of 4.17.

Those **pairwise differences** whose absolute **mean rank difference** is greater than 1.920 (emboldened in Table 5.22) have had a significant effect on the response time data. In this case, the following pairwise significances are found: DC/all other conditions, WF/NP, and WF/DZ.

---

[32] Corresponding tables for independent measures analysis appear in Appendix A1 as Tables A1.12 and A1.13.

[33] A nonparametric pairwise comparisons independent measures example is given in Section A1.2.3 of Appendix A1.

In SPSS, the "All pairwise" option for a single-step Related Samples nonparametric test produces the pairwise differences in mean ranks (as in Table 5.22), as well as a matrix of adjusted p-values. Those p-values $<.05$ indicate the significant pairwise differences, giving the same results as the Nemenyi analysis (Table 5.23).

Table 5.23: *Matrix of adjusted* p-*values produced by SPSS*

	BP	CC	DC	DZ	NS	NP	WF
BP		1.000	**.000**	1.000	1.000	1.000	.762
CC			**.000**	1.000	1.000	1.000	.306
DC				**.003**	**.000**	**.022**	**.000**
DZ					1.000	1.000	**.045**
NS						1.000	1.000
NP							**.006**
WF							

These results can be reported as follows:

There were significant differences in performance as represented by the response time data according to condition under a Friedman test:
$\chi^2(6) = 53.844 > \chi^2 (6, p = .05) = 12.59$.

A post-hoc Nemenyi pairwise test ($p = .05$) revealed where the differences lie:

- tasks on diagrams with duplicated curve labels (DC) took longer than tasks on diagrams with all other properties;
- tasks on diagrams with either disconnected zones (DZ) or n-points (NP) took longer than tasks on well-formed (WF) diagrams.

5.4 Analysis of preference data

So far in this chapter, we have concentrated on analysis of quantitative data, with the focus on *performance* data. If the performance data are normally distributed, then parametric methods are used and, if not, then nonparametric methods are used.

The other common quantitative data are *preference* data, which are collected by asking participants to rank or rate conditions or stimuli according to their preference. *Rating* means associating a value with each item, for example, indicating the relative difficulty of tasks by giving each a number within a given range (e.g., 1 for "very easy," 10 for "very difficult"): more than one item may have the same rating. *Ranking* means putting the items in order to indicate how they differ, for example, sorting a set of conditions in order of complexity, and thus allocating a rank number to each condition: ideally, no two items may have the same rank (although in practise, ranks may be shared).

There is an important distinction between the nature of performance and preference data. Performance data are measured on an *interval scale*; that is, the numbers used to represent the data points are equally distant from each other, with the distance between consecutive numbers always representing the same value difference. Thus, for error data, the difference in performance between making twelve errors and fifteen errors is the same as the difference in performance between seven errors and ten errors (i.e., three errors).

Preference data are not measured on an interval scale, as it is, by its nature, *relative* – the preference rank or rating given to a condition depends on the participant's opinion of the other conditions.

Because the data points collected in these cases are subjective, they cannot be assumed to be on an interval scale. There is also no guarantee that the "preference distance" between consecutive preference ratings is the same – the difference in a participant's preference between a condition given a 7 rating and one given an 8 rating is not necessarily the same as the difference in preference between conditions given ratings of 2 and 3.

Similarly, in a ranking task, if 1 represents "worst," 2 represents "middle," and 3 represents "best," then it cannot be said that the difference in preference between "worst" and "middle" is always the same as the difference between "middle" and "best," even though the difference between 1 and 2 is always the same as the difference between 2 and 3. For such noninterval data, nonparametric methods should be used.

When applying the nonparametric methods described previously, the performance data needed to be ranked before the methods were applied. For *ranked* preference data, this initial ranking step has already been done, and nonparametric methods can be directly applied to the raw data. For *rated* preference data, the ratings need to be ranked as a first step (as with performance data).

In the Web Page Aesthetics experiment (Example 2, p 12), twenty-one participants were asked to **rank** fifteen colour screenshots of web pages according to their perception of "good aesthetic," where 1 represents "best" aesthetic and 15 represents "worse" aesthetic. The data are shown in Table 5.24 and Figure 5.11.

Table 5.24: *Ranked data for fifteen web sites according to "good aesthetics"*

	p1	p2	p3	p4	p5	p6	p7	p8	p9	p10	p11	p12	p13	p14	p15	p16	p17	p18	p19	p20	p21	Rank Sum
Procricket	14	6	12	7	14	2	7	7	7	2	10	5	8	8	12	15	10	11	8	3	12	180
Borders	11	1	1	1	7	1	1	1	2	1	2	1	2	2	3	1	1	4	2	5	11	61
Our Players	3	5	2	3	2	3	9	6	8	3	9	4	3	7	5	2	4	10	7	4	13	112
Google	2	13	3	10	3	12	6	3	1	14	12	13	14	1	1	7	2	3	11	1	8	140
UniSat	7	10	8	5	1	9	5	4	11	6	6	8	9	5	4	3	9	14	6	9	6	145
UOA News	15	15	15	12	5	15	11	9	14	15	15	10	11	9	8	8	8	9	5	15	2	226
ASB	6	7	6	6	8	8	3	8	10	4	1	3	4	6	7	6	7	2	10	2	7	121
SE	13	4	4	4	12	5	10	13	15	11	7	2	7	15	6	11	15	15	3	12	1	185
Te Mata Cheese	1	3	7	8	10	4	2	2	3	8	5	7	1	4	14	5	5	13	1	14	14	131
Foodtown	9	2	14	2	13	6	4	11	12	10	3	6	5	13	15	4	14	5	9	13	15	185
Seek	8	12	5	11	6	11	8	10	6	9	11	9	13	3	11	10	13	8	14	8	5	191
ECE	10	8	11	13	11	7	12	14	13	7	8	12	6	14	9	9	11	6	4	11	3	199
Telecom	12	9	9	9	9	10	15	15	4	12	4	11	10	11	13	12	12	1	15	10	10	213
Windows Live	5	14	13	14	15	14	13	5	9	5	14	15	15	12	2	13	3	12	13	7	4	217
Gmail	4	11	10	15	4	13	14	12	5	13	13	14	12	10	10	14	6	7	12	6	9	214
Rank totals	120	120	120	120	120	120	120	120	120	120	120	120	120	120	120	120	120	120	120	120	120	

Each cell is the unique ranking given by the participant to the web page.

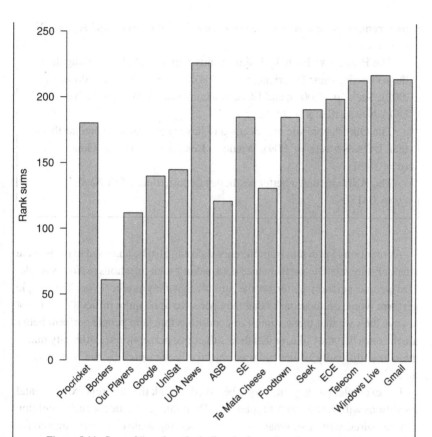

Figure 5.11: Sum of "good aesthetics" ranks for each web page.

We used the **Friedman** test, the first step of which (ranking the data points within each participant) was unnecessary in this case because the data had already been collected as ranks. Application of the Friedman formula (Appendix A2, Table A2.9) produces an χ^2-*value* of 75.224; this is greater than the critical χ^2-value (23.68), $df = 14$, $p = .05$.

SPSS produces the same χ^2-*value* of 75.224, as well as a p-value of .000. We can therefore say that the web sites display significantly different aesthetic appeal when judged by participants.

A **Nemenyi pairwise** analysis could be used to determine the specific **pairwise differences**, but it is easier to use a statistical package when there are so many conditions. The SPSS All Pairwise option for a Related Samples nonparametric test reveals the following significant **pairwise**

differences. Note that this is a one-step pairwise analysis and so $p = .05$ can be used.

The Borders web site had significantly better aesthetics ranking than the following sites: Procricket ($p = .004$); SE ($p = .002$); Foodtown ($p = .002$); Seek ($p = .001$); and ECE, Telecom, Gmail, Windows Live, and UOA News (all at $p < .000$).

The Our Players site was deemed to have significantly better aesthetics than UOA News ($p = .009$), Windows Live ($p = .031$), and Gmail ($p = .045$).

The ASB site had a better aesthetics ranking than UOA News ($p = .031$).

As mentioned previously, preference data can also be analysed to investigate whether they relate to performance data, asking such questions as, for example, "Do people perform better on the stimuli that they prefer?", or "Do people perform worse on those tasks that they perceive to be more difficult?" It is not always the case that those stimuli or conditions that help people perform better are the ones that they like, or that their subjective perceptions of difficulty match the actual difficulty of the tasks as objectively measured by the performance data.

For example, participants might be asked to rank the different experimental conditions with respect to "complexity." Their ranking value for each condition can be paired with a summary value representing their own performance for that condition. A correlation coefficient can then be determined over all participants to determine whether participants performed worse (or better) with those conditions that they believed were more complex (or whether there is no relationship between these subjective and objective measures).

Statistical and spreadsheet software will calculate the correlation coefficient between two sets of paired data: the result will range between -1 and 1, with 1 representing a perfect positive relationship, -1 representing a perfect negative relationship, and 0 representing no relationship.[34] The statistical significance of a correlation coefficient depends on the number of participants, and can be read off a correlation statistical table.[35] Note that it is therefore possible for

---

[34] There are two types of correlation coefficient than can be calculated: the Pearson correlation indicates whether there is a linear relationship between the two sets of values, and the Spearman's rank correlation indicates whether the two sets of values follow the same increasing/decreasing trend (and, as its name suggests, uses ranked data).

[35] For example, if there are twenty-two participants, then a correlation coefficient greater than 0.4227 (or less than -0.4227) is significant at the $p = .05$ level.

a correlation to be strong and not significant (a high correlation value from a small number of participants), or small and significant (a low correlation value from a large number of participants).

5.5 Further analyses

The analysis done so far may be all you need to do – it may be sufficient for answering your research question about the relative performance of different conditions. You could simply stop right here.

However, there are additional analyses that may be useful or interesting, which this section covers. In particular, we look at what you might do if different performance measures give conflicting results, or if you believe that different experimental objects or tasks (or other factors) might have affected the performance data.

5.5.1 Comparing Results from Different Dependent Variables

The first optional step in the analysis sequence is as follows:

STEP 3: In the case of there being more than one dependent variable, investigate any relationship between them.

In many cases, more than one dependent variable may be measured. Indeed, it is common to collect data on both errors and response time, with response time considered an indication of the cognitive cost of completing a task, and errors indicating the difficulty of the task. Note that in this case, each individual trial will contribute both an *error* data point and a *response time* data point, regardless of whether a between- or within-participants experimental design is used.

In many cases, these two dependent measures can be analysed independently. However, sometimes the significant results from one analysis may contradict those of the other; for example, the response time data may show that the Green condition produced significantly *better* performance than the Blue condition, whereas the error data show that the Green condition produced significantly *worse* performance than the Blue condition.

For instance, consider the bar charts in Figure 5.12 showing (fabricated) results for an experiment comparing three different graph layout algorithms (an improved version of the Graph Algorithms experiment (Example 4, p 19)).

The results in Figure 5.12 indicate the following:

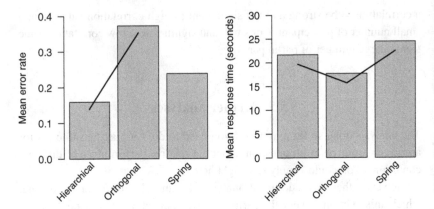

Figure 5.12: Example bar charts showing seemingly contradictory results. The lines indicate where there is statistical significance between the conditions.

- The Hierarchical condition is easier than the Orthogonal condition.
- The Hierarchical condition takes longer that the Orthogonal condition.
- The Spring condition takes longer than the Orthogonal condition.

There is a contradiction here: Hierarchical is shown to be "better" than Orthogonal in terms of errors, but "worse" in terms of response time.

In cases like this, we have to consider the possibility that when participants respond quickly, they may be more likely to make errors (and vice versa – if they take a long time, they may be more likely to get the answers correct). Thus, there is a potential "trade-off" between time and accuracy

If there has been a time/accuracy trade-off, then the two contradictory Hierarchical/Orthogonal results are suspicious because they may simply "cancel each other out"; that is, the Hierarchical condition was shown to be easier than the Orthogonal condition with respect to errors only because participants took longer over answering the Hierarchical tasks then they did when answering the Orthogonal tasks.

This time/accuracy trade-off could be investigated by looking at the relationship between time and accuracy for data from the individual trials, with no aggregation according to condition, participant, task, or experimental object. However, because the error data for each trial is only a 0 or a 1, and it is preferable to use continuous rather than binary data in correlation calculations, some aggregation may be appropriate. It seems appropriate to aggregate according to participant because some may have deliberately worked quickly and erroneously, whereas others took their time to get correct answers. And because we are interested in results according to condition, the data can also be aggregated according to condition. Thus, for each participant, we have an aggregated (usually the mean) value for response time, as well as an aggregated error value, for each condition. These paired time/error values are the ones used in the calculation of the correlation coefficient.

The correlation coefficient will indicate whether there has been a trade-off between response time and errors:

- If the correlation is negative and significant [i.e., a short (low) response time results in high error], then the two contradictory results should be presented with caution because it is indeed the case that there has been a time/accuracy trade-off.
- If the correlation is positive, then errors are not a consequence of fast response times, and both these seemingly contradictory results can stand independently. This is also the case if the correlation is negative, but small and not significant.[36]

In the Small Multiples/Animation experiment (Example 12, p 41), the results for task 3 showed that

- Small Multiples is faster than Animation ($p < .001$).
- Small Multiples is more difficult than Animation ($p = .013$).

The aggregated data collected in this experiment are shown in Table 5.25. They show the results of the trials using task 3 ("Which two edges appear together exactly once?").

The **correlation coefficient** between the fifty-six pairs of time/error values is –0.076, with a significance of $p = .576$. This is a **negative correlation**, suggestive of faster responses leading to more errors (and vice versa); it is, however, very small and not statistically significant.

We can therefore state both results: Small Multiples leads to both faster *and* more erroneous performance than Animation. This would typically be reported as follows:

- Small Multiples results in significantly faster performance than Animation ($p < .001$).

---

[36] My experience has been that seemingly contradictory results are seldom due to a time/accuracy trade-off; usually, the correlations show that the trials with longer response times also tend to be erroneous (and vice versa). This is good news because it means that the two results can stand independently.

Table 5.25: *Data for the Small Multiples/Animation experiment for task 3*

	Mean response time: Animation	Mean response time: Small Multiples	Mean error rate: Animation	Mean error rate: Small Multiples
p1	32.00	19.50	0.00	0.25
p2	29.50	13.25	0.00	0.00
p3	31.00	26.00	0.25	0.25
p4	30.25	23.75	0.50	0.00
p5	34.25	19.00	0.25	0.50
p6	19.75	20.50	0.00	0.00
p7	33.00	23.25	0.25	0.25
p8	34.00	31.25	0.00	0.50
p9	32.00	19.75	0.00	0.00
p10	23.75	21.00	0.00	0.75
p11	32.00	34.00	0.25	0.25
p12	34.50	29.25	0.50	0.00
p13	30.50	19.25	0.025	0.50
p14	32.50	21.00	0.00	0.25
p15	25.25	24.75	0.00	0.25
p16	32.25	18.75	0.00	0.25
p17	27.75	26.25	0.25	0.25
p18	21.50	18.50	0.00	0.25
p19	26.75	32.25	0.00	0.25
p20	33.50	23.00	0.00	0.25
p21	24.25	17.25	0.00	0.25
p22	31.00	24.50	0.25	0.25
p23	29.75	17.25	0.00	0.25
p24	32.00	27.75	0.00	0.25
p25	29.25	24.00	0.00	0.25
p26	31.00	17.75	0.25	0.25
p27	30.75	29.75	0.25	0.25
p28	32.50	28.25	0.25	0.25

- Small Multiples is significantly more difficult than Animation ($p = .013$).
- The correlation between time and error is -0.076 ($n = 56$, $p = .576$). Because this correlation is small and not significant, this indicates that faster responses did not lead to more errors (and vice versa).

5.5.2 Factor Analysis

In the final optional analysis step, the effect of factors other than the independent variable can be investigated.

> **STEP 4:** Split the data so as to investigate more specific research questions (factor analysis).

The analysis so far has focussed on determining whether the set of predefined conditions (the independent variable) has had any effect on performance. In this section, we consider extending the definition of independent variable to include other *factors*. In doing so, we define the *primary independent variable* as the set of conditions relating to the original research question to distinguish it from other factors.

Factor analysis allows for a more in-depth investigation of the data according to the different tasks and experimental objects. Recall from Section 2.4 that the reason why it is a good idea to use different experimental objects and tasks is to permit generalisation of the results, ensuring that any significant results do not hold for only one type of task and only one type of experimental object. The experimental results can therefore be generalised within the definitions of all tasks and experimental objects used, making them more useful.

However, it may be the case that the effect of the conditions is more marked for particular tasks or experimental objects; for example, the experimental conditions may not have had an overall effect, but may have had an effect only on task 1 or only on the largest of the experimental objects. This means that there are two additional factors to be investigated: the effect of the tasks and the effect of the experimental objects.

Indeed, any aspect of the experiment that the experimenter has had control over and that has had varied values can be considered a relevant *secondary factor*. These factors may include, for example, the gender of the participants, the time of day when the experimental sessions took place, or different computing equipment used for different participants. Any of these factors could have affected the results: we call these *secondary independent variables*.

Note, however, that only those factors (and their values) that can be clearly described and differentiated are appropriate secondary independent variables – there must be a clear *qualitative difference* (i.e., difference in quality) between the values that the factor can take. Examples of inappropriate factors with no qualitative difference include three randomly generated graphs of similar size, four identical experimental rooms differing only in room number, a bus timetable for three consecutive Wednesdays, and the telephone numbers for 100 people with the surname Smith living in Glasgow. We cannot distinguish the values of these factors in a meaningful and relevant way.

In contrast, qualitative differences can be described, for example, for three data sets of different size or different structure; the interfaces for three mobile devices produced by different companies; the bus timetables for Friday, Saturday, and Sunday; and experimental rooms with different size windows. It is meaningless to investigate factors for which there are no relevant qualitative differences between their values because any results will be impossible to interpret. If it is discovered that random graph 1 has had an effect on performance, whereas random graph 2 has not, unless there is some relevant way in which these two graphs can be distinguished from each other, this result holds no meaning.

Our main research question is still focussed on whether the primary independent variable (the set of conditions) has had an effect on the dependent variable (the performance). In analysing the data further to determine whether other factors have had an effect on performance, there are two approaches[37]:

- Producing all possible statistics for all combinations of factors, and investigating those that are interesting (i.e., performing a *multiway factor analysis*). This approach, which can only be used for data that are normally distributed, is the method typically favoured by psychologists.
- Focussing on the primary research question first, and then investigating other factors as necessary (i.e., performing a *selective factor analysis*). This approach entails devising appropriate and interesting second-level research questions, and investigating each of these in turn, producing only those statistics relevant to these second-level research questions. If factor analysis is to be performed on nonnormal data, then this is the approach that must be used because there are no nonparametric equivalents to the parametric multiway analysis methods.[38]

5.5.2.1 Multiway Factor Analysis

In this approach, other relevant factors are considered as independent variables in addition to the primary independent variable (the set of conditions) on which the research question is based.

In the context of the types of experiments described here, the most obvious relevant factors are the tasks and the experimental objects. Recall that

---

[37] And, in the battleground that is statistical analysis, people will have different views as to the best approach.
[38] An extensive example demonstrating both approaches is given in Appendix A3.

these were chosen to ensure generalisability of the conclusions of the primary research question (the effect of the conditions on performance): they are controlled by the experimenter and take on different values during the experiment. If their values can be qualitatively distinguished, then they can be considered as additional independent variables. Thus, a three-way factor analysis can be performed with three independent variables (condition, task, and experimental object) for *each* dependent variable (typically, response time and error).[39]

The analysis will not only consider the effect of each factor on the performance data, but will also provide information about the interactions between the three factors (i.e., the extent to which the value of the dependent variable depends on a combination of factors). This means that all combinations of factors are subject to pairwise analysis; in the case of three factors (condition, task, and experimental object), there will be seven significance tests for each dependent variable, each returning a p-value:

1. the *main* effect of condition,
2. the *main* effect of task,
3. the *main* effect of experimental object,
4. the *two-way interaction* effect of condition and task,
5. the *two-way interaction* effect of condition and experimental object,
6. the *two-way interaction* effect of experimental object and task,
7. the *three-way interaction* effect of condition, experimental object, and task.

In the more common case of two factors (e.g., condition and task), only items 1, 2, and 3 are relevant. A statistically significant two-way interaction (item 4) would indicate that the effects of the primary independent variable (the conditions) are different for each of the different tasks.

The hard line on interpreting these values is that the *main* effect of the primary independent variable conditions (item 1) is meaningless (even if significant) if *any* of the interaction effects associated with these conditions (i.e., items 4–6) are significant. Thus, you should not report the conditions as having had a significant effect if their performance has been affected by other factors.

A more practical approach focuses on the nature of the original primary research question, the purpose of the additional factors, and the usefulness

---

[39] The discussion in the rest of this section refers to error data as the dependent variable, although, of course, any quantitative data (including response time) can be investigated in this manner.

of the results. The varied tasks and experimental objects were included to ensure generalisation of the result, not because there was any expectation that any qualitative differences between them would affect performance. The main effect of the condition is therefore the most important result of the experiment, regardless of the interactions with other factors.

Another important issue to consider is that, in most cases, the eventual use of the HCI idea being tested is unknown. It is not known what experimental objects or tasks the eventual user will employ, and it is probable that they will be different from those used in the experiment. Strict application of the multiway approach may prevent the reporting of any overall conclusion about the primary independent variable (which has formed the basis of the initial research question) and may mean that the only results reported are those that are constrained by other factors.

For example, if we are attempting to prove the worth of a new graph layout algorithm by comparing it with another, and a multiway factor analysis indicates that the algorithm is only good for one type of task, then this does not help a tool designer decide whether the algorithm should be included in a graph drawing tool. The designer does not know the full range of tasks the user might want to perform; indeed, the task that has produced the significant experimental result may ultimately be rarely used.

If we are attempting to demonstrate the usefulness of a mobile device for navigation as opposed to a traditional map, then a result that indicates that it is only useful for novice users of large maps does not help in making a decision about whether it is appropriate to deploy, because it is not known what type or size of maps users will load into the new mobile device and how much navigating experience they will have. For this reason, although a multiway factor analysis might reveal effects between secondary factors, if it does not allow for the initial overall research question (based on the primary independent variable) to be answered, then it may not produce the desired overall conclusion.

Multiway factor analyses are useful when data incorporating several factors have been collected, with no clear suggestion in advance as to which of the factors is a main focus of the investigation. For example, if investigating the use of different interface designs, then relevant factors could be the screen colour, font, animation effects, and size of images, and the experimenter may be interested in results arising from any of these factors. Note that investigations like these are contrary to the approach suggested in this book, which encourages the clear specification of which set of conditions are to be investigated as part of the main research question that is defined at the start.

Multiway factor analyses are also useful if you believe that there may have been some confounding factors that have affected your results (see Section 2.3). These factors are aspects of the experiment that varied (which you know varied and which you can clearly define with a qualitative difference), but which you did not *deliberately* vary as part of the experimental definition. Examples of confounding factors might be the experimenter (if the experiment was conducted by more than one person due to unexpected absence), different computing equipment (if the experiment was run by necessity on whatever equipment was available at the time), or unexpected interruptions or noise that occurred during the experiment. Doing a factor analysis would identify whether such factors had an effect on the results.

It does no harm to perform a multiway factor analysis for normally distributed data, but beware of being side-tracked into focussing on interactions between factors that were never part of your original research question. It might be best to only do this method if you anticipate in advance that there will be interesting interaction effects that you want to investigate and report, and if it does not matter if you do not get an overall answer for the primary independent variable.

In the Spring Dynamic Graph experiment (Example 10, p 33), the research question focussed on whether maintaining the mental map between time slices in a dynamic graph layout algorithm affected participants' performance in interpreting the information represented: the independent variable consisted of three conditions: High, Medium, and Low Mental Map. Three tasks and three experimental objects were used to ensure some generalisability of the results.

The graphs were generated randomly, and so there is no definable qualitative difference between them: the only criterion for creation was that they be roughly the same size. We can, however, describe the difference between the three tasks because each requires a different visual process.

Although Samra did not do a **two-way factor analysis** at the time, the statistics for a repeated measures multiway factor analysis (the Within-Subjects Effects) of the error data from this experiment (calculated by SPSS) are given in Table 5.26.

Because $0.267 > 0.05$, there was **no interaction** between mental map and task, so the main research question can be answered: there was an effect of mental map condition on performance as measured by error.

Table 5.26: *Multiway factor analysis of error data*

	df	F	p-value
Mental Map condition	2,58	15.656	<.001
Task	2,58	8.050	.001
Mental Map/task	4,116	1.318	.267

A further **pairwise analysis** (with a Bonferroni confidence interval adjustment) shows that there were significant interactions between all three conditions. The means of the three conditions are shown in Figure 5.13.

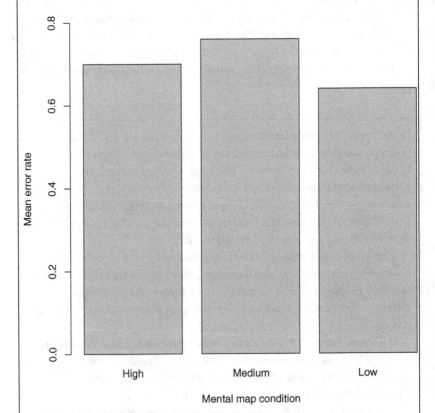

Figure 5.13: Bar chart showing the overall means of the three conditions.

The results can be reported as follows:

There were significant differences in performance as represented by the error data according to mental map condition: $F(2,58) = 15.66$, $p < .001$. Pairwise analysis (adjusted for the Bonferroni correction) showed that Low Mental Map condition produced better performance than both High ($p = .021$) and Medium ($p = .043$) Mental Map conditions, and High Mental Map produces better performance than Medium ($p < .001$) Mental Map.[40]

Because there is **no significant interaction** between the two factors (mental map and task), this overall result can be reported with the confidence that the mental map effect does not differ significantly for each task. It can be useful to look at the interaction of the two factors graphically (Figure 5.14). Parallel trend lines would indicate no interaction because it would mean that the ordering of the mental map trend lines is the same for each task. Here, this is almost the case, apart from when the performance for the Medium Mental Map condition dips only slightly below that of the High Mental Map for task 2.

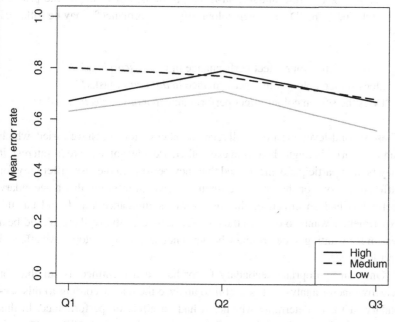

Figure 5.14: Chart showing the interaction between conditions and tasks.

---

[40] This result was reported in the article arising from the research as 'Extremes are Better' (Purchase and Samra, 2008).

5.5.2.2 Selective factor analysis

The approach taken to experimental design in this book is to clearly define, and focus on, a primary research question and a set of experimental conditions to be investigated. The title of this section is therefore "selective factor analysis" because it focusses on the initial research question first, and then selects appropriate additional factors to investigate by posing *second-level research questions*.

Under this approach, the data are first analysed using *t*-tests/ANOVA/ pairwise tests (or their nonparametric equivalents) according to the primary independent variable. This allows for an overall result to be reported for the effect of the conditions on performance. The interpretation of this primary result is, of course, constrained by the nature of the tasks and experimental objects chosen; however, it is at least generalisable over these tasks and objects (which would not be the case if the experiment used only one task and object).

After the main question about the primary independent variable has been answered, then, if desired, other selected interesting factors can be investigated by posing a set of relevant *second-level questions*. For example, the primary research question, "Does screen colour affect performance?" may be followed by

- "Does screen colour affect performance in *visual search* tasks?"
- "Does screen colour affect performance in *data entry* tasks?"
- "Does the screen colour affect performance in *mouse selection* tasks?"

These second-level questions will relate to other factors that have varied, which can be clearly distinguished from each other, are relevant, and are of interest. It may be that participants mentioned that they performed the task differently for different factors, or that the experimenters have an intuition that a secondary factor has had an effect, or that no overall significance was found but the experimenter wants to explore the data further – essentially, there should be a reason for wanting to determine whether other secondary factors have affected performance.

Once an appropriate secondary factor has been identified as suitable for selective factor analysis, it is useful to analyse the data according to this secondary factor to determine whether it had an effect on performance. In this case, no distinction is made between the data arising from different conditions: the aggregations are done over all trials with respect to the secondary factor. The same *t*-test/ANOVA/pairwise tests (or nonparametric equivalents) discussed previously can be used to analyse with respect to the secondary factor.

Table 5.27: *Form of data for investigating effect of tasks*

Mean ERRORS	task1	task2	task3	task4
p1				
p2				
p3				
p4				
. . .				
pn				
Mean				

The data are aggregated over all experimental objects and conditions.

For example, if the nature of the task has been chosen as the secondary factor, then the form of the data will be as shown in Table 5.27, and tests can be performed to determine whether the different tasks have produced significant differences. The results of these tests will suggest whether the proposed secondary factor analysis is likely to reveal interesting results.

Assuming that the selected factor is "task," our second-level research questions will focus on the effect of the primary independent variable with respect to task. This results in a second-level, task-focussed analysis. The data can be split and analysed separately; thus, for example, the data for task 1 can be analysed, and then the data for task 2, task 3, etc. The data points are aggregated over experimental objects for each participant, and the form of the data are as shown in Table 5.28.

Secondary factor analysis entails performing *t*-test/ANOVA/pairwise (or nonparametric equivalent) tests on the data for each task independently. You would hope that the same pattern of results that you obtained for the overall analysis (which considered the overall effects of the primary independent variable) would be repeated for each of the tasks, thus confirming the overall result. This may not be the case because the results could show, for example, that one of the conditions produces better performance than another for one of the tasks, but that the contrary is true for a different task. Different results would then be reported separately for each task.

Other secondary factors can also be analysed in this way. For example, a secondary analysis may be performed with experimental objects as the selected factor, or the time of day that the experiment was run. The data would be similarly split, but with respect to the chosen secondary factor. For example, in the case of experimental objects as the secondary factor, the data are aggregated over the different tasks, and separate analyses are performed for each

Table 5.28: *Form of data for second-level factor analysis, considering the data with respect to different tasks*

TASK 1 Mean ERRORS	cond1	cond2	cond3
p1			
p2			
p3			
. . .			
pn			
mean			
TASK 2 Mean ERRORS			
p1			
p2			
p3			
. . .			
pn			
mean			
TASK 3 Mean ERRORS			
p1			
p2			
p3			
. . .			
pn			
mean			

experimental object. It would be done if it were suspected that the primary independent variable had an effect on performance for one or more of the experimental objects, but not for others.

However, as discussed in Section 5.2.3, we need to consider that multiple analysis of data will always give us a better chance of getting significant results, simply because statistics is based on probabilities.

We therefore need to apply a Bonferroni adjustment to each of our second-level analyses. If the data have been divided into n data sets, the required p-value for each of the subsequent n ANOVA/pairwise analyses will be $0.05/n$ (thus making it harder to find significance).

For example, consider an experiment with four conditions, three tasks, and five experimental objects:

- The top-level analysis would be done according to condition, aggregating over all experimental objects and tasks, using $p = .05$ for the ANOVA and post-hoc pairwise analyses.

- A second-level analysis considering the effect of the conditions for each of the three tasks would divide the data into three subsets (one for each task), and use $p = .05/3 = .017$ for each of the three ANOVA and post-hoc pairwise analyses.
- A second-level analysis considering the effect of the conditions for each of the five experimental objects would divide the data into five subsets (one for each experimental object), and use $p = .05/5 = .01$ for each of the five ANOVA and post-hoc pairwise analyses.
- A third-level analysis considering the effect of *both* the five experimental objects *and* the three tasks would divide the data into 15 subsets, and use $.05/15 = .0033$.[41] In this case, very specific results may be obtained of the form: "The orthogonal layout algorithm produced better performance than the spring layout algorithm for shortest path tasks using graphs with a high *node:edge ratio*."[42]

Note that this p-value adjustment does not apply when the data are split and analysed separately as part of the process of investigating interactions revealed by multiway factor analysis. In that case, $p = .05$ can be used for analysing the second-level data sets. This is because in multiway analyses, no overall analysis of the primary independent variable has been performed in advance of the second-level analysis, and the second-level analysis is therefore not considered as an instance of multiple data analysis.

Selective factor analysis is useful if answering the main research question, "Has the primary independent variable had an effect on performance?",

- is of key importance,
- is the main focus of the research, and
- is the result you want to report.

Performing subsequent analysis on selected relevant factors can then reveal additional useful results. This may be particularly useful if you have first discovered that there has been no significant overall effect of your primary independent variable.

---

[41] Few statistical tables will give the values for p-values as low as this, but tools like SPSS will produce the appropriate p-values for both multiway factor or selected-factor analyses.

[42] The application of these statistical adjustments is a subtle point. I have, at various times, published experimental results where I have applied erroneous adjustments. Although my reviewers have not objected, as the field matures and HCI researchers learn more about statistical analysis, getting these details correct is becoming more important.

In the Clustering experiment (Example 18, p 72) our **primary analysis** revealed (see Section 5.3.1):

> A Wilcoxon test indicated that there were no significant differences in performance as represented by the error data between the Path-preserving Cluster and No Cluster conditions: $T(23) = 83, p = .094$.

There were six experimental objects used in this experiment, each defined as either "high connectivity" or "low connectivity" (Table 5.29). Anticipating that the connectivity of the graphs might have had an effect on performance, we performed a **selective factor analysis** on the data.

Table 5.29: *Definitions of "low" and "high" connectivity in the Clustering experiment*

	Ratio of nodes to edges
High connectivity (IMDB data)	Ranges from 1.68 to 1.86
Low connectivity (Internet data)	Ranges from 1.21 to 1.31

First, we analysed the data according to connectivity, using the Wilcoxon test (because there are only two connectivities), and $p = .05$. We found that there was a significant difference between graphs of high and low connectivity with respect to performance as measured by the error ($p < .001$), with high connectivity graphs producing more errors than low connectivity graphs.

We then performed a selective factor analysis on the data from each of the connectivities separately, looking to determine whether the **primary independent variable** (the two conditions: Path-preserving Cluster and No Cluster) had an effect on error performance for either of the connectivities when analysed as a separate **second-level analysis**.

Although the **primary research question** is "does using path-preserving clusters in the depiction of large graphs improve the readability of graphs?", there are now two **second-level research questions:**

- Does using path-preserving clusters in the depiction of large graphs improve the readability of graphs with a *low ratio of nodes to edges*?
- Does using path-preserving clusters in the depiction of large graphs improve the readability of graphs with a *high ratio of nodes to edges*?

For each of these research questions, we need to use a *p*-value adjusted by the number of values the secondary factor can take: .05/2 = .025.

We divided the data into two data sets, one for each of the connectivities. Figure 5.15 shows the mean error data for each connectivity.

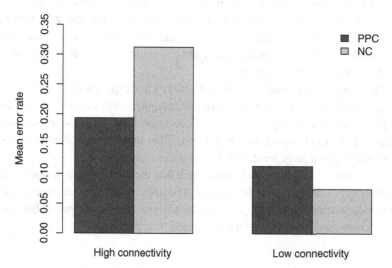

Figure 5.15: Mean errors for the Path-preserving Clusters and No Clusters conditions, separated by the connectivity of the graphs.

Analysing each of the two data sets using a Wilcoxon test revealed:

- For high connectivity, there is a significant difference in error performance between the Path-preserving Clusters and No Clusters conditions, with No Clusters producing worse performance ($p = .003$). We can state this as a result because .003 < .025.
- For low connectivity, there is no significant difference in error performance between the Path-preserving Clusters and No Clusters conditions ($p = .279$).

5.5.3 Investigating demographic factors

The demographic profiles of the participants provide additional secondary factors that could be investigated (e.g., gender, age, experience in a particular area, cultural background). Recall that your sample set of participants is intended to be representative of your population, to permit generalisability; ideally, the experimental results should apply to all participants equally.

However, there may be good reasons for investigating the effect of demographics. For example, observations of participants in a sketching experiment might suggest that some participants were more comfortable in using a pen-based stylus that others; this might lead to a secondary factor analysis with respect to the extent of experience of pen-based technology. Questionnaire or interview data might suggest, for example, that female participants were more confident with the more abstract tasks, and this could lead to a secondary factor analysis with respect to gender.[43]

Demographic information can be collected by postexperiment questionnaire. Any analysis performed on demographic categories will be more robust for objective categories (e.g., gender, age, education level) than subjective ones (e.g., extent of experience, use, or interest)[44] because the latter depend on the participant's own judgement, which may differ from others'.

If secondary analysis is performed such that the data are split according to demographic category, then there needs to be sufficient numbers of participants within each demographic category to make analysis feasible and generalisations appropriate, and p-value adjustments should be applied.

5.6 Role of qualitative data

It is easy to get excited about statistical analyses and the hard facts that they produce, and to focus entirely on the numbers and what they reveal. However, it is important not to forget the role of qualitative data, which can both guide the analyses and help in interpreting the quantitative results.

Qualitative data obtained by interview or questionnaire, or by observation of the participants, can help in guiding the analysis by

- *Identifying potential outliers.* For example, a participant who was particularly confused about how to perform the tasks may say so in an interview, and one who is not taking the experiment seriously could be identified by

---

[43] Some experimenters *always* analyse their data according to demographic profiles. My personal view is that this is inappropriate unless the research question explicitly addresses demographic factors (e.g., "Does expertise in navigation using a mobile device differ with ethnicity?") or if the qualitative data gathered during the experiment suggest that there may be interesting demographic influences.

[44] For example, participants may be asked to indicate the extent of their experience with pen-based technology as "none," "infrequent use," "frequent use," or "extensive use."

the experimenter's observations. It may then be reasonable to eliminate these data.

- *Revealing potentially important secondary factors.* For example, if participants said they found one task more difficult than the others, then selective factor analysis can be guided by knowledge of what factors (in this case, the task) might produce interesting results.
- *Revealing possible confounding factors.* For example, if some participants reported that the light in the experimental room made it difficult to see the images on the screen in early morning sessions, then a factor analysis could reveal whether the results were affected by the confound.

The qualitative data can therefore help in justifying your statistical approach, as well as in interpreting the results (as discussed in Section 4.4).

Analysis of data is more interesting and robust if a broad approach is taken, considering all possible sources of information: hard numbers and bare statistics paint a limited picture if not supplemented by anecdotes, quotes, and qualitative impressions or opinions.

5.7 Evaluations

It is unlikely that a full statistical analysis will be required for an evaluation that takes place as part of an iterative design cycle. Indeed, the analyses presented in this chapter assume the presence of an independent variable and a comparison between the values of the dependent variables associated with a set of conditions. In the case where the system designers are interested in comparing different design decisions (e.g., whether the users should input information using text or drop-down combo boxes), then the evaluation may include a comparative method and analysis. It is unlikely, however, that a full and rigorous statistical experiment will be required for such software design decisions. Qualitative feedback from participants is likely to be much more useful than statistical analysis in informing subsequent design decisions.

5.8 Summary

Any measure that can be quantified and interpreted as a measurement of performance can be subject to the analysis procedures described in this chapter. It is important to recall, though, that these quantitative measures are only indicative of the comprehension and problem-solving processes of the participants and do not truly represent cognitive activity or comprehension (we cannot get inside our participants' heads!), and that a rigorous quantitative analysis needs to be supplemented by qualitative data.

It is easy to let getting statistical significance become the most important goal of your study, and to celebrate when the hard numerical data give you the magic $p < .05$ value. However, a small significant effect should be treated with caution: if there is a statistically significant difference between the mean error rate of two conditions of 0.03 (say, 0.90 vs. 0.87), then although this shows that condition A may be better than condition B, it is only a small improvement. This may not mean that condition A should always be recommended over B because any gains will be minimal. Similarly, a significant correlation coefficient of 0.15 represents only a small relationship between the two variables (even if it is significant).

In the Aural Tables experiment (Example 8, p 31), the repeated measures two-tailed t-test produced a p-value of .019 for response time data, indicating statistical significance. The mean response time for the Sonification condition was 7.19 seconds and the mean for the Speech condition was 7.36 seconds: a difference of only 0.17 seconds. Despite the **significant results**, it would be strange to recommend that sonification be the only means of access to aural tables for the visually impaired because the response time gain is very small indeed.

Recall that the typical steps of quantitative data analysis (see Section 5.1.3) are as follows:

STEP 1: Analyse the data to determine whether the different conditions had any effect on the data when there are
- only two conditions, or
- more than two conditions.

STEP 2: In the case of there being more than two conditions, determine which conditions performed better or worse than other conditions by comparing pairs of conditions.

STEP 3: In the case of there being more than one dependent variable, investigate any relationship between them.

STEP 4: If appropriate, split the data so as to investigate more specific research questions.

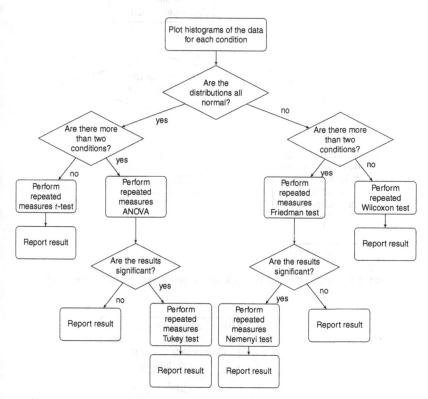

Figure 5.16: Steps 1 and 2 of repeated measures analysis, which should be performed for each dependent variable.[45]

Figures 5.16, 5.17, and 5.18 illustrate these four steps.

It is easy to make mistakes in performing statistical analysis. In fact, it is a good idea for two members of a research team to do the analyses in parallel, perhaps using different statistical tools, because it is surprising how trivial errors can make a substantial difference to the final results.[46] This parallel analysis method will ensure you can have complete confidence in your results.

Many decisions need to be made on how to conduct a statistical analysis of experimental data, and, as mentioned, different people will have different views on what is appropriate. This chapter is not intended to be the only and final word on how to conduct statistical analyses; its intention is to describe some

---

[45] The corresponding independent measures flowchart appears in Appendix A1 as Figure A1.3.

[46] I have used this method of analysing the data in parallel with collaborators on many occasions; in all cases, our initial analyses did not agree, and we needed to undergo a few iterations together before we produced exactly the same results.

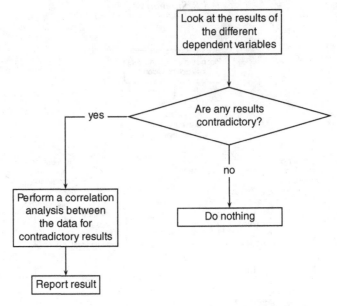

Figure 5.17: Step 3 of the analysis (repeated measures and independent measures).

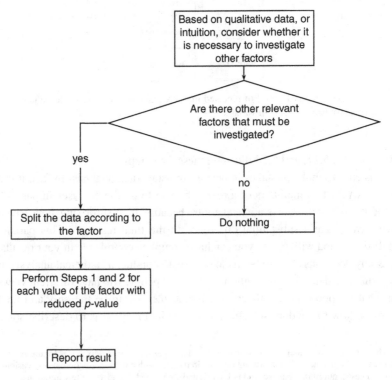

Figure 5.18: Step 4 of the analysis (repeated measures and independent measures).

basic tools for simple analyses and equip the reader with sufficient knowledge to investigate further, if required.

Analysing the data and answering your research question does not indicate the end of the process – you now need to tell the world about it. The next chapter considers how best to report both the experiment and its results.

6

Reporting

So, now you have your results, and you want to tell everyone about them. This chapter discusses the way in which you report your research, typically in a research article for an academic conference or journal, or in a dissertation for assessment. In all cases, you need to keep in mind that *someone else* will be reading what you write, and that this person has not been party to your decision-making process. It is easy to leave information out because it appears obvious.

6.1 Reviewers' concerns

It is the job of reviewers or assessors to make a judgement on the worth of your research, and it is your job to make sure that you have presented it sufficiently well that they can do so.[1] This is true of all research; however, writing experimental papers brings with it its own particular issues:

- *An experiment focuses on addressing specific research questions:* reviewers may not believe that these questions are interesting or important.
- *An experimental research question could be addressed in many different ways:* everyone will have their own idea as to how best to address it.
- *Different statistical methods are favoured by different people:* beware the reviewers who are well versed in statistics when you have not analysed your data using their favoured method!
- *No experiment can ever be perfect:* reviewers can easily find faults on which to base a negative judgement if they want.

[1] This chapter does not claim to cover *all* categories of possible reviewer concerns, simply those that I have come across so far (I have no doubt that I will get many more in my lifetime!).

- *Many reviewers have never actually designed and conducted an experiment themselves:* they do not always appreciate the amount of work required for running experiments, the difficulty in making appropriate design decisions, or the constraints that apply to experimental design.

Writing to address these problems requires that the decision-making process is, as far as is possible, described in detail. It is not sufficient to explain *what* you did, you also need to explain *why* you did it.

6.2 Justifying design decisions

6.2.1 The research question

First, a case needs to be made as to why the research question you are addressing is important and interesting – this is typically done with reference to previous research, experimental or otherwise. Identifying specific prior research that makes a clear case for the question to be addressed is useful. For instance, the research question for the Euler Diagrams experiment (Example 6, p 24) is an obvious further step that builds on the work of Flower et al. (2008), who first defined the well-formedness properties, but did not consider any issues regarding the ease with which they can be interpreted by users.

More difficult is the case when the research question arises from ideas spread across different research areas. For instance, the research question for the Mental Model experiment (Example 17, p 62) arose from our knowledge of graphs and the principles underlying graph algorithms, previous experiments on graph layout, our experience with sketch-based experiments, and existing psychological theories of perception. A clear case needed to be made as to why these areas were worth bringing together and how the research question emerged from a consideration of how they linked together.

Typical reviewer comments on the motivation for the research include "the authors need to make clearer the case for doing this study," "the whole context of the experiment was flawed to begin with," "the authors need to reframe this research some other way," "combining [two areas of research] into a body of work is not necessarily the only reason to do it," or "I am left with one question: so what?"[2]

---

[2] All reviewer comments quoted are from reviews of my own papers – I have not identified the projects that they are associated with so as to spare the blushes of my collaborators!

6.2.2 The experimental method

Next, all experimental design decisions need to be justified. That is, the reader needs to know why the experiment has been designed this way and why other possible options were not chosen. This is particularly difficult when there are restrictions on the maximum number of pages allowed for the article because you need to be both comprehensive and succinct. In the (usually rare) case that the method is similar to one that has been previously published, then it may be possible to refer to this prior work as an indirect means of justifying the method. However, this would need to be a popular and well-known experiment, and you would need to be sure that the readers will know about it. Not explaining design decisions leaves you vulnerable to reviewers who are looking for reasons to reject your paper.

It is useful to remember that the experiment is a single point in a multidimensional design space, where each dimension represents a decision that has been made, and that there are many dimensions of choice, including (but not limited to) the following:

- conditions,
- experimental objects,
- tasks,
- within- or between-participants method,
- pre- and postexperiment activities,
- location of the experiment,
- nature of participants,
- equipment used,
- number of participants,
- experimental timing,
- data collection methods,
- data analysis methods.

Some of these decisions are relevant to the research question and obviously need to be justified, for example,

- in the Screen Layout experiment (Example 9, p 32), we needed to justify our use of triangles as targets,
- in the Metro Maps experiment (Example 21, p 84), the location of the participants during the experiment was an important decision.

Other decisions are trivial:

- in the Shortest Path experiment (Example 7, p 27), the colour used to highlight the nodes was not important.

The trick is to ensure that you justify important decisions and not waste precious space on trivial decisions – having said this, it can sometimes be surprising which decisions reviewers want to know about!

The choice of conditions, experimental objects, and tasks are the most obvious decisions on which to focus. Other choices such as experimental method, timing, and nature and number of participants also require attention, especially if they are unusual or affected your results in any noticeable way.

The choice of conditions should be related to the research question, and so should be justified as part of the case made for addressing the question itself.

The choice of experimental objects will be related to your choice of domain (see Section 2.8). It is common for reviewers to complain that the objects are too abstract and that the results thus have no "real world" applicability (e.g., "limited generalizability to typical interfaces").[3] This is a difficult issue to address. In breaking new experimental ground, using an abstract domain in a preliminary experiment enables important experience to be gained before experimenting using real world scenarios, and reviewers need to be persuaded of the importance of an initial (abstract) step in guiding the design of a second (applied) experiment. A clear case therefore needs to be made for an abstract experiment: this may be easier if it is clear that either the results are in a never-before-explored area (and are thus interesting regardless of the nature of the domain) or the experiment and its results are obviously necessary to inform the design of a later real world experiment.[4]

The most common criticism from reviewers tends to concern the tasks chosen for the trials (e.g., "It remains unclear how the questions were chosen for the three data sets").[5] You would have chosen your tasks from a vast number of possibilities – some of which you may have thought of, but many of which you would not have even considered. Often, the task choice has been constrained by the choice of conditions and experimental objects, the nature of the research question, the form of the data required for analysis, the need to use tasks of similar or different difficulty, and prior experience in the research area. It is the

---

[3] Other comments include "bring real users and real tasks" and "narrow focus and [...]lack of concrete examples."

[4] Note that subsequent experiments in a real world domain may require an entirely different experimental method than the initial abstract one that you used because participants' prior knowledge needs to be considered, as does the complexity and scale of real world tasks. So, an abstract experimental method cannot always be simply reused with real world experimental objects.

[5] Other comments include "lack of strong motivation for choosing the questions," "I think the two tasks only cover a small set of real world tasks," and "I'd like to know what's good for all of the types of tasks."

interaction between these decisions that is most difficult to explain succinctly when justifying the choice of tasks.

Timing is also a common query, especially if you have chosen to limit the time for each trial (see Section 3.2.1), for example, "I have trouble understanding why the task completion time needs to be limited to 20 seconds."[6] You would usually have a good reason for limiting the time for the trials: this decision may interact with other decisions and should be explained clearly. Because one reason for limiting the time for each trial is to keep the experiment at a reasonable length, this should be stated, particularly if your timing choices have been based on experiences in pilot experiments.

The nature and number of participants should always be reported, as well as the means of recruiting them. Comments on this issue are sometimes associated with the choice of research question and the experimental objects; for example, "The experiment did not include software engineers, which might have different results." In other cases, there may be comments on the nature of the participants (in particular the use of computing science students); for example, "The use of a narrow spectrum sample group, although providing an adequate depth to the results, does limit the relevance of results to a small demographic of users, and as such the judgements cannot be applied to the broader population."[7] The number and nature of participants is sometimes a consequence of practical constraints that are not always appreciated by those who have not had to deal with such constraints themselves.

In general, reviewers typically want more information about the experimental design than they have been given (although seldom suggesting, of course, which aspects of the article could be reasonably omitted to make space for this additional information!).[8] Many criticisms of experimental papers are a result of the reviewer not being given sufficient information to understand the complexity and nature of the design decisions, and the way that they interact with each other. Because many decisions are a result of experiences of pilot experiments (see Section 3.3), it may be useful to include a section that briefly discusses what occurred in the pilots as a way of justifying subsequent decisions.

---

[6] Other comments include "The authors should also explain why did they allow [sic] the participant to look at the drawing for only 3 seconds and not 5 or 10 seconds" and "The time limit on individual tasks did not seem to be very successful."

[7] Reviewers sometimes query the gender or age profile of the participants and whether the experimental results differ according to these profiles. Demographic data should always be reported, and they may be analysed in a secondary research question if it appears that interesting results may emerge (see Section 5.5.3).

[8] For example, "Further clarity over the approach taken and tools/techniques used would aid in establishing the usefulness and credibility of the study."

6.3 Presenting results and conclusions

6.3.1 Analysis and results

There are three aspects to presenting results:

- describing the method of analysis used,
- presenting the results of applying the method, and
- explaining the results.

For quantitative data, the statistical analysis methods that have been used should be clearly stated.

When qualitative data have been analysed, the methods used need to be described, including information about how many independent people took part in the coding analysis and what process was followed to reach agreement.

Many reviewers know a great deal about statistics (more than you and I). Some will get excited about your data and suggest other possible analyses that could be performed. Some will complain that you have not done your statistical analysis the way that they would have done it (and therefore the entire research is questionable). Conversely, many reviewers know little about statistics and will simply accept what is presented.

My approach is to focus on the research questions (rather than on the data), to let the questions guide the analysis, and not to perform any analyses that are not required for shedding light on the research questions (even if the data permit). This approach is not always agreed on, and reviewers may question why further analyses were not performed (e.g., "as there are quite a few independent variables, it would be interesting to see a complete model comprising all independent variables and all interaction effects"). If your research questions are clearly listed at the start of the paper, and your description of the analysis method is clearly related to each research question, you should be able to mitigate against comments like this by making sure your article tells a complete "research story."

The results section itself can be short and concise by presenting just the statistical facts, and providing summary bar charts (indicating where significant differences have been found on these charts themselves). The outcome of qualitative analysis can be usefully summarised in tables.

Being clear about the research questions and describing the structured approach to analysing the data to address these specific questions is essential: it should not look like you simply collected a lot of data and then analysed it in every way you could think of!

6.3.2 Presenting the data

It is common to use data visualisation techniques for presenting the quantitative data (e.g., bar charts, scatter plots, box plots, histograms) (as shown in Figure 5.3). Some simple rules will help ward against criticism:

- bar charts representing similar data should have the same scales;
- bar charts should always have a zero origin (or if it is necessary to shift the origin, then this should be clearly highlighted in the caption);
- line charts should only be used for data where the x-axis represents ordered categories (not nominal data);
- pie charts and 3D graphics should be avoided;
- all axes should be labelled, and the units used should be clear;
- don't clutter the graphic with unnecessary clutter (as advocated by Tufte (2001).

6.3.3 Making conclusions: separating fact from opinion

It is easy to (consciously or unconsciously) overgeneralise the experimental results when stating conclusions, and thus mislead readers (Zhai, 2003). However, if all experimental facts (tasks, experimental objects, procedure, analysis) are described completely, clearly, and unambiguously, then the readers will be able to form their own conclusions. Your conclusion is simply one possible interpretation of these facts.

The data and its analysis are therefore the objective facts, whereas the conclusions are *your* interpretation of the facts. It is therefore useful to clearly separate the presentation of the hard facts from your opinion of what they mean. By doing so, you acknowledge that your conclusions are your interpretation of the facts, and you therefore make it possible for other readers to interpret the facts in their own way. This means that readers who do not agree with your interpretation can clearly identify the facts and make their own judgement, independent of their disagreement with your opinion. Allowing a reader to make their own judgement of the facts is difficult if the fact is not clearly distinguished from the opinion in the report.

It is useful, therefore, to make sure that there is a point in the paper where "the fact" ends and "the opinion" begins.

6.3.4 Making conclusions: acknowledging limitations

It is important that the limitations of the experiment are faithfully acknowledged. All experiments are limited, and no experiment is perfect. The limitations may be caused by the choice of tasks, experimental objects, participants, unexpected incidents that occurred in the experimental process, confounding factors, etc. These limitations will constrain the boundaries within which your conclusions can be generalised.

Two concepts that are sometimes used in discussing limitations are *reliability* and *validity*, and particularly in the empirical software engineering literature, limitations are often discussed in terms of "threats to reliability" and "threats to validity."

Reliability (precision) is the extent to which an experiment will give the same result if performed again (i.e., its consistency). If someone else were to repeat the experiment exactly, would they get the same conclusions?

The reliability of an experiment can be improved by the following:

- gathering more data using the same experimental method (although the effort required for HCI experiments means that replications are uncommon);
- obtaining many different types of data using different techniques and methods – for example, using several different tasks and experimental objects, or collecting additional qualitative data (the "mixed methods approach" advocated in Section 4.4).

Validity (accuracy) is the extent to which the experiment correctly addresses the specified research questions. Has the experiment been conducted in a manner that allows appropriate conclusions to be made?

There are two types of validity: internal and external. They are defined as follows:

- *Internal validity* relates to the design of the experiment. Has it been designed appropriately with respect to randomisation, controls, data collection methods, and experimental process? Can the effect on the dependent variable(s) be attributed to the changes in the independent variables (and not to any other intervention)?
- *External validity* relates to the generalisation of the results. Would these results hold for other participants, or to other experimental objects and tasks? The external validity of an experiment can be improved by:
  o using large random samples from the population as the participants and employing wide advertising methods for recruiting participants;
  o increasing the number and range of tasks and experimental objects used in the experiment.

An experiment may be *reliable* and may be *internally valid*, but its results may not be generalisable to other situations (e.g., those involving different tasks or experimental objects), or to populations other than the one from which the participants were recruited – this is a problem with *external validity*.

Identifying the limitations is an important step towards preempting the criticisms of the reviewers – make sure you point out the constraints of your experiment before they do!

A careful balance is needed, however, between acknowledging limitations (and the extent to which these limitations constrain the usefulness of the results) and being so negative about the experiment that it seems that you have discovered nothing useful at all! Don't overstate your conclusions; rather, highlight the importance of what you have discovered and the opportunities for building on these conclusions in further work. And always note that limitations are also opportunities because they identify avenues for future research.

6.3.5 Explaining the results

Having made conclusions based on your results, it is important to relate them, as much as possible, to the world outside your particular experiment: you need to provide some explanation as to why you believe that your results are the way they are. It may be useful to explain the results by referring to existing theoretical models (typically, psychological, perceptual, or interaction models) and discussing how your experiment has reinforced them (or not). Similarly, your results may be discussed in relation to prior experimental results in the same or a similar area. Doing this may be tricky if your results do not say what you expected or appear to conflict with prior results. In these cases, addressing obvious limitations and constraints may help with explaining the results obtained. Explaining your results allows you to show how they contribute to an exploration of ideas that is wider than your own specific research question.

6.4 The overall story

As for all papers, experimental articles need to tell a story: it should be clear to the readers as they read the paper why each step of the process was conducted in the way it was. A suggested structure for reporting experiments is as follows:

1. *Aim of the experiment.* This will include a clear statement of the research question, a description of the independent variable (and its conditions), and an explanation as to why this question was an interesting one to investigate. It will usually include reference to previous research work so as to motivate the research question.

2. *Experimental method.* This will include description and justification of two aspects of the experimental design:
   - the form of the experiment: tasks, experimental objects, questionnaires, types of data collected, etc.;
   - the nature of the experimental process: tutorials, software, randomisation, timing, allocation of conditions, etc.

   This section may include discussion of the pilot experiments, as well as any important outcomes that arose from them that influenced the design decisions.
3. *Procedure.* These are the hard facts of what occurred: what computing equipment was used, where the experiment took place, how many experimenters took part, the number of participants, how they were recruited (and, where appropriate, other relevant demographic information about them). This section should also state whether any problems arose during the experiments.
4. *Data and analysis.* The analysis methods (both quantitative and qualitative) should be described, and then the results of the analysis presented. Bar charts showing the data should be included here. The end of this section is a good point for the separation between fact and opinion.
5. *Conclusions.* This is where your conclusions are stated, based on the results of the analysis, in the context of the overall aim of the experiment and the research questions. It is here that you might extrapolate from the sample results to make general claims about the population.
6. *Discussion.* Here the wider implications of the conclusions can be discussed. What do the conclusions mean to the specific area of study and to wider HCI research? This is a good place to discuss the limitations of the experiment and how they can inform interesting future research.

6.5 Evaluations

The desired output of an evaluation which takes place as part of an iterative design cycle is rarely a formal article – it is typically a report of the outcomes of the evaluation and suggestions for improvement that can inform the design of the next iteration. This does not release evaluators from clearly describing what has been done, but it does mean that their report is unlikely to be subject to the scrutiny of independent reviewers.

The nature of the evaluation report will differ according to the size of the software product, and the number of people involved in the project and its management. For a one-person software development project, formal reports of the evaluation may not be necessary; for a larger team, they will probably be essential for reporting purposes. In the latter case, a full account of the method, data collected, and analysis may be requested to motivate the design changes recommended, especially if these changes will be expensive.

This is not to say that evaluations cannot be written up formally and submitted to an academic conference or journal, and much of the information in this chapter is relevant to doing so. Rather, the problem comes in successfully motivating the evaluation: "I built this system, and I wanted to see what happened when other people used it" is rarely sufficient motivation for publication in top-quality journals nowadays, even if the outcomes demonstrate that other people used it successfully. However, it all depends on the area of research, and the nature and status of the conference or journal. Chances are that if the conference or journal has recently accepted evaluation papers, then they might accept yours, too. However, reviewers may still insist that a comparative experiment be performed to demonstrate that your system is an improvement over a similar alternative.

6.6 Summary

This chapter provides advice on how to report the results of experiments for publication, focussing on some typical concerns of reviewers. However, reviewers are wide ranging in nature, having their own interests, agendas, and biases, experiencing both good days and bad days,[9] so it is impossible to preempt all criticisms that might come your way.

By first showing that a research question (or questions) is interesting and worth investigating, and then maintaining the focus of the paper on that research question, you will ensure that a good story is told. Justifying the important design decisions and acknowledging limitations will help alleviate reviewers' concerns about the validity and reliability of the experiment.

Like all research projects, experiments do not always go as planned. Chapter 7 addresses problems and pitfalls of experiments, suggesting preparations that can be made in advance to avoid them and actions that can be taken afterward to try to repair them.

---

[9] I can say this because I am a reviewer, too!

7

Problems and pitfalls

So far, we have assumed that everything will go smoothly; however, in practise, this is rarely the case. All will not go as planned, especially if this is your first experiment. Thus, this chapter discusses some of the things that can go wrong, and gives suggestions as to how to prevent them occurring, or how to deal with them if they do. Problems can be prepared for, and in many cases, following the advice given in this and previous chapters will put you in a good position to address them (be forewarned!). Pitfalls are those events for which you cannot prepare but that must be dealt with in order to rescue the situation.

7.1 Problems

Pilot tests show that the experimental design is fundamentally flawed. You may have put a great deal of work into preparing the experimental objects, tutorials, etc., only to discover that the task given to the participants is simply too difficult and takes too long, that the participants cannot understand what is expected of them, or that the tasks are actually inappropriate for the different conditions. The concept of pre-pilots (and even pre-pre-pilots!) is useful here. Piloting is an iterative process. Although you must pilot at least once with the full experimental method before running it, it is useful to run smaller, partial pilots on some aspects of the experiment before putting it all together. For example, get feedback on the tutorial from a colleague to find out whether it is clear, or ask someone to perform the tasks on the experimental objects on paper to determine whether they are appropriate. By the time you get to running the final pilots, many of the potential problems will have already been addressed.

Ethics approval is not granted. It can be frustrating to wait for a response from an ethics committee, only to find that the response is a negative one and that you need to resubmit your ethics application. If this is your first ethics application, then it is a good idea to look at examples of successful applications and to read the ethics guidelines for your institution. If possible, ask a member of an ethics committee to look at your application before sending it. The turnaround time for ethics committees can be long, so begin the process early. Even if the specific details of your experiment are not finalised, most committees will permit minor amendments after approval is given.

The experimenter leaves before all data have been collected. It is better to have the same experimenter for all participants so that they have the same experimental experience, thus avoiding confounding factors that might affect the results. Preparing a clear and detailed procedure document (see Section 3.6.7) will help ensure that the participants taking the experiment with the new experimenter will be treated as equally as possible.

Participants make an appointment for an experiment, but do not show up. Many frustrating hours can be lost waiting for "no shows." This problem can be mitigated to some extent by reminding the participant of the appointment via email or text message the day before the experimental session; in fact, emailing or texting the afternoon or evening before is likely to be more effective than emailing the morning before. The message should be explicit about time and provide directions to the venue. It is a good idea to ask participants for their mobile phone number when they register for the experiment. And, of course, the experimenter should have something worthwhile to do while waiting.

Participants arrive late for their experiments. Having only one participant show up late can offset the timing of a whole day's sessions, and later participants may have to opt out because they cannot wait. When giving participants time and venue information, make it clear that if they arrive, say, more than 15 minutes late, the experiment will be abandoned. They will then be more likely to arrive on time, especially if they have been promised a financial reward!

You cannot recruit enough participants. Giving a small financial reward can help, as can wide advertising. Some institutions have measures in place that make it easy for recruiting participants – one university I know has an "Experiments Seeking Volunteers" section in their weekly email newsletter to students and staff, and many psychology students require first-year students to do experiments for course credits. Other institutions have regulations that make recruiting participants difficult – for example, not being permitted to use student mailing lists for recruiting purposes. One thing to keep in mind, though, is the power of word-of-mouth and social networking: if your experiment is fun, not too demanding, and interesting, then participants will tell their friends – if it isn't, then they won't!

7.2 Pitfalls

It seems that some participants have not taken the experiment seriously. This is a difficult call to make because it may be that the participants have actually been taking the experiment seriously, but your impression is otherwise. It is useful to take observational notes during the experiment – a good way to do this is to annotate a copy of the procedure document for each participant, noting your impression of the participant's commitment. If you have concerns, then you could ask the participant whether they believed that they took the experiment seriously enough at the end of the postexperiment interview. If your impression was of lack of commitment, and this is supported by the data (e.g., all responses are provided in an impossibly short length of time), then that participant's data should be discarded.

If several participants are deemed to have not taken the experiment seriously, then you need to look carefully at the experiment. Perhaps it is too difficult, too easy, or too long. Perhaps the experimental room is too hot or too cold. Perhaps the content of the experimental objects is too boring or offensive. It does not make sense to continue an experiment if most participants are not providing useful data.

Equipment breaks midexperiment. If the equipment breaks during an experimental session, then it will need to be abandoned, and the participant sent away. It would probably not be appropriate to use that participant for "real" data collection again, although, if the participant is willing, he or she could take part in another pilot. Once the equipment is fixed (assuming it can be), you will need to consider whether later participants will have the same experience as earlier ones – this may not be the case if fixing the equipment has required, for example, a change to the interface, the use of a larger mobile device, or a different speaker system. Continuing the experiment with altered equipment may introduce confounding factors, so it may be better to start the data collection over again. If fixing the equipment has resulted in nonperceptible changes, then previous data can be retained.

There are several unexpected external confounding factors. Some serious external factors might affect the collection of data: the sun obscuring the screen at certain times of day, distracting noise from adjacent rooms, frequent interruptions, rain leaking through the ceiling, etc. If these factors only affect a few initial experimental sessions, then restarting the experiment in a more controlled environment might be wise. If these factors are only discovered after the data have been collected, then they would need to be taken into account when analysing the data and reporting the conclusions. Conducting the pilot experiments in the same environment as is intended for the real experiment will help identify these unwelcome external factors in advance.

The data collected prove to be insufficient or inappropriate for answering the research question. This should never be the case for a well-planned experiment, but it can indeed happen [and it is for this reason that it is advisable to fabricate data before starting the experiment (see Section 4.1) to ensure they are sufficient for the required analysis]. For example, some excellent product and process data may have been collected about how people draw schematic diagrams based on rigorous specifications, but unless we also collected data on how they drew such diagrams without these specifications, we may find that we have nothing with which to compare the participants' data, and thus we have no obvious means of analysis. This is a tricky situation because it is rare that you can reasonably get the additional data required from the same participants. You can either throw the data away (and put the event down to experience), or examine the data to determine whether they can be used to answer any other interesting research questions.[1] This may mean changing your approach to the area of research, looking at different previously published work, and investigating aspects of the research area that you had not focussed on before.

Unwelcome significance is found in the data. This is always disappointing. For example, let's say that you wanted to prove that your HCI idea is better than two comparators of equivalent functionality, and the data show that one of the comparators actually produces significantly *better* performance than the other conditions. All is not lost – and so much effort has gone into producing these results that you do not want to ignore or waste the data.

The key issue to think about is "why"? If your results had shown that your HCI idea is better than the others, then you would usually have plenty of reasons why this is the case: it is novel, it is yours, it is the outcome of years of research, it has a whole range of features and new ideas that no one else has ever used before, it builds on the work of other famous researchers, etc. If a comparator is found to be better, then you need to answer the question "why"? What is it about the other system that enabled it to performe better? It is here that qualitative data are important: the comments from the participants in questionnaires or interviews may reveal other factors that you had not thought about that make it clear why the comparator performed better. It may simply be that the comparator device was, for example, lighter in weight than yours, rather than that the features enabled better performance.

If your research question is interesting and important, then *any* results will be interesting to a reader and can be discussed in a way that the reader will

---

[1] The key word, of course, is *interesting*: it doesn't make much sense to analyse data unless they will answer an interesting question.

find interesting. Remember that, regardless of the result, you have discovered something that no one else knew before!

There are not enough participants to allow for statistical analysis. Despite your recruitment efforts, you may not get enough participants for valid statistical analysis. This is again a situation where the collection of qualitative information may save the day – you may be able to report trends in the quantitative data that are supported by participants' comments or by observation, even if these trends cannot be verified by statistical analysis.

No significance is found in the data. This is always very disappointing! It is a sorry fact that positive results are always easier to publish than negative ones, and if no significance is found, then you cannot make any firm conclusions. There are a few issues to think about here:

- This is a clear case for ensuring that extensive qualitative data are collected during the experiment – if the quantitative data do not reveal significant results, then looking at the qualitative data will provide interesting insights that can be discussed alongside the quantitative analysis.
- You should try to explain why there is no significance – it may be because of ceiling or floor effects (see Section 2.6), because of substantial confounding factors that affected the results, or simply because the conditions are not themselves different in any substantial way.
- Setting up a "straw man" in your experiment may ensure that you will always get significant results! For example, if you want to look at the effect of different colour (red, blue, green) screens on people's preference, then including a black-and-white condition (which you have every expectation will perform poorly) may give you a better chance of getting significant results that you can discuss. This is not always a wise approach: a reader will notice it as an obvious tactic if the straw man is not chosen carefully, and if the straw man is the only condition that produces significant data, then you haven't really answered the question you wanted to answer anyway. Use with caution.

Do remember, though, that significance is not the only thing that matters; it is better to address an interesting question (and to not get significant results) than to address a question that no one cares about. Ellis and Dix (2006) distinguish between evaluating "aspects that are questionable" (when you are likely to get problematic conclusions) and evaluating "aspects that you are pretty sure are okay" (when you are more likely to get clear significance). The former are definitely more interesting!

Reviewers don't like the paper. Many of the issues that reviewers raise are discussed in Chapter 6. When reading the reviews, it is useful to identify and list exactly what they don't like (e.g., research question, conditions, choice of tasks and experimental objects, experimental process, form of data collected, analysis method, results, conclusions). Some of these issues will be based on fundamental differing opinions; that is, some reviewers will not agree that your research question is interesting or that the choice of conditions is appropriate. Some of the objections will be a consequence of the fact that there are many different ways to skin a cat: reviewers will not like your choice of tasks, experimental process, or analysis method. These will require further justification. Some aspects you cannot do anything about – the actual results are hard facts over which you have no control. Some issues are a result of practical considerations and constraints that may not be fully understood by the reviewer: the nature of the participants, the location of the experiment, or the equipment used. And, finally, reviewers may not agree that your conclusion is a reasonable interpretation of the data; therefore, it is essential that you use careful wording to make sure that it is clear that any conclusions are your own opinion.

7.3 Evaluations

Many of the problems and pitfalls mentioned are also relevant to evaluations. The main difference is that the consequences are less serious because of the iterative nature of evaluations and the less formal reporting requirements. If your equipment breaks midexperiment, this will not invalidate evaluation data in the same way that it would for an experiment; if the responses to the results are negative, these can be discussed within the software development team. The main challenges will be recruiting and managing suitable potential users and ensuring that they provide valid data that will appropriately inform the next round of design decisions.

7.4 Summary

This chapter is not an exhaustive list of the problems and pitfalls you will experience; however, it does discuss the most obvious and most likely ones. Taking note of them before even starting to plan an experiment is a good idea – forewarned is forearmed!

8

Six principles for conducting experiments

To conclude, this chapter summarises the contents of this book by presenting a model and six key principles for designing and conducting experiments.

8.1 A model of the experimental process

The model, presented in Figure 8.1, shows the main stages of the experimental process and the important considerations that need to be addressed at each stage.

8.2 Six key principles for conducting experiments

This book presents specific advice to guide the researcher through the experimental process, and, subsequently, six key general principles emerge. These are listed as follows:

Principle 1: **Define a clear research question and answer it.** Doing so will provide a useful focus throughout the process and will ensure that a good "story" can be told at the end. Many decisions need to be made, and making them within the context of a clearly phrased research question will make them easier to decide on and justify.

Principle 2: **Plan, prepare, and pilot.** Participant time is a scarce resource: insufficient preparation will simply result in wasting the participants' time. You cannot do too much preparation!

Principle 3: **Only collect, analyse, and present data that are meaningful to the research question.** Experimenter time is also a scarce resource. Like Principle 1, this principle ensures that your efforts are focussed, that

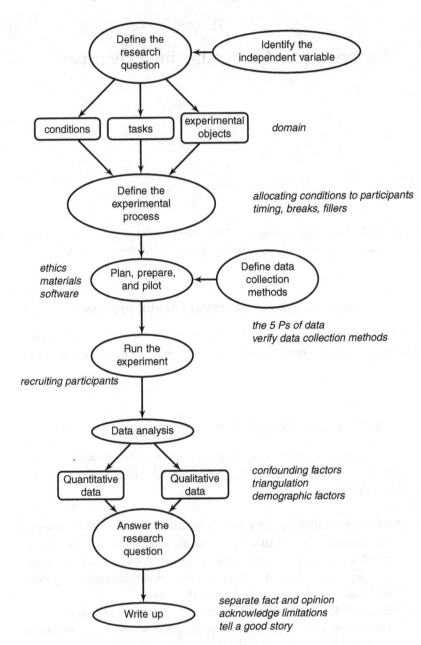

Figure 8.1: Model of the HCI experimental process.

you are not sidetracked into addressing interesting (but irrelevant) issues, and that your own time is not wasted.

Principle 4: Apply the planned analysis method on fabricated data before running the experiment. Collecting data that are not sufficient for answering your research question wastes your time and the participants' time. Identify the form of data required for answering the research question *before you start the experiment.*

Principle 5: Collect and use both quantitative and qualitative data. The temptation is to focus on the numbers, whereas "softer" data are often much more revealing. Qualitative data are also useful when the numbers do not tell you what you wanted to hear.

Principle 6: Acknowledge the limitations of the experiment. Doing so is not only honest, but ensures that you do not overstate the conclusions. It also helps preempt the criticisms of reviewers.

8.3 Concluding remarks

Although this book presents only one, there are many ways to test the value of an HCI idea. McGrath (1995) presents a useful model of the range of strategies that can be employed (including respondent, field, and theoretical strategies). Several other methods are also discussed in Dix et al. (2004): cognitive walkthrough, heuristic evaluation, review-based evaluation, field studies, think aloud, observational studies, cooperative evaluations, etc. Each method has its own advantages and disadvantages, and each its own secrets of success, secrets that are typically only discovered through experience.

This book attempts to pass on secrets of success for conducting formal experiments, based on my own experience, so that other researchers will not make the same mistakes as I have. Conducting experiments is difficult and time consuming, and it is my hope that this book will make doing so less painful and more rewarding.

Much of the specific and detailed advice given may seem to the first-time experimenter to be a set of hard-and-fast, inflexible, constraining and unnecessary rules: experience will help in identifying when these rules can reasonably be bent or broken while still conducting a reliable and valid experiment. HCI experimentation of the form described here has been criticised for being too narrow, with an inappropriate focus on small, discrete research questions rather than on a broader picture. Because small questions can be addressed in a controlled manner and larger ones cannot, broader questions cannot be easily answered using this method. I take the view that every experimental result is a useful small step: I have been chipping away at the marble block that is the useful design of graph layout algorithms for many years now, taking off small chips one at a time and getting closer to general conclusions with every use of the chisel.

Although Roosevelt (1932) was primarily offering advice at a time of economic uncertainty in his Commencement Address at Oglethorpe University, he could just as easily have been encouraging a generation of HCI researchers: "The country needs . . . bold, persistent experimentation. It is common sense to take a method and try it; if it fails, admit it frankly and try another. But above all, try something."

So . . . give it a try – and good luck!

Appendix A1
Independent measures examples

This appendix includes independent measures counterparts to the repeated measures tables and examples given in Chapter 5.

A1.1 Parametric analysis

A1.1.1 Two conditions (*t*-test)

Table A1.1: *Form of data for* t-*test (independent measures) with example data*

| | Mean error for each condition | |
	condition 1	condition 2
p1	0.45	
p2		0.32
p3	0.55	
p4		0.54
. . .		
pn		0.33
Mean (over all participants)		

It is not necessarily the case that half the participants use condition 1 and the other half condition 2. The number of participants per condition may be different, but would usually only vary by 1

The Small Multiples/Animation experiment (Example 12, p 41), had two conditions, and data for this experiment are presented in Table A1.2 and Figure A1.1.[1] Sixteen participants did the tasks under the Animation condition, and a different seventeen participants used the Small Multiples condition.

Table A1.2: *Data for the Small Multiples/Animation experiment*

Participant number	Average time: Small Multiples	Participant number	Average time: Animation
p1	27.20	p2	32.05
p3	23.35	p4	30.70
p5	30.20	p6	32.25
p7	29.50	p8	30.30
p9	23.90	p10	32.50
p11	32.00	p12	27.05
p13	28.00	p14	36.40
p15	32.90	p16	34.10
p17	28.50	p18	34.15
p19	29.15	p20	29.40
p21	34.90	p22	32.15
p23	28.35	p24	34.25
p25	24.20	p26	30.55
p27	26.10	p28	32.45
p29	27.30	p30	29.40
p31	25.85	p32	33.85
p33	24.35		

Each data point is the mean response time for all trials relating to the specified condition.

An **independent samples *t*-test** in SPSS gives the following information:

$t(31) = 3.996$, two-tailed significance $p = .000$, degrees of freedom $= 31$

[1] The data presented for this example have been slightly adapted and reduced for the purposes of effective illustration of an independent measures *t*-test. The real experiment was a within-participants experiment, but these data have been adapted to illustrate data analysis for a between-participants experiment. In addition, several data points in the Small Multiples data have been altered to ensure that the data used here are normally distributed.

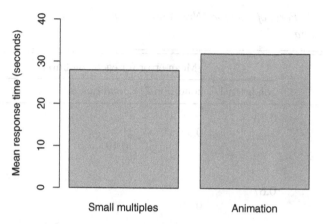

Figure A1.1: Bar chart showing the overall response time means for each condition. The mean for the Small Multiples condition is 27.99, and for the Animation condition it is 31.97.

We can therefore say that there is a significant difference between the performance from the Small Multiples condition and the Animation condition (with a significance level of $p < .001$).

Observation of the bar chart showing the means for each condition (Figure A1.1) confirms that the Animation condition took longer time than Small Multiples. This can be reported as a result in the following manner:

There were significant differences in performance as represented by the response time data according to condition under a two-tailed independent measures t-test, with the Animation condition taking significantly longer than the Small Multiples condition: $t(31) = 3.998, p < .001$.

Table A1.3: *Form of data for ANOVA test (independent measures), with example data*

	condition 1	condition 2	condition 3	...	condition k
		Mean error for each condition			
p1	0.52				
p2		0.57			
p3			0.49		
...					
pk					0.39
pk + 1	0.67				
pk + 2		0.66			
...					
pn		0.59			
Mean (over all participants)	0.53	0.60	0.52		0.44

The participants have been divided into groups, with each group using just one of the k conditions. Note that the number of participants (*n*) does not necessarily need to be divisible by the number of conditions (*k*).

A1.1.2 More than two conditions (analysis of variance)

The Orthogonal Corners experiment (Example 1, p 11) was a repeated measures experiment with **three conditions**. For the purposes of illustration of independent measures analysis, we consider fabricated data as if they had been collected in a between-participants experiment (with unequal sample sizes), as presented in Table A1.4 and Figure A1.2.

An **independent measures (One-Way) analysis of variance (ANOVA)** in SPSS gives the following information:

$F = 3.871$, $p = .036$. The degrees of freedom values are 2 and 22.

Because .036 < .05, the results are significant. This means that the type of corner used for bends in orthogonal graph drawings significantly affected the number of errors, and the probability of the differences in performance being due to chance is less than .05.

This can be reported as a result in the following manner:

There were significant differences in performance as represented by the error data according to condition under an independent measures ANOVA test: $F(2,22) = 3.871, p = .036$.

Table A1.4: *Fabricated data for the Orthogonal Corners*
experiment

Participant	90-degree bends	Smoothed	Quadratic
p1	0.45		
p2	0.18		
p3	0.23		
p4	0.77		
p5	0.30		
p6	0.07		
p7	0.17		
p8	0.79		
p9		0.31	
p10		0.31	
p11		0.59	
p12		0.19	
p13		0.16	
p14		0.14	
p15		0.46	
p16		0.29	
p17			0.73
p18			0.46
p19			0.48
p20			0.68
p21			0.67
p22			0.54
p23			0.31
p24			0.59
p25			0.56

Each data point is the mean number of errors made over the nine trials
for each condition: there were three tasks and three experimental
objects per condition.

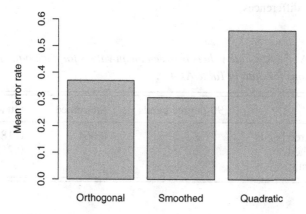

Figure A1.2: Bar chart showing the overall means for each condition.

A1.1.3 Post-hoc pairwise comparisons (Tukey)

We revisit the independent measures ANOVA calculation for Orthogonal Corners experiment. Having determined that the type of corner (90-degree, Smooth, Quadratic) had a significant effect on the errors, we now try to find out which **pairs of conditions** produced significantly different performances.

The **absolute differences** between the mean values for each pair of conditions can be calculated and represented in a diagonal matrix (Table A1.5).

The manual **Tukey** calculation (using the formula in Appendix A2, Table A2.6) returns an HSD of 0.242, having used a q-value from the Studentised range statistic table ($k = 3$, $dfError = 22$, $p = .05$) of 3.58. Looking at the matrix of pairwise differences, we can conclude that there is a significant difference between the mean error rate for the Quadratic and Smoothed corner conditions because $0.252 > 0.242$. However, we cannot conclude anything about the performance associated with the 90-degree bends condition.

An **independent measures (One-Way) ANOVA** in SPSS gives the following information: $F(2,22) = 3.871, p = .036$ (as before). SPSS gives the p-values for the post-hoc Tukey pairwise multiple comparisons in a diagonal matrix (Table A1.6). Because Tukey is a **one-step pairwise analysis** method, we can use $p = .05$, and so conclude that there is a significant difference between the mean error rate for the Quadratic and Smoothed conditions because $.037 > .05$, but that there are no other pairwise differences.

Table A1.5: *Absolute values between mean values for each pair of conditions for data in Table A1.4*

	90-degree bends	Smoothed	Quadratic
90-degree bends		0.064	0.188
Smoothed			0.252
Quadratic			

Table A1.6: *p-values for each pair of conditions for data using Tukey post-hoc analysis in SPSS (One-Way ANOVA)*

	90-degree bends	Smoothed	Quadratic
90-degree bends		.140	.792
Smoothed			.037
Quadratic			

Observation of the bar chart (Figure A1.2) shows that the average errors were greater for the Quadratic condition than for the Smoothed. This can be reported as follows:

There were significant differences in performance as represented by the error data according to condition under an independent measures ANOVA test: $F(2,22) = 3.871, p = .036$. A post-hoc Tukey test revealed where the differences lie: the Smoothed method produced better performance than the Quadratic method ($p = .037$). There were no other significant pairwise differences.

A1.2 Nonparametric analysis (for nonnormally distributed data)

Table A1.7 demonstrates the ranking process for independent measures data, using four conditions (c1–c4). On the left is the original (fabricated) response time data; on the right, the same data transformed into ranks. Note how tied values for p4 and p6 are treated (shaded): the total of the ranks must be 21.

Table A1.7: *Example of transformation of data into ranks for independent measures data: data on the left, ranks on the right*

	c1	c2	c3	c4		c1	c2	c3	c4
p1	14.7				p1	1			
p2		25.3			p2		3		
p3			18.3		p3			2	
p4				27.4	p4				4.5
p5	30.1				p5	6			
p6		27.4			p6		4.5		

A1.2.1 Two conditions (Mann-Whitney)

Table A1.8: *Form of ranking data required for Mann-Whitney test: data on the left, ranks on the right*

	Condition 1	Condition 2		Ranked (Condition 1)	Ranked (Condition 2)
p1		153	p1		8
p2	182		p2	9	
p3		106	p3		6
p4	112		p4	7	
p5		43	p5		2
p6	97		p6	5	
p7		81	p7		3.5
p8	204		p8	10	
p9		81	p9		3.5
p10	22		p10	1	

Note that all data (over both conditions) are ranked together.

For the Mann-Whitney example, we consider an adaptation of the Smalltalk experiment (Example 16, p 53) using only **two conditions** (a high number of edge bends, and a low number of edge bends) and fabricated response time data for a **between-participants** experiment, as shown in Table A1.9.

The **Mann-Whitney** statistic calculated from these data is 59.5 (using the formula in Appendix A2, Table A2.8). The value read from the two-tailed Mann-Whitney table for $p = .05$ and the numbers of participants (12 and 13) is 41. As 59.5 is not less than 42, there is no significant difference between the performance (as measured by response time) resulting from the extent of bends in the Smalltalk diagram.

Using these data with the SPSS nonparametric independent samples analysis, the value of the larger Mann-Whitney U statistic is presented (96.5), as well as a *p-value* (0.314), which indicates no significance.

This can be reported as follows:

There were no significant differences in performance as represented by the response time data according to the number of bends under a two-tailed independent measures nonparametric Mann-Whitney test: $U(12,13) = 96.5$, $p = .314$.

Table A1.9: *Fabricated response time data for Smalltalk between-participant experiment: data on the left, ranks on the right*

Participant	Few Bends	Many Bends	Participant	Few Bends	Many Bends
p1	41.54		p1	8	
p2	53.88		p2	17	
p3	58.86		p3	19	
p4	48.53		p4	14	
p5	26.38		p5	1	
p6	67.07		p6	25	
p7	41.56		p7	9.5	
p8	32.41		p8	4	
p9	29.81		p9	3	
p10	29.44		p10	2	
p11	43.11		p11	11	
p12	67.00		p12	24	
p13		52.63	p13		16
p14		65.41	p14		22
p15		43.88	p15		12
p16		50.59	p16		15
p17		35.63	p17		6
p18		63.55	p18		20
p19		66.36	p19		23
p20		41.56	p20		9.5
p21		63.86	p21		21
p22		55.70	p22		18
p23		41.41	p23		7
p24		33.00	p24		5
p25		47.19	p25		13

Table A1.10: *Form of ranking data required for Kruskal-Wallis test: data on the left, ranks on the right*

	Condition 1	Condition 2	Condition 3		Condition 1 rank	Condition 2 rank	Condition 3 rank
p1	11.06			p1	5.5		
p2	4.94			p2	2		
p3		2.49		p3		1	
p4		14.99		p4		7	
p5			11.06	p5			5.5
p6			9.70	p6			3
p7			10.67	p7			4
				Rank Totals	7.50	8.00	12.50
				Rank Means	3.75	4.00	4.17

A1.2.2 More than two conditions (Kruskal-Wallis)

The Metabolic Pathways experiment (Example 3, p 13) was a repeated measures experiment with **three conditions**. For the purposes of illustration of independent measures analysis, we consider fabricated response time data as if they had been collected for a between-participants experiment (Table A1.11).

Using the **Kruskal-Wallis** formula of Appendix A2, Table A2.10, the Kruskal-Wallis statistic (H) can be calculated as 8.295. The critical χ^2-value from the statistical table for the χ^2 distribution ($df = 2$, $p = .05$) is 5.99. Because the *H-value* (8.295) is greater than the critical χ^2-value (5.99), there are significant differences between the performances relating

Table A1.11: *Fabricated between-participants response time data for the Metabolic Pathways experiment: data on the left, ranks on the right*

	MetaViz	GEM	Hierarchical		MetaViz	GEM	Hierarchical
p1	47.56			p1	2		
p2	82.59			p2	17		
p3	68.78			p3	10		
p4	57.56			p4	5		
p5	94.00			p5	22		
p6	50.89			p6	3		
p7	63.44			p7	7		
p8	65.44			p8	9		
p9		74.00		p9		11	
p10		64.33		p10		8	
p11		78.22		p11		12	
p12		41.44		p12		1	
p13		91.67		p13		21	
p14		81.56		p14		15	
p15		56.67		p15		4	
p16		61.78		p16		6	
p17			83.89	p17			20
p18			82.56	p18			16
p19			121.67	p19			24
p20			83.62	p20			18
p21			81.44	p21			14
p22			96.11	p22			23
p23			78.28	p23			13
p24			83.67	p24			19
				Rank Totals	75.0	78.0	147.0
				Rank Means	9.38	9.75	18.38

to the method used for presenting the metabolic pathways. The degrees of freedom = 2, which is one less than the number of conditions.

Using the Kruskal-Wallis option in SPSS (independent samples, nonparametric analysis), the Kruskal-Wallis statistic is produced (8.295) with a *p-value* of .016.

This result can be reported as follows:

> There were significant differences in performance as represented by the response time data according to condition under a Kruskal-Wallis test: $H(2) = 8.295 > \chi^2 (2, p = .05) = 5.99$.

Or, as follows:

> There were significant differences in performance as represented by the response time data according to condition under a Kruskal-Wallis test: $H(2) = 8.295, p = .016$.

A1.2.3 Post-hoc pairwise comparisons (Nemenyi and Dunn)

Table A1.12: *Ranks for independent measures data, using fabricated data for purposes of illustration: data on the left, ranks on the right*

	Condition 1	Condition 2	Condition 3		Condition 1 rank	Condition 2 rank	Condition 3 rank
p1	28			p1	3		
p2	84			p2	8.5		
p3	70			p3	7		
p4		22		p4		1	
p5		90		p5		10	
p6		27		p6		2	
p7		84		p7		8.5	
p8			55	p8			5
p9			45	p9			4
p10			61	p10			6
				Rank Totals	18.5	21.5	15
				Rank Means	6.17	5.38	5.00

Table A1.13: *Pairwise mean rank differences for data in Table A1.12*

	Condition 1	Condition 2	Condition 3
Condition 1		0.79	1.17
Condition 2			0.38
Condition 3			

There are two statistics applicable for independent measures post-hoc pairwise comparisons: the independent measures version of the Nemenyi test (only appropriate when the sample sizes are equal), and the Dunn test (appropriate when the sample sizes are not equal).

Continuing with the Metabolic Pathways experiment, we first determine the **absolute difference between the mean ranks** for each pair of conditions (Table A1.14)

The manual independent measures **Nemenyi calculation** (using the formula in Appendix A2, Table A2.12) returns a *critical difference* of 8.28, having used a q-value from the Studentised range statistic ($k = 3$, *dfError* = infinity, $p = .05$) of 3.31.

Those pairwise differences whose absolute mean rank difference is greater than 8.28 have had a significant effect on the response time data. In this case, the following **pairwise significances** are found: Hierarchical/MetaViz; Hierarchical/GEM.

In SPSS, the All Pairwise option for a Kruskal-Wallis independent samples test produces the pairwise differences in mean ranks (as in Table A1.14), as well as a matrix of adjusted p-values. Those p-values < .05 indicate the significant pairwise differences, giving the same results as the manual Nemenyi analysis (Table A1.15).

Table A1.14: *Absolute values between mean rank values for each pair of conditions for data in Table A1.11*

	MetaViz	GEM	Hierarchical
MetaViz		0.37	9.00
GEM			8.63
Hierarchical			

Table A1.15: *Matrix of adjusted p-values produced by SPSS*

	MetaViz	GEM	Hierarchical
MetaViz		1.00	.033
GEM			.044
Hierarchical			

This result can be reported as follows:

There were significant differences in performance as represented by the response time data according to condition under an independent measures nonparametric Kruskal-Wallis test: $H(2) = 8.295, p = .016$. An adjusted post-hoc pairwise comparison test ($p = .05$) revealed where the differences lie: the Hierarchical method produced worse performance than both the GEM ($p = .044$) and MetaViz methods ($p = .033$).

A1.3 Summary

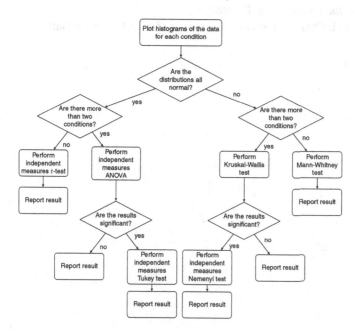

Figure A1.3: Steps 1 and 2 of independent measures analysis, which should be performed for each dependent variable.

Appendix A2
Statistical formulae

This appendix presents the formulae for all the statistical tests described and used in Chapter 5 (repeated measures) and Appendix A1 (independent measures). These formulae have been taken from, and cross-checked between, the following books:

- Hinton, P. (2004). *Statistics Explained: A Guide for Social Science Students* (2nd ed.). Routledge.
- Cook, P.A., Wheater, C.P., and Wright, J. (2000). *Using Statistics to Understand the Environment*. Routledge.
- Zar, J.H. (2009). *Biostatistical Analysis* (5th ed.). Prentice Hall.

A2.1 Parametric tests

A2.1.1 Two Conditions (*t*-Test)

Table A2.1: *Formula for repeated measures t-test, with two conditions, X and Y*

n	Number of participants, each of whom did trials for both condition X and condition Y	
df	Degrees of freedom	$n - 1$
XBar	Mean of all data points for condition X	$\sum_{j=1}^{n} \frac{X_j}{n}$
YBar	Mean of all data points for condition Y	$\sum_{j=1}^{n} \frac{Y_j}{n}$
D_p	Difference between X data value and Y data value for participant *p*	$X_p - Y_p$
SumSqD	Sum of square of all differences between X data value and Y data value for all participants	$\sum_{j=1}^{n} D_j^2$
SqSumD	Square of sum of all differences between X data value and Y data value for all participants	$\left(\sum_{j=1}^{n} D_j \right)^2$
Numerator	Numerator for *t*-value formula	$\lvert XBar - YBar \rvert$
Denominator	Denominator for *t*-value formula	$\sqrt{\dfrac{SumSqD - \frac{SqSumD}{n}}{n(n-1)}}$
t-value	*Numerator/Denominator*	
Critical *t*-value	This value is read off the statistical table for the *t*-distribution, using *p*-value (usually .05) and *df*. There will be different values for one- or two-tailed *t*-tests.	If *t*-value > critical *t*-value, then result is statistically significant.

The data value for participant *p* for condition X is denoted X_p, and the data value for condition Y is denoted Y_p.

Table A2.2: *Formula for independent measures* t-*test, with two conditions,*
X and Y

n_x	Number of participants who did trials for condition X	
n_y	Number of participants who did trials for condition Y	
df	Degrees of freedom	$(n_x - 1) + (n_y - 1)$
XBar	Mean of all data points for condition X	$\sum\limits_{j=1}^{n_x} \frac{X_j}{n_x}$
YBar	Mean of all data points for condition Y	$\sum\limits_{j=1}^{n_y} \frac{Y_j}{n_y}$
SumSqX	Sum of square of all data points for condition X	$\sum\limits_{j=1}^{n_x} X_j^2$
SumSqY	Sum of square of all data points for condition Y	$\sum\limits_{j=1}^{n_y} Y_j^2$
SqSumX	Square of sum of all data points for condition X	$\left(\sum\limits_{j=1}^{n_x} X_j\right)^2$
SqSumY	Square of sum of all data points for condition Y	$\left(\sum\limits_{j=1}^{n_y} Y_j\right)^2$
Numerator	Numerator for *t*-value formula	$|XBar - YBar|$
Denominator1	First factor of denominator for *t*-value formula	$\sqrt{\dfrac{\left(SumSqX - \frac{SqSumX}{n_x}\right) + \left(SumSqY - \frac{SqSumY}{n_y}\right)}{df}}$
Denominator2	Second factor of denominator for *t*-value formula	$\sqrt{\dfrac{1}{n_x} + \dfrac{1}{n_y}}$
t-value		$\dfrac{Numerator}{Denominator1 \times Denominator2}$
Critical *t*-value	This value is read off the statistical table for the *t*-distribution, using *p*-value (usually .05) and *df*. There will be different values for one- or two-tailed *t*-tests.	If *t*-value > critical *t*-value, then result is statistically significant.

The data value for participant number *p* for condition X is denoted X_p, and the
data value for participant number *q* for condition Y is denoted Y_q.

A2.1.2 More Than Two Conditions (Analysis of Variance)

Table A2.3: *Formula for repeated measures ANOVA, with k conditions*

k	Number of conditions	
n	Number of participants, each of whom did trials from all conditions	
N	Total number of scores	$k \times n$
$dfBetCond$	"Between conditions" degrees of freedom	$k - 1$
$dfError$	"Error" degrees of freedom	$(n - 1)(k - 1)$
$SumData$	Sum of all data points	$\sum_{i=1}^{k} \sum_{j=1}^{n} X_{ij}$
$SqSumData$	Square of sum of data points	$(SumData)^2$
$SumSqData$	Sum of square of all data points	$\sum_{i=1}^{k} \sum_{j=1}^{n} X_{ij}^2$
TC_c	Sum of all data points for condition c, over all participants	$\sum_{j=1}^{n} X_{cj}$
$SumSqConds$	Sum of square for all conditions	$\sum_{j=1}^{k} TC_i^2$
TP_p	Sum of all data points for participant p, over all conditions	$\sum_{j=1}^{k} X_{ip}$
$SumSqPart$	Sum of square for all participants	$\sum_{j=1}^{n} TP_i^2$
$SumSqTotal$	Total sum of squares	$SumSqData - SqSumData/N$
$SumSqBetCond$	Sum of squares between conditions	$SumSqConds/n - SqSumData/N$
$SumSqWithCond$	Sum of squares within conditions	$SumSqTotal - SumSqBetCond$
$SumSqBetPart$	Sum of squares between participants	$SumSqPart/k - SqSumData/N$
$SumSqError$	Sum of square of the error	$SumSqWithCond - SumSqBetPart$
$MSBetCond$	Mean square, between conditions	$SumSqBetCond/dfBetCond$
$MSError$	Mean square, error	$SumSqError/dfError$
F-value	Variance ratio	$MSBetCond/MSError$
Critical F-value	This value is read off the statistical table for the F-distribution, using the p-value (usually .05) and $dfBetCond$ and $dfError$.	If F-value > critical F-value, then result is statistically significant.

The data value for participant p for condition 1 is denoted X_{1p}, and the data value for condition X_i as X_{ip}.

Table A2.4: *Formula for independent measures ANOVA, with k conditions*

k	Number of conditions	
n_c	Number of participants who did trials for condition c	
N	Total number of scores	$\sum_{i=1}^{k} n_k$
T_c	Sum of all data points for condition c, over all participants who did trials for condition c	$\sum_{j=1}^{n_c} X_{cj}$
dfTotal	Total degrees of freedom	$N-1$
dfBetCond	"Between conditions" degrees of freedom	$k-1$
dfError	"Error" degrees of freedom	*dfTotal – dfBetCond*
SumData	Sum of all data points	$\sum_{i=1}^{k} \sum_{j=1}^{n_i} X_{ij}$
SqSumData	Square of sum of data points	$(SumData)^2$
SumSqData	Sum of square of all data points	$\sum_{i=1}^{k} \sum_{j=1}^{n_i} X_{ij}^2$
SumSqConds	Sum of square for all conditions	$\sum_{i=1}^{k} \frac{T_i^2}{n_i}$
SumSqTotal	Total sum of squares	*SumSqData – SqSumData/N*
SumSqBetCond	Sum of squares between conditions	*SumSqConds – SqSumData/N*
SumSqError	Sum of square of error	*SumSqTotal – SumSqBetCond*
MSBetCond	Mean square, between conditions	*SumSqBetCond/dfBetCond*
MSError	Mean square, error	*SumSqError/dfError*
F-value	Variance ratio	*MSBetCond/MSError*
Critical *F*-value	This value is read off the statistical table for the *F*-distribution, using *p*-value (usually .05) and *dfBetCond* and *dfError*.	If *F*-value > critical *F*-value, then result is statistically significant.

The data value for participant p for condition 1 is denoted X_{1p} and the data value for participant q for condition X_i is denoted X_{iq}.

A2.1.3 Post-Hoc Pairwise Comparisons (Tukey)

Table A2.5: *Formula for calculating critical difference using Tukey's honestly significant different statistic (repeated measures)*

k	Number of conditions	
n	Number of participants, each of whom did trials from all conditions	
$dfError$	"Error" degrees of freedom	$(n-1)(k-1)$
$MSError$	Mean square, error	$SumSqError/dfError$ (as in previous repeated measures ANOVA calculation; Table A2.3)
q-value	This value is read off statistical table for Studentized range statistic, using p-value (usually .05), number of conditions k, and $dferror$.	
Critical difference	Honestly significant difference: pairwise differences with absolute values > *critical difference* are statistically significant.	$q\text{-value} \times \sqrt{\frac{MSError}{n}}$

Table A2.6: *Formula for calculating critical difference using Tukey's honestly significant different statistic (independent measures)*

k	Number of conditions	
n_k	Number of participants who did trials for condition k	
n	Approximation of simple "average"	$\frac{k}{\sum_{i=1}^{k} n_k}$
N	Total number of scores	$\sum_{i=1}^{k} n_k$
$dfError$	Error degrees of freedom	$(N-1)-(k-1)$
$MSError$	Mean square, error	$SumSqError/dfError$ (as in previous independent measures ANOVA calculation; Table A2.4)
q-value	This value is read off statistical table for Studentized range statistic, using the p-value (usually .05), number of conditions k, and $dfError$.	
Critical difference	Honestly significant difference: pairwise differences with absolute values > *critical difference* are statistically significant.	$q\text{-value} \times \sqrt{\frac{MSError}{n}}$

A2.2 Nonparametric tests

A2.2.1 Two Conditions (Wilcoxon and Mann-Whitney)

Table A2.7: *Formula for Wilcoxon repeated measures test*

n	Number of participants, each of whom did trials for both conditions
nNT	Number of participants without ties (i.e., those for whom data values for both conditions are different)
PositiveRankSum: R^+	Sum of all ranks for which difference between two data values is positive
NegativeRankSum: R^-	Sum of all ranks for which difference between two data values is negative
	Note that $R^+ + R^- = \frac{nNT(nNT+1)}{2}$
T-value	Smaller value between R^+ and R^-
Critical T-value	This value is read off the statistical table for Wilcoxon T-distribution, using p-value (usually .05) and nNT. There will be different values for one- or two-tailed Wilcoxon tests. The T-value must be less than or equal to the critical T-value for significance.

Table A2.8: *Formula for Mann-Whitney independent measures test*

n_x	Number of participants who did trials for condition X
n_y	Number of participants who did trials for condition Y
$nProduct$	$n_x \times n_y$
$XRankSum$	Sum of all ranks for condition X
$YRankSum$	Sum of all ranks for condition Y
$XTerm$	$\frac{n_x(n_x+1)}{2}$
$YTerm$	$\frac{n_y(n_y+1)}{2}$
XU-value	$nProduct + XTerm - XRankSum$
YU-value	$nProduct + YTerm - YRankSum$
U-value	Smaller of XU-value and YU-value
Critical U-value	This value is read off the statistical table for the Mann-Whitney T-distribution, using p-value (usually .05) and n_x and n_y. There will be different values for one- or two-tailed Mann-Whitney tests. The U-value must be less or equal to the critical U-value for significance.

A2.2.2 More Than Two Conditions (Friedman and Kruskal-Wallis)

Table A2.9: *Formula for Friedman repeated measures test, with k ranked conditions*

n	Number of participants, each of whom did trials for all conditions	
k	Number of conditions	
df	Degrees of freedom	$k - 1$
T_c	Total rank for condition c, over all participants	$\sum_{j=1}^{n} R_{cj}$
SumSqRanks	Sum of squared rank totals, over all conditions	$\sum_{i=1}^{k} T_i^2$
χ^2-value		$\frac{12 \times Sum\,Sq\,Ranks}{nk(nk+1)} - 3n\,(k+1)$
Critical χ^2-value	This value is read off the statistical table for the χ^2 distribution, using p-value (usually .05) and df.	If χ^2-value > critical χ^2-value then conditions have had effect on performance.

The rank of participant p's data for condition 1 is denoted R_{1p} and for condition R_i as R_{ip}.

Table A2.10: *Formula for Kruskal-Wallis independent measures test, with k ranked conditions*

k	Number of conditions	
n_k	Number of participants who did trials for condition k	
N	Total number of ranks	$\sum_{i=1}^{k} n_k$
df	Degrees of freedom	$k-1$
T_c	Total rank for condition c, over all participants	$\sum_{j=1}^{n} R_{cj}$
WT_c	Squared total rank for condition c, inverse weighted by number of participants who did trials for condition c	$\frac{T_c^2}{n_c}$
$WeightedSumSqRanks$	Sum of weighted squared rank totals, over all conditions	$\sum_{i=1}^{k} WT_i$
H-value		$\frac{12 \times WeightedSumSqRanks}{N(N+1)} - 3(N+1)$
Critical χ^2-value	This value is read off the statistical table for the χ^2 distribution, using the p-value (usually .05) and df.	There are no tables specifically for the H statistic; χ^2 table is used. If H-value $>$ critical χ^2-value, then conditions have had effect on performance.

The rank of participant p's data for condition 1 is denoted R_{1p}, and the rank for participant q's data for condition R_i is denoted R_{iq}.

A2.2.3 Post-Hoc Pairwise Comparisons (Nemenyi and Dunn)

Table A2.11: *Formula for Nemenyi multiple comparisons test (repeated measures), with k ranked conditions*

k	Number of conditions	
n	Number of participants, each of whom did trials from all conditions	
df	Infinity	
SE	Standard error	$\sqrt{\frac{k(k+1)}{12n}}$
q	This value is read off the statistical table for the Studentized range statistic, using the p-value (usually .05), number of conditions k, and $df = infinity$.	
Critical difference	Honestly significant difference: mean rank pairwise differences with absolute values > *critical difference* are statistically significant	$q \times SE$

Table A2.12: *Formula for Nemenyi multiple comparisons test (independent measures), with k ranked conditions and equal sample sizes*

k	Number of conditions	
n	Number of participants for each condition	Sample sizes are equal
df	Infinity	
SE	Standard error	$\sqrt{\frac{k(nk+1)}{12}}$
q	This value is read off the statistical table for the Studentized range statistic, using the p-value (usually .05), number of conditions k, and $df = infinity$.	
Critical difference	Honestly significant difference: mean rank pairwise differences with absolute values > *critical difference* are statistically significant	$q \times SE$

Table A2.13: *Formula for Dunn multiple comparisons test (independent measures), with k ranked conditions and unequal sample sizes*

k	Number of conditions	
n_c	Number of participants who did trials for condition c	Sample sizes are not equal
N	Total number of data points	$\sum_{i=1}^{k} n_i$
df	Infinity	
$SE_{c,d}$	Standard error for conditions c and d	$\sqrt{\frac{N(N+1)}{12}\left(\frac{1}{n_c} + \frac{1}{n_d}\right)}$
q	This value is read off the statistical table for the Studentized range statistic, using p-value (usually .05), number of conditions k, and $df = infinity$	
Critical difference(c,d)	Honestly significant difference for conditions c and d: if absolute value of mean rank pairwise difference between means of conditions c and d > *critical difference(c,d)*, then that difference is statistically significant.	$q \times SE_{c,d}$

Appendix A3
Factor analysis example

To illustrate the two approaches to factor analysis, consider a within-participant experiment that aims to answer the research question, "Which visual form of an image best supports visual search?" The independent variable is the visual form of an image with three conditions: Black and White (BW), Colour (C), and Grey-scale (GS).

Each screen presents forty items, and there is only one task – identify the largest image. To ensure generalisability of the results, there are three experimental objects, each using a different type of image: images of the environment (photographs, P), paintings (photographs of paintings, PP), and graphics (images created using a digital imaging tool, G). Error and response time data are collected, but only error data are analysed here. Data for this experiment (fabricated for the purposes of illustration) are shown in Table A3.1.

The *primary independent variable* is visual form (BW, C, GS) because this is directly related to the research question. A *secondary independent variable* is image type (with three secondary conditions, P, PP, G).

A3.1 Multiway factor analysis

A two-way factor analysis of the error data (calculated by SPSS using Repeated Measures ANOVA) for visual form and image type is shown Table A3.2.

There is an interaction between visual form and image type ($p < .001$). So, although we may want to answer our primary research question by reporting that overall the visual form had a significant effect on performance (with $p = .003$) and then determining the pairwise differences, we cannot do so because we must look further at the interaction with the other factor, the image type. The line chart (Figure A3.1) shows the interactions.

Table A3.1: *Data used for demonstrating two approaches to factor analysis*

	Black and white			Colour			Grey scale		
	P	PP	G	P	PP	G	P	PP	G
p1	0.69	0.59	0.07	0.36	1.00	0.55	0.64	0.38	0.40
p2	0.40	0.20	0.43	0.27	0.51	0.79	0.53	0.34	0.42
p3	0.76	0.50	0.39	0.34	0.80	0.60	0.67	0.33	0.35
p4	0.76	0.03	0.76	0.27	0.48	0.58	0.59	0.33	0.57
p5	0.72	0.74	0.00	0.33	0.63	0.92	0.63	0.56	0.07
p6	0.69	0.08	0.75	0.36	0.95	0.91	0.37	0.52	0.75
p7	0.72	0.67	0.05	0.42	0.64	0.96	0.77	0.40	0.25
p8	0.70	0.04	0.67	0.51	0.83	0.95	0.53	0.36	0.39
p9	0.43	0.75	0.21	0.55	0.70	0.96	0.15	0.60	0.60
p10	0.23	0.02	0.51	0.42	0.63	0.96	0.47	0.58	0.35
p11	0.39	0.76	0.54	0.43	0.80	0.90	0.20	0.51	1.00
p12	0.53	0.55	0.55	0.40	0.61	0.92	0.46	0.51	0.37
p13	0.08	0.87	0.74	0.56	1.00	0.87	0.74	0.54	0.67
p14	0.10	0.55	0.90	0.25	0.66	0.94	0.65	0.52	0.06
p15	0.09	0.52	0.33	0.26	0.82	0.57	0.48	0.52	0.73
p16	0.69	0.01	0.53	0.38	0.81	0.71	0.59	0.52	0.10
p17	0.59	0.58	0.22	0.40	0.67	0.76	0.63	0.52	0.34
p18	0.39	0.19	0.55	0.35	0.43	0.60	0.65	0.56	0.09
p19	0.18	0.57	0.22	0.54	1.00	0.55	0.03	0.57	0.72
p20	0.22	0.18	0.53	0.50	0.97	0.60	0.63	0.40	0.22
p21	0.02	0.51	0.22	0.33	0.67	0.57	0.45	0.42	0.21
p22	0.07	0.21	0.50	0.35	0.61	0.75	0.34	0.39	0.03
p23	0.06	0.58	0.25	0.54	0.65	0.75	0.65	0.38	0.73
p24	0.23	0.42	0.60	0.19	0.63	0.75	0.53	0.33	0.24
p25	0.19	0.60	0.50	0.36	0.49	0.61	0.34	0.41	0.06
p26	0.37	0.09	0.25	0.53	0.28	0.72	0.60	0.21	0.60
p27	0.08	0.60	0.42	0.38	0.63	0.77	0.74	0.52	0.67
p28	0.05	0.20	0.38	0.35	0.46	0.54	0.42	0.40	0.40
p29	0.19	0.37	0.22	0.19	0.64	0.93	0.61	0.57	0.51
p30	0.51	0.25	0.41	0.36	0.61	0.75	0.60	0.92	0.54

Table A3.2: *Table of interactions between visual form and image type*

	df	F	p-value
Visual Form	2,58	6.58	.003
Image Type	2,58	46.07	<.001
Visual Form/Image Type	4,116	11.29	<.001

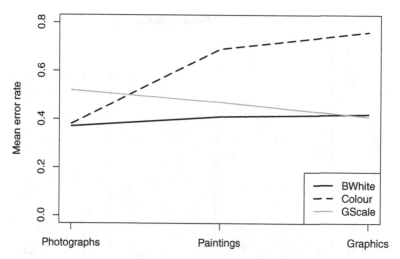

Figure A3.1: Line chart showing the interaction between Visual Form and Image Type.

We investigate the interactions by splitting the data into three separate data sets according to image type, and then perform three *separate* ANOVA/single-step pairwise analyses (each using $p = .05$), one for each image type, and *report a separate result for each image type.*

The results of the analysis for this experiment would be reported as four separate results:

1. A repeated measures two-way ANOVA revealed a significant interaction between visual form and image type, $F(4,116) = 11.29, p < .001$.
2. **For Photographs** (Figure A3.2), there were significant differences in performance as represented by the error data according to visual form: $F(2,58) = 6.152, p = .004$. A single-step pairwise comparison test ($p = .05$) revealed where the differences lie: the Grey-scale condition produced significantly worse performance than both Black and White ($p = .021$) and Colour ($p = .005$).
3. **For Paintings** (Figure A3.3), there were significant differences in performance as represented by the error data according to visual form: $F(2,58) = 20.525, p < .001$. A single-step pairwise comparison test ($p = .05$) revealed where the differences lie: the Colour condition produced significantly worse performance than both Black and White ($p < .001$) and Grey-scale ($p < .001$).
4. **For Graphics**, (Figure A3.4) there were significant differences in performance as represented by the error data according to visual form: $F(2,58) = 26.316, p < .001$. A single-step pairwise comparison test ($p = .05$) revealed

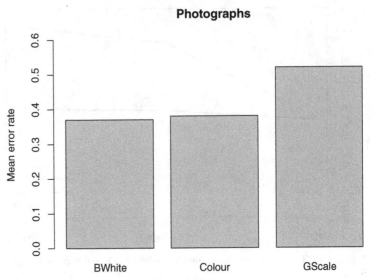

Figure A3.2: Mean error rate for Photographs.

where the differences lie: the Colour condition produced significantly worse performance than both Black and White ($p < .001$) and Grey-scale ($p < .001$).

Note that no result for the overall effect of visual form is reported; thus, the primary research question remains unanswered.

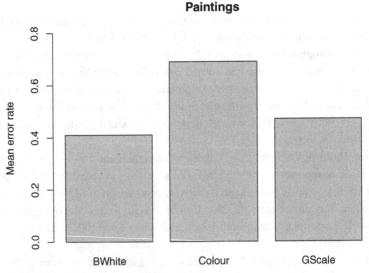

Figure A3.3: Mean error rate for Paintings.

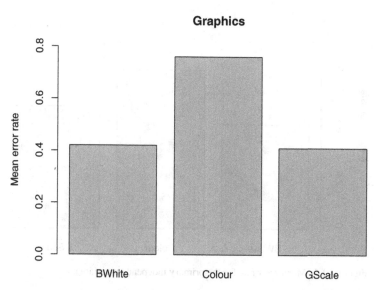

Graphics

Figure A3.4: Mean error rate for Graphics.

A3.2 Selective factor analysis

Here, we take a "selective factor" approach to the same visual form experiment and data, ensuring that we get an overall result that answers our primary research question first, before looking at other selected factors.

First, we look at the independent variable in which we are interested (the three visual forms) and perform an ANOVA/single-step pairwise test (Figure A3.5).

We then report our primary result:

1. There were significant differences in performance as represented by the error data according to visual form: $F(2,58) = 46.067, p < .001$. Single-step pairwise comparison tests ($p = .05$) revealed pairwise differences: the Black and White condition resulted in fewer errors than Colour ($p < .001$) and Grey-scale ($p = .028$), and Grey-scale resulted in fewer errors than Colour ($p < .001$).

The visual form conditions can therefore be ranked in order best to worst: Black and White, Grey-scale, and Colour.

Having answered our main research question with respect to the primary independent variable, we may be interested to see if the image type affected the relative performance of the different visual forms. This may be because of our own intuition as to the different nature of the image type, observation

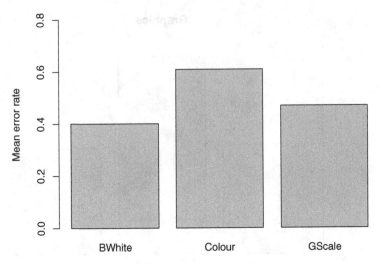

Figure A3.5: Mean error rate for the primary independent variable.

of the participants while they did the different tasks, or comments made by the participants in the postexperiment interviews. We can therefore investigate further to see if there was any effect of image type on the performance (Figure A3.6), and report this result:

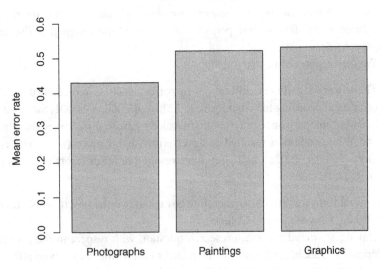

Figure A3.6: Mean errors for the three different types of image, where Image Type is a secondary factor in the experiment.

2. There were significant differences in performance as represented by the error data according to image type: $F(2,58) = 6.576$, $p = .003$. There are pairwise differences between the Photograph condition and Paintings ($p = 0.021$) and between the Photographs and Graphics conditions ($p = .008$).

This result confirms any intuition that it might be useful to investigate each type of image separately.

  We can then pose three second-level research questions:

- "Which visual form of an image best supports visual search for photographs?"
- "Which visual form of an image best supports visual search for paintings?"
- "Which visual form of an image best supports visual search in graphics?"

  Answering these questions requires performing a selective factor analysis on the data, with respect to the image type secondary factor. We use a Bonferroni adjustment to reduce the p-value according to the number of separate data sets analysed; that is, $p = .05/3 = .0167$.

  We split the data into three sets according to image type, perform three separate ANOVA/Tukey analyses (each using $p = .0167$), one for each image type, and report a separate result for each image type. Note that this is exactly the same process followed in the preceding multiway factor analysis, except that we are required to use a reduced p-value.

  We can then report these three results:

3. **For Photographs**, there were significant differences in performance as represented by the error data according to visual form: $F(2,58) = 6.152$, $p = .004$. A single-step pairwise comparison test (with adjusted $p = .0167$) revealed that the Grey-scale condition produced significantly worse performance than Colour ($p = .005$).

4. **For Paintings**, there were significant differences in performance as represented by the error data according to visual form: $F(2,58) = 20.525, p < .001$. A single-step pairwise comparison test (with adjusted $p = .0167$) revealed where the differences lie: the Colour condition produced significantly worse performance than both Black and White ($p < .001$) and Grey-scale ($p < .001$).

5. **For Graphics**, there were significant differences in performance as represented by the error data according to visual form: $F(2,58) = 26.316$, $p < .001$. A single-step pairwise comparison test ($p = .0167$) revealed where the differences lie: the Colour condition produced significantly worse performance than both Black and White ($p < .001$) and Grey-scale ($p < .001$).

Note that we have lost one of the significant results that we reported in the two-way factor analysis: the result that the Grey-scale condition produced significantly worse performance than Black and White for photographs. This is because the p-value for this pairwise difference (.021) is greater than the Bonferroni-adjusted probability that we need to use for this second-level analysis (.0167).

These are deliberately extreme data designed to illustrate a subtle interaction effect; for more realistic data, the reduced p-value used in selective factor analysis might have a more radical effect on the number of secondary-level analyses that can be reported.

Bibliography

This book addresses formal experiments in HCI, but there are many other HCI evaluation methods (e.g., heuristic evaluation, cognitive walkthrough, collaborative think aloud, usage studies). Any good HCI textbook will give a reasonable introduction to these. See, for example,

- Preece, J., et al. (1994). *Human-Computer Interaction*, Addison Wesley.
- Dix, A., et al. (2007). *Human-Computer Interaction*, 4th ed. Prentice Hall.

A seminal paper providing a useful overview of the dimensions of HCI evaluation, with comparisons of different evaluation methods, is as follows:

- McGrath, J.E. (1995). Methodology matters: Doing research in the behavioral and social sciences. In R.M. Baecker, J. Grudin, W.A.S. Buxton, and S. Greenberg (eds.), *Readings in Human-Computer Interaction: Toward the Year 2000*, 2nd ed., Morgan Kaufmann, pp. 152–169.

Anyone working with statistics has their own favourite statistics text. Mine is as follows:

- Hinton, P. (2004). *Statistics Explained: A Guide for Social Science Students*, 2nd ed. Routledge.

Hinton also has a useful companion book for those wanting to use SPSS (although be wary of the fact that several new versions of SPSS have been released since this book was written):

- Hinton, P., Brownlow, C., and McMurray, I. (2004). *SPSS Explained*. Routledge.

References

Archambault, D., H.C. Purchase, and B. Pinaud, "The readability of path-preserving clusterings of graphs," *Computer Graphics Forum*, 2010; 29(3):1173–1182.

Archambault, D., H.C. Purchase, and B. Pinaud, "Animation, small multiples, and the effect of mental map preservation in dynamic graphs," *IEEE Transactions on Visualization and Computer Graphics*, Washington, 2011; 17(4):539–552.

Auber, D., "Tulip – a huge graph visualisation framework," in *Graph Drawing Software*, P. Mutzel and M. Junger, eds. Spinger Verlag, Berlin Heidelberg, 2003, pp. 105–126.

Bourqui, R., H.C. Purchase, and F. Jourdan, "Domain specific vs generic network visualization: an evaluation with metabolic networks," in *Australasian User Interface Conference*, Perth, January 2011, Conferences in Research and Practise in Information Technology, vol. 117 C. Lutteroth and H. Shen, eds, Australia: Australian Computer Society (ACS), Sydney, 2011, pp. 9–18.

Bourqui, R., et al., "Metabolic network visualisation using constraint planar graph drawing algorithm," in *Information Visualisation Conference*, London, IEEE Computer Society, Washington, 2006, pp. 489–496.

Brown, L.M., S.A. Brewster, and H.C. Purchase, "A First Investigation into the Effectiveness of Tactons," paper presented at First Joint Eurohaptics Conference and Symposium on Haptic Interfaces for Virtual Environment and Teleoperator Systems, World Haptics 2005, Pisa, March 18–20, 2005, IEEE, Washington, pp. 167–176.

Cairns, P. and A. Cox, *Research Methods for Human–Computer Interaction*, Cambridge University Press, Cambridge, 2008.

Chen, P.P.-S., "The entity-relationship model – toward a unified view of data," *ACM Transactions on Database Systems*, New York, 1976; 1(1):9–36.

Cook, P.A., C.P. Wheater, and J. Wright, *Using Statistics to Understand the Environment*, Routledge, London, 2000.

Dix, A., et al., *Human–Computer Interaction*, 3rd ed., Prentice Hall, Harlow, 2004.

Ellis, G. and A. Dix, "An explorative analysis of user evaluation studies in information visualisation," in *Proceedings of the 2006 AVI Workshop on Beyond Time and Errors: Novel Evaluation Methods for Information Visualization*, Venice, E. Bertini, C. Plaisant, and G. Santucci, eds. New York: ACM Press, 2006, pp. 1–7.

Erten, C., et al., "GraphAEL: graph animations with evolving layouts," in *Graph Drawing*, G. Liotta, ed. LNCS 2912, Springer Verlag, Berlin Heidelberg, 2004, pp. 98–110.

Field, A. and G. Hole, *How To Design and Report Experiments*, Sage, London, 2003.

Flower, J., F. Fish, and J. Howse, "Euler diagram generation," *Journal of Visual Languages and Computing*, 2008; 19(6):675–694.

Frick, A., A. Ludwig, and H. Mehldau, "A fast adaptive layout algorithm for undirected graphs," in *Graph Drawing*, R. Tamassia and I.G. Tollis, eds. LNCS 894, Springer Verlag, Berlin Heidelberg, 1994, pp. 388–403.

Frishman, Y. and A. Tal, "Online dynamic graph drawing," *IEEE Transactions on Visualization and Computer Graphics*, 2008; New York, 14(4):727–740.

Fruchterman, T.M.J. and E.M. Reingold, "Graph drawing by force-directed placement," *Software – Practice and Experience*, 1991; 21(11):1129–1164.

Greenberg, S. and W. Buxton, "Usability evaluation considered harmful (some of the time)," in *CHI '08 Proceedings of the Twenty-Sixth Annual SIGCHI Conference on Human Factors in Computing Systems*. New York: ACM Press, 2008, pp. 111–120.

Grundon, S. and H.C. Purchase, "Using Graph Drawing Aesthetics in Class Diagrams," University of Queensland, Department of Computer Science, 1996.

Hamer, J. and H.C. Purchase, "Usability Evaluation of Aropä, the Peer Assessment System," University of Auckland, Department of Computer Science, 2009.

Himsolt, M., "GraphEd: A graphical platform for the implementation of graph algorithms," in *Graph Drawing*, R. Tamassia and I.G. Tollis, eds., LNCS 894, Springer Verlag, Berlin Heidelberg,1994, pp. 182–193.

Hinton, P., *Statistics Explained: A Guide for Social Science Students*, Routledge, London, 1995.

Hinton, P., *Statistics Explained: A Guide for Social Science Students*, 2nd ed. Routledge, London, 2004.

Hinton, P., C. Brownlow, and I. McMurray, *SPSS Explained*, Routledge, London, 2004.

Hoggan, E. and H.C. Purchase, "Corners in Orthogonal Graph Drawings," University of Glasgow, Computing Science Department, 2005.

International Standards Organization (ISO), "ISO 9241-11:1998: Ergonomic Requirements for Office Work with Visual Display Terminals (VDTs) – Part 11: Guidance on Usability," Geneva, Switzerland, 1998.

Kildal, J. and S. Brewster, "Non-visual overviews of complex data sets," in *Human Factors in Computing Systems (CHI Extended Abstracts)*, ACM, New York, 2006, Montreal, pp. 947–952.

Koenig, P.-Y., "DAGMap: un outil d'exploration adapté aux relations d'heritages multiples," in *HM '07 Proceedings of the 19th International Conference of the Association Francophone d'Interaction Homme-Machine*, New York: ACM Press, 2007, pp. 237–240.

Lieberman, H., "The tyranny of evaluation," in *Human Factors in Computing Systems*, CHI Fringe 2003, Fort Lauderdale, 2003.

McGee-Lennon, M.R., M. Wolters, and T. McBryan, "Audio reminders in the home environment," in *Proceedings of the 13th International Conference on Auditory Display*, Montreal: Schulich School of Music, McGill University, 2007, pp. 437–444.

McGrath, J.E., "Methodology matters: doing research in the behavioral and social sciences," in *Readings in Human-Computer Interaction: Toward the Year 2000*, 2nd ed., R.M. Baecker, J. Grudin, W.A.S. Buxton and S. Greenberg, eds., Chapter 2, pgs 152–169 San Francisco, CA, Morgan Kaufmann, 1995.

Ngo, D., L. Teo, and J.G. Byrne, "Modelling interface aesthetics," *Information Sciences*, 2003; 152:25–46.

Nielsen, J., "Why you only need to test with 5 users," *Jakob Nielsen's Alertbox*, March 19, 2000. Available at: www.useit.com/alertbox/20000319.html.

Preece, J., et al., *Human-Computer Interaction*, Addison Wesley, Wokingham, 1994.

Purchase, H.C., "Which aesthetic has the greatest effect on human understanding?" in *Graph Drawing Conference*, G. Di Battista, ed., LNCS 1353, Springer Verlag, Berlin Heidelberg, 1997, pp. 248–261.

Purchase, H.C., "Performance of layout algorithms: comprehension, not computation," *Journal of Visual Languages and Computing*, 1998; 9(6):647–657.

Purchase, H.C., R.F. Cohen, and M. James, "Validating graph drawing aesthetics," in *Graph Drawing Symposium*, F.J. Brandenberg, ed., LNCS 1027, Springer Verlag, Berlin Heidelberg, 1995, pp. 435–446.

Purchase, H.C., E. Freeman, and J. Hamer, "An Exploration of Visual Complexity," Proceedings of the Diagrams Conference, P. Cox, and B. Plimmer, eds., LNCS, Springer Verlag, Berlin Heidelberg, 2012 (to appear) In press.

Purchase, H.C. and J. Hamer, "Generating Sets of Alphabetic Letters of 'Equal Difficulty,'" University of Glasgow, School of Computing Science, 2010.

Purchase, H.C. and A. Samra, "Extremes are better: investigating mental map preservation in dynamic graphs," in *Diagrammatic Representation and Inference*, G. Stapleton, J. Howse, and J. Lee, eds., LNAI 5223, Springer Verlag, 2008, pp. 60–73.

Purchase, H.C., et al., "UML class diagram syntax: an empirical study of comprehension," in *Australian Symposium on Information Visualisation, Sydney, December 2001. Conferences in Research and Practice in Information Technology*, vol. 9, P. Eades and T. Pattison, eds. Australian Computer Society (ACS), 2001, pp. 113–120.

Purchase, H.C., et al., "Comprehension of diagram syntax: an empirical study of entity relationship diagram notations," *International Journal of Human-Computer Studies*, 2004; 61(2):187–203.

Purchase, H.C., et al., "Investigating objective measures of web page aesthetics and usability," in *Australasian User Interface Conference*, Perth, January 2011, Conferences in Research and Practise in Information Technology, vol. 117 C. Lutteroth and H. Shen, eds., Australia: Australian Computer Society (ACS), Sydney, 2011, pp. 19–28.

Purchase, H.C., et al., *An investigation of graph layout aesthetics based on perceptual theory*. University of Glasgow, School of Computing Science, 2012.

Rodgers, P., L. Zhang, and H.C. Purchase, "Wellformedness properties in Euler diagrams: which should be used?" *IEEE Transactions on Visualization and Computer Graphics*, Washington, 2011 (preprint).

Roosevelt, F.D., "Commencement Address at Oglethorpe University, Atlanta, Georgia," The American Presidency Project: Papers of Franklin Roosevelt, University of California, Santa Barbara, 1932.

Salimun, C., et al., "The effect of aesthetically pleasing composition on visual search performance," in *Nordic Human Computer Interaction*, ACM, New York, 2010, pp. 422–431.

San Augustin, J., et al., "Low cost gazing and EMG clicking," in *Human Factors in Computing Systems* (CHI Extended Abstracts), ACM, New York, 2009, pp. 3247–3252.

Shneiderman, B., "Tree visualisation with tree maps: 2-d space-filling approach," *ACM Transactions on Graphics*, 1992; 11(1):92–99.

Stott, J., et al., "Automatic metro map layout using multicriteria optimization," *IEEE Transactions on Visualization and Computer Graphics*, Los Alamitos, CA, 2011; 17(1):101–114.

Tufte, E.R., *The Visual Display of Quantitative Information*, 2nd ed. Graphics Press, USA, 2001.

Tullis, T. and L. Wood, "How many users are enough for a card-sorting study?", in *Proceedings UPA 2004*, Bloomingdale, IL: Usability Professionals' Association, Minneapolis, 2004.

Ware, C., et al., "Cognitive measurements of graph aesthetics," *Information Visualization*, 2002; 1(2):103–110.

Weaver, P.L., *Practical SSADM Version 4 – A Complete Tutorial Guide*, Pitman, London, 1993.

yWorks, *yEd Graph Editor*, 2012

Zhai, S., "Evaluation Is the Worst Form of HCI Research Except All Those Other Forms That Have Been Tried," paper presented at CHI 2003 Conference on Human Factors in Computing Systems, Fort Lauderdale, FL, April 5–10, 2003.

Index

Printed in the United States
by Baker & Taylor Publisher Services